nicholas of cusa on god as not-other

nicholas of cusa on god as not-other

a translation and an appraisal

of de li non aliud

third edition

by jasper hopkins

the arthur j. banning press, minneapolis

Nicholas of Cusa on God as Not-other
Third edition, 1987
(First edition published by the University of Minnesota Press, 1979)

Library of Congress Catalog Card Number

ISBN 0-938060-38-4

Printed in the United States of America

Ita omnes veritate afficimur quod, ipsam undique reperibilem scientes, illum habere magistrum optamus, qui ipsam nostrae mentis oculis anteponat.

De Li Non Aliud 1

pReface

American and British students of Nicholas of Cusa seem seldom
to advance beyond familiarizing themselves with the system of
thought contained in *De Docta Ignorantia*. This failure of
movement is not necessarily a failure of progress. For given the
wealth of content of that magnificent but cryptic work, our
understanding of its central ideas can only be progressive. Still,
there comes a time when we need to move onward to a careful
consideration of Nicholas's other philosophical works as well—
if only to afford ourselves the opportunity of viewing *De Docta
Ignorantia* in a different light when we subsequently return to
reexamine it. In particular, the time has come to explore more
fully such later works as *De Possest* and *De Li Non Aliud*. I
previously have made available an English translation of the
former;[1] I now present an equally close rendering of the latter.[2] I
am grateful to both Karsten Harries of Yale University and
Thomas P. McTighe of Georgetown University, who read
through the entire manuscript and offered helpful suggestions for
its improvement. I cannot be certain, however, that either of
them would sanction all aspects of the final product.

De Li Non Aliud is not an easy work. (Indeed, even its main
theme has sometimes been misunderstood.)[3] Nor is it a work
which can suitably stand alone, as can *De Possest*. Rather, if it is
to be appreciated at all, it must be read against the backdrop of
De Docta Ignorantia. And it must be approached with some
allowance for its conceptual style—i.e., with no expectation of
its being anything other than what it is: viz., a highly original
speculation. In breaking away from the conceptual constraints

vii

Preface

of Scholasticism, Nicholas sometimes, as in the present dialogue, gives only light rein to his metaphysical musings. In the present instance he guides his meditation along a single path: viz., the pathway to God through the signification of the symbolic name "Not-other."

The importance of this dialogue will, I suspect, be best discerned by the intellectual historian, who will be able to recognize its proper place within the long and pervasive tradition of medieval Neoplatonism. The intellectual historian will see too, no doubt, the significance of Chapter 14 as a source-book of themes which motivate certain forms of Renaissance reasoning.

My introductory appraisal of the dialogue aims at being concise and evenhanded; it is an appraisal and not a summary, a commentary, or an appreciation. A student of the present dialogue should already be familiar with the Platonic and the Aristotelian traditions and with the complex metaphysical problems about being and not-being, singularity and plurality, sameness and otherness, substance and accident, form and matter, universality and particularity—some of which topics reached early focal points in Plato's *Parmenides* and *Sophist* as well as in Aristotle's *Metaphysics*. The reader of *De Li Non Aliud* may well be amazed at how many of these themes the single motif of *non-aliud* manages to encompass. Nicholas's extensive exploration of this rich motif—his relating of it to the views of Plato, Aristotle, Proclus, Dionysius, and David of Dinant—testifies amply to his imaginativeness and ingenuity. Once we realize that he is exploring a motif rather than formulating lines of argument, we will understand why we may need to approach his text more as historians than as philosophers and theologians.

Jasper Hopkins
Professor of Philosophy
University of Minnesota

PREFACE TO THE THIRD EDITION

This edition improves upon the two previous ones in important ways. The Latin text here presented is my own transcription of Codex Latinus Monacensis 24848, folios 1ᵛ - 54ʳ. It is published by permission of the Department of Manuscripts at the Bavarian Staatsbibliothek, Munich, Germany. I am grateful to Dr. Hermann Hauke for his advice.

In preparing the present edition, I also examined, on site, Latin Ms. 19-26 (folios 55ʳ - 76ʳ) of the Cathedral Library in Toledo, Spain. This manuscript, which includes many works of Cusanus, is extremely unreliable—as evidenced, for example, by comparing its version of *De Visione Dei* with the other available versions. In the case of *De Li Non Aliud* the readings of the Toledo manuscript are of interest only where an editor has independent grounds for believing that the Munich manuscript is incorrect. I list Toledo's many variants in an appendix—only exceptionally incorporating any of them into the apparatus that accompanies the printed Latin text. A detailed description of Toledo 19-26 was given by Klaus Reinhardt in *Mitteilungen und Forschungsbeiträge der Cusanus-Gesellschaft*, 17 (1986), 96-141.

contents

nicholas of cusa on god as not-other

INTRODUCTION

1. Enigmatic Character of the Dialogue

When Nicholas of Cusa wrote the dialogue *De Li Non Aliud*, he was sixty years old and had long been a master of speculation.[1] Over the years his intellect had learned to soar upward with conceptual wings borrowed from the writings of Pseudo-Dionysius, Proclus, Erigena, Thierry of Chartres, and Meister Eckhart—the more important of those by whose aid he ascended. Having left behind both the *via antiqua* and the *via moderna*, he ventured upon the *via speculativa* in open disregard of the fears earlier expressed by such fifteenth-century thinkers as John Gerson. Although Gerson and others had warned against *curiositas vana*, Nicholas scarcely regarded any of his own writings as falling under this rubric. For whether the epithet be construed as signifying "distorting intellectualism," "idle curiosity," or "pointless speculation," Nicholas would, in any event, have protested that his intellectualism—if such it can be called—was not distorting, his inquisitiveness not idle, his reflection not pointless. And yet, any contemporary reader of the present dialogue— even the most sympathetic reader—will more than once be tempted to employ the labels "*Wortspielerei*," "triviality," "confusion," and "obscurantism." By all means, *curiositas vana*!

Still, there is something boldly imaginative about this speculative venture—something which signals us to approach the work in a way other than usual. The usual way would be to point out a host of philosophical difficulties which Nicholas either ignorantly rushes into or cunningly detours around. For example,

3

there is the problem of equivocation—as in Chapter 3, where we read: "Since everything which exists is not other than itself, assuredly it does not have this fact from any other. Therefore, it has it from Not-other." Inasmuch as "Not-other" is a name for God, the inference is a *non sequitur*. For there is a difference between asserting that something is derived from no other and asserting that it is derived from Not-other. Second, someone can point to the confusion, prevalent throughout the work, between *using* an expression and *mentioning* it. For instance, Ferdinand asks: "Does *Not-other* posit something, or does it remove something?" And Nicholas answers: "It is seen prior to all positing and removing."[2] In the question, "Not-other" is mentioned; in the answer, it is used. Thus, the answer seems not to correspond to the question.

Third, Nicholas's notion of definition is bizarre. We cannot seriously regard as a definition the sentence "The sky is not other than the sky" or the sentence "The earth is not other than the earth."[3] Moreover, no one could rightly agree with the unqualified claim, advanced in Chapter 1, that "definition defines everything." And derision is surely invited by Ferdinand's suggestion, in Chapter 19, that if Aristotle had understood the truth about Not-other, he would "not have had need either of an elaborate logic or of the difficult art of definition . . . . "

Fourth, some of the reasoning appears simplistic, not to mention specious. Thus, in Chapter 10, the following line of consideration occurs: "You do not doubt that Not-other is indestructible. For if it were destroyed, it would become other. But as soon as other is posited, Not-other is posited. Hence, Not-other is not destructible." This reasoning does not *demonstrate* that God, who is Not-other, exists and is indestructible. Nor, for that matter, does Nicholas suppose that it does. Instead, he seems to be intimating that if Not-other exists and is God, then God is unchanging; so God cannot cease existing, since cessation is a change. But, of course, the interesting issue is *whether or not* God exists and is absolutely unchanging, i.e., is absolutely Not-other—*whether or not* other presupposes an existent Not-other. But this existence is the very point which is assumed. Another instance of bypassing an important issue is found in Chapter 7, where chaos is referred to as "intelligible nothing" but where we are left without any explication of this intriguing statement. Finally, in much of Nicholas's reasoning a fifth problem is inherent: viz., that closely related concepts are not carefully distinguished. For example, the uses of the word "*ratio*" often are not precise enough to make clear to the reader which one of its twenty or so different meanings is operative in the context at hand.

In short, philosophers or theologians can readily locate and call attention to such defects as the foregoing. And, indeed, they are obliged to do so. But once having registered these objections, should they not then begin to wonder whether *De Li Non Aliud* ought to be viewed in another light as well? For does not this work represent, in its broader sweep, a self-conscious attempt to transcend the usual conceptual confines in order to attain a reality regarded as inaccessible in the former way? That is, granted that this writing does contain some glaring conceptual confusions, does it not perhaps also contain some striking intellectual transformations with an intelligibility of their own? And, if so, do these not also deserve special attention?

Like Pseudo-Dionysius before him, Nicholas revels in paradoxical expression. And, to be sure, the intelligibility of these expressions cannot be grasped through a literalistic approach. For example, Nicholas speaks of Magnitude which is "comprehended incomprehensibly and is known unknowably, even as it is seen invisibly."[4] Again, he maintains that our knowledge of God is perfect ignorance.[5] And the names of God are said to signify a "participation in Him who cannot be participated in."[6] Similarly, God is not only "all in all" but is also "nothing in nothing."[7] He is not only the "Being of being" but is also the "Not-being of not-being."[8] Likewise, He is "not the sky, which is an other; nonetheless, in the sky God is not an other; nor is

He *other* than the sky."⁹ That is, in an other Not-other is this other.

Whatever may be the correct verdict about the truth or falsity of these and other such statements, one thing must be insisted upon: viz., that in the contexts in which the statements are embedded, they are not altogether unintelligible. Let us consider several of them. In *De Possest* 2 even Bernard and John express perplexity over the statement that "invisible things are seen." This fact shows that Nicholas is not unaware that the statement is problematical. He makes the following response: "They are seen invisibly—just as when the intellect understands what it reads, it invisibly sees the invisible truth which is hidden behind the writing. I say 'invisibly' (i.e., 'mentally') because the invisible truth, which is the object of the intellect, cannot be seen in any other way." Here the paradox has been dissolved.

By comparison, the statement that God is known unknowably or known through ignorance presents a paradox which Nicholas then goes on to dissolve. For when we come to recognize that God is undifferentiated Being itself, we come to recognize that His "nature" cannot be intellectually known by us—either in this lifetime or in the next. So in knowing that He is not a differentiated being, we know something about Him which informs us that we cannot know anything determinate about Him. But even more, we cannot know anything at all about Him as He is in Himself. To know that He is not a differentiated being is in no respect to know what He is. For we cannot at all conceive of what it is like to be undifferentiated Being itself. And if we cannot conceive of it, then *a fortiori* we cannot have knowledge of it. Hence, to know *that* God is Being itself is not tantamount to knowing *what* God is. Similarly, to conceive of God as inconceivable is, in an important sense, not to conceive of God. For though we conceive *that* God is inconceivable, we do not rightly conceive of what the inconceivable God either is or is like. Thus, to comprehend Him incomprehensibly is (1) to comprehend that He is incomprehensible and (2) to compre-

hend Him either through various symbolisms, such as occur in
the present dialogue, or through the "revelation" of Christ, even
though the form in which He appears in Christ is totally other
than He is in Himself.[10]

In *De Li Non Aliud* Nicholas does not confuse (1) participating in God and (2) signifying a participation in God. Strictly
speaking, God cannot be participated in. Nonetheless, the names
of God can *signify* a participation in Him. For instance, in calling God the Omnipotent One we signify in Him a power which
bears some resemblance—however dim—to power which we
experience. In accordance with one version of the metaphysical
doctrine of participation, it follows that in calling things which
we experience *powerful*, we signify that they participate in the
power of God, in Powerfulness as such. But in Himself God is
not Powerfulness, because He is beyond the distinction between
the determinations "powerful" and "powerless." Nonetheless, we
are able to signify as being the case what, in fact, is not the case.
Indeed, as Richard Campbell rightly points out, some expressions—
such as the expression "that which destroys this book"—"must
signify an existing thing, but there might not really be such a
thing. It is this insight which underlies and justifies the general
medieval distinction between *existentia ut significata* and *existentia ut exercita.*"[11]

Nicholas also struggles to explain the sense in which "in an
other Not-other is this other." To indicate his meaning he has
recourse to analogies.[12] These analogies are illustrative rather
than argumentative: they do not try to establish a point but only
to render it more plausible. Thus, in Chapter 16 Ferdinand
makes a comparison with time:

> In time an understanding of Not-other is especially manifest. For exam-
> ple, in an hour |time| is the hour; in a day it is the day; in a month, the
> month; in a year, the year. And as |time| is seen before all these things,
> |so| in time they are time—just as in all things time is all things. And
> although in all the things which partake of time time is all things, and
> although time proceeds to all things and remains with them inseparably

and defines them and delimits them, nonetheless within itself it remains fixed and immovable . . . .

In a sense, Ferdinand's illustration produces more puzzles than it solves, since the notion of time is itself in need of analysis. But the thrust of his point is clear enough to be clearly wrong. For time is not "in" an hour or a day or a month; for an hour, say, does not last an hour, does not last sixty minutes. Rather, an activity or a process, etc., lasts an hour. Although an hour is a measure of time, it does not itself *take* time—does not *partake* of time. Indeed, no passage of time—whatever the unit of measure—takes time. Nor, on the other hand, does time remain fixed and immovable; for the future can become present, and the present can become past. If we say that the whole of time remains fixed and unchangeable, then it is no longer obvious that we are saying anything meaningful, since it is not clear what it would be like for the whole of time *not* to be unchangeable.

However, another of Nicholas's illustrations is more interesting: light is not color, he says; and yet, in color light is not anything other than color. Similarly, God, who is Not-other, is not the sky, which is an other—even though in the sky God is not anything other than the sky. Nicholas is aiming to show how God transcends the world while remaining immanent in it. As immanent, He is the unopposing sustaining power of every differentiated thing; as transcendent, He is unqualifiedly undifferentiated. Now, if color is a modification of light—as indeed it is—then, in accordance with the analogy, it seems that Nicholas must be prepared to say that the universe and anything within it are modifications of God. And this indeed is what some people have interpreted him as teaching. According to them the universe is a modification of God and yet is not itself God, since God *can* (though He never *does*) exist without the universe (just as light can exist without color). Nonetheless, so the interpretation continues,

if the determinations were removed from the being of the universe, the being of the universe would coincide with the being of God.[13] Moreover, the universe is, in Nicholas's words, an *emanation from God*. Although its oneness of being is other than the oneness of God, its very being *is* God's being. For in the universe God is the universe. In subscribing to the doctrine of emanation, Nicholas does not mean to deny that God created the world *ex nihilo*—i.e., from no preexisting substance. In fact, precisely because creation is emanation, it is *ex nihilo nisi deo*.

However, Nicholas does not seem to have adopted the foregoing position. That is, he seems *not* to have taught that 'the universe in its very being (i.e., apart from all determinations) is God, because God is Being itself.' What he says is that just as apart from a physical object the mirror image thereof is nothing, so apart from God the universe (i.e., creation, which is in some sense the image of God) is nothing.[14] Similarly, just as apart from God the universe is nothing, so it is also nothing apart from all its determinations. To say (as Nicholas does) that God is the being itself (*entitas*) of all things does not commit him to saying (as he does not) that any given thing, in its being, is God. Similarly, to say that God is the essence of all things does not commit him to saying that any given thing, in its essence, is God. For God is the essence of a given thing in that He is the Essence of all essences,[15] including that thing's essence. And He is the being of a given thing in that He is the Being of all being, including that thing's being. *That* thing's being, however, is always differentiated; and undifferentiated being is never *that* thing's being.

2. Relation to Predecessors

In Chapter 14 Nicholas characterizes the author of *The Celestial Hierarchy, The Ecclesiastical Hierarchy, The Divine Names*, etc., as *theologorum maximus*: the greatest of the theologians.[16] He regards him as the Areopagite converted by St. Paul. Today we know that this author dates from a later period and wrote under the pseudonymn "Dionysius the Areopagite." His influence on Nicholas was profound. In fact, it would be no exaggeration to maintain that Nicholas's very philosophical style is derived from this predecessor; for Dionysius glories in paradoxical language, cryptic metaphor, and redolent imprecisions. From this source, too, comes the *via negativa* as well as the extensive discourse both about not-being and about the infinite distance between God and man. In Dionysius, too, Nicholas encountered a contagious enthusiasm regarding the possibility of a mystical vision of the Beautiful and the Good. Moreover, the very notion of *non-aliud* was suggested to him from *The Mystical Theology*.[17] And the doctrine that all things are contained in God before all times is adapted from *The Divine Names*.

According to Dionysius God is beyond existence, i.e., beyond being insofar as it is distinct from not-being. Because God transcends the distinction between being and not-being, He is the Being of beings only insofar as He is also the Not-being of not-beings. To Dionysius (as to Paul Tillich in our time) God is the Power-of-being which supports all beings; "for what is not at all supported by any power does not exist . . . ."[18] Nicholas himself uses the term *"ratio essendi,"* or "Ground of being."[19]

The extensive excerpts that *De Li Non Aliud* 14 cites from the works of Dionysius constitute the passages deemed by Nicholas to be the most important and the most concise. These are drawn from Ambrose Traversari's Latin translations, which were completed by 1436. Also available to Nicholas, however, were the earlier Latin translations by John Scotus Erigena, John Sarrazin, and Robert Grosseteste.[20] We may justifiably conclude—with Martin Honecker—that Nicholas knew a little Greek but not enough to read with discernment the original text of Dionysius's works.[21] So Nicholas was dependent upon the aforementioned translations, none of which are without serious problems. For example, the renderings by Traversari and by Erigena are often neither sufficiently literal nor sufficiently clear; and there are systematic mistranslations.[22]

From Thierry of Chartres Nicholas adopts the expression *"forma essendi."*[23] Sometimes he even says *"universal* Form of being": *"Deus igitur est universalis essendi forma, quia dat omnibus esse."*[24]

God is not, then, the form of earth, of water, of air, of aether, or of any other thing. Rather, He is the absolute Form of the form of earth, or of air, [etc.] Therefore, God is not the earth or any other thing. Rather, earth is earth, air is air, aether is aether, and man is man—each through its own form.[25]

As Form-of-being, then, God is the Form of the forms of particular elements, substances, and accidents. He is Form-of-forms in the sense that He is Form which gives form, Form which bestows being. In last analysis, to call God "Form of forms" is tantamount to calling Him "Being of beings," since in God Form *is* Being.

At first glance, Nicholas's metaphysics appears to leave room for a version of exemplarism, though not the version of Thomas Aquinas, who in the *Summa Contra Gentiles* objected to a plurality of divine Ideas.[26] According to Thomas there is but one Form of creation, viz., the Word of God, who is God's Understanding of Himself; for in understanding Himself God understands the varying degrees of likeness which created things—of which He is the Cause—bear to Him. Just as in the order of dependency a cause is prior to what it causes, so also, explains Thomas, God's Understanding (i.e., the Form of creation) is ontologically prior to creation. Nicholas goes beyond Thomas by contending that God has no knowledge of the ways in which creatures *resemble* Him—since creatures do not resemble Him. Hence, strictly speaking, there is no divine Idea. Yet, Nicholas *calls* God the "triune, most true, and most congruent Exemplar," the *exemplar absolutum*, the "truest formal (or truest exemplary) Cause." And he regards the Word of God as the "Concept both of itself and of the universe." But this naming and this viewing are conceded by him to be only "ignorance." For creation does not *conform* to God in the sense of resembling Him as Creator. Rather, it conforms to Him in the reduced sense of according with His will—i.e., being identical with what He wills for it to be.

In the light of the fact that Nicholas uses the *language* of exemplarism and of *analogia entis vel cognoscentis*, we may now address ourselves to Josef Koch's distinction between a *Seinsmetaphysik* and an *Einheitsmetaphysik*:

> To the metaphysic-of-being (*Seinsmetaphysik*) belongs the distinction between Being (i.e., God) and beings. To it also belongs the analogy of being, the distinction of degrees of being, the doctrine that all beings are composed of essence and act of being, and |the doctrine| that the essence of all material objects consists of form and matter. Thereto belongs also the acceptance of the principle of contradiction as an onto-logical law, etc. None of these |points| are now either mentioned or disputed by Cusanus; instead, they are replaced—point for point—by his metaphysic-of-oneness (*Einheitsmetaphysik*)."[27]

Koch also expresses this contrast in terms of the metaphor of direction:

> According to its nature the metaphysic-of-being is a metaphysics from below: i.e., it proceeds from beings (among which we find ourselves), and with the aid of analogical concepts (*being, one, true, good*, etc.) it attempts to mount up to Being itself (i.e., God) and to make predica-tions regarding Him. The metaphysic-of-oneness, which is of Neopla-tonic character, is always a metaphysic from above: i.e., it proceeds from Absolute Oneness, as that which is the very first given thing, and from there it descends to an understanding of the world.[28]

According to Koch Nicholas sets forth a *Seinsmetaphysik* in *De Docta Ignorantia*, and an *Einheitsmetaphysik* in *De Coniec-turis*. Yet, this distinction—be it ever so intriguing—cannot be supported.[29] Characteristic of a *Seinsmetaphysik* is supposed to be acceptance of the doctrine of *analogia entis*. But there is no more reason to suppose that Nicholas subscribed to this doctrine in the former treatise than there is to think that he subscribed to it in the latter. Likewise, there is no more reason to suppose that he was attempting to establish the existence of God in the former than there is to believe that he was endeavoring to do so in the latter. Moreover, the latter distinguishes being (*das Sein*) from beings (*das Seiende*) just as surely as does the former.[30] And it does not dispense with the principle of noncontradiction any more than does the former.

Let us go beyond the mere comparison of *De Coniecturis* with *De Docta Ignorantia*. If one notices anything about the later works *De Possest* and *De Li Non Aliud*, in comparing them with *De Docta Ignorantia*, it is that they do not veer from the main directions of the earlier philosophical system. Thus, if Nicholas moved from a *Seinsmetaphysik* in *De Docta Ignorantia* to an *Einheitsmetaphysik* in *De Coniecturis*, then he later reverted to a *Seinsmetaphysik*. But it is more reasonable to suppose that these developments did not occur—especially since, as Koch himself observes, Nicholas in *De Coniecturis* does not *dispute* any of his theses from *De Docta Ignorantia*. Nor do the theses seem to be, *pace* Koch, "*Stück für Stück ersetzt.*"

Although Nicholas stands in the Neoplatonic tradition, he is not altogether uninfluenced by Aristotle. Still, he does not claim extensive familarity with Aristotle's thought[31]—though he does, nevertheless, make a point of disparaging the *Metaphysics*.[32] Nicholas's own doctrine of substance differs even in its terminology from Aristotle's. By "primary substance" Aristotle meant those beings—composed of form and matter—that exist more or less independently. By "secondary substance" he meant the species or the genus to which a primary substance belongs. By contrast, Nicholas's terminology is extremely loose. In Chapter 12 of *De Li Non Aliud* it shifts repeatedly. Thus, what Aristotle called "primary substance" Nicholas calls "perceptible substance." And perceptible substance is composed of matter (confusedly called, within the space of a few paragraphs, "substantial matter," "substantial possibility," "specifiable matter," and "possibility-of-being") and of form (called "specific substance," "specific form," "intelligible substance," and "form-of-being").

Clearly, however, Nicholas teaches that the specific form never exists apart from specifiable matter, though it can be conceived as distinct therefrom.[33] And he maintains that the universe is a plurality of substances. For were it a single substance, this substance would not be other than anything—i.e., would be Not-other, or God. But this view, he believes, is absurd. Instead of there being a substance-of-the-universe which is God, there is a God who is the Substance of the substances within the universe. That is, God is the *ratio essendi* of all substantially existing things. If *per impossibile* the Substance of substances were removed, no substances could remain.[34]

We might indeed wish that Nicholas's terminology were more precise and that his position were less sketchily presented. At times he seems to use terms deliriously, almost defying them to be meaningful. At other times he senses a deeply significant point but seems unconcerned about developing it further. An instance of this insight and refusal can easily be found in his brief treatment of the *moment* as the substance of time. Being indivisible and unchangeable, it is reminiscent of God, to whom Dionysius even gave the name "the Moment." When we remember how important and how multifaceted this notion becomes within the philosophy of someone such as Hegel, we can readily conjecture that a more elaborate discussion by Nicholas might well have been profitable.

3. Faith and Reason

Given the highly speculative character of *De Li Non Aliud*, a reader might deem ironic the stipulation laid down by Nicholas at the beginning of the dialogue: "I shall speak and converse with you Ferdinand, |but only| on the following condition: viz., that unless you are compelled by reason, you will reject as unimportant everything you will hear from me."[35] Does Nicholas really aim to establish all his points on a *rational* basis? If he does, his notion of *ratio* must be functioning in a greatly attenuated way.[36] In fact, it is so attenuated that it scarcely qualifies as *ratio*. For example, his brief excursus on the Trinity propounds theses which, *prima facie*, do not seem to be based on rational considerations. Indeed, Nicholas speaks of the *mystery* of the Trinity—a mystery received by faith. Nonetheless, he regards the names "Oneness," "Equality," and "Union" as more suitable names for the Trinity than "Father," "Son," and "Holy Spirit."

"For these are |the terms| in which Not-other shines forth clearly. For in *oneness*, which indicates indistinction from itself and distinction from another, assuredly Not-other is discerned. And, likewise, in *equality* and in *union* Not-other manifests itself to one who is attentive."[37] But we are not given any further reason for accepting this view. Ought we, therefore, to "reject |it| as unimportant" since we are not "compelled by reason" to accept it? Revealingly, at the beginning of this very segment in Chapter 5, Nicholas explicitly mentions his recourse to reason: "All things are seen from what has been said—seen on the basis of a single rational consideration (*unica ratione*)." This rational consideration turns out to be the recognition that Not-other is not other than Not-other. Through this consideration, says Nicholas, we see *Not-other* defining itself; through it we see a Unity which is trine and a Trinity which is one.

We are now in a position to realize that Nicholas's conception of the relationship between faith and reason is not as Anselmian as the quotation from *De Li Non Aliud* 1 may have led us to suppose. For a *rational* consideration turns out to be— on his understanding of it—any consideration which elucidates an issue by rendering it in some respect more plausible. Thus, analogies, symbolisms, similes—in short, all kinds of similitudes— will count as *rationes*. (And all will be deemed *prima facie* "compelling.") Nicholas seeks these *rationes* in the common occurrences of life rather than in the esoteric teachings of the philosophers. In *Idiota de Sapientia* he rejects the Orator's contention that wisdom is so related to learning, and learning so related to the study of authorities, that wisdom cannot be attained by the unschooled. Instead, he sides with the simple Layman, who believes that wisdom cries out in the very streets and is therefore available to all who truly desire it. This belief explains why Nicholas uses such object lessons as that of the ruby (*De Li Non Aliud* 11) to illustrate certain points he wants to make about the notion of intelligible (as distinguished from perceptible) substance. Similarly, he develops an entire treatise around various comparisons which arise in regard to eyeglasses (*De Beryllo*) or in regard to an artist's painting of an omnivoyant visage (*De Visione Dei*).

Like Augustine and Anselm, Nicholas is fond of quoting Isaiah 7:9: "Unless you believe, you will not understand."[38] Like Augustine and Anselm, he does not present a precise analysis of *faith*. Instead, he is content with metaphor: "Faith enfolds within itself everything which is understandable. But understanding is the unfolding of faith. Therefore, understanding is guided by faith, and faith is increased by understanding."[39] (Here used as metaphors, the words *"complicans"* and *"explicatio"* are elsewhere used as technical terms with respect to the relationship between God and the universe. For the universe, as enfolded in God, is said to be unfolded from Him at creation.) Faith—whether the act of faith or the content of faith—is belief, but not irrational belief, thinks Nicholas. Were the content irrational, faith could not be said to be the enfolding of everything understandable; were the act irrational, the unfolding of faith could not be called understanding. The emphasis here is upon the continuity between *fides* and *intellectus*: rather than being diametrically opposed, they interpenetrate each other. Faith without understanding is blind; understanding without faith is empty and vain. The most that faith can hope for in this life is a transient *visio mystica dei*.[40] Only in the next life will there come an abiding *visio intellectualis dei*,[41] without which no mind can be at rest. But the promise of an intellectual vision of God is not the promise of a knowledge of God as He is in Himself. Rather, this vision will yield a fuller knowledge of Christ, who is the Word of God and the Concept both of Himself and of the universe.[42] Insofar as Christ is *deus revelatus*, our knowledge of Him is a knowledge of God; but it is not a knowledge of *deus absconditus*, who is Being itself, inconceivable, unknowable, and ineffable—except to Himself.[43]

We also need to consider whether or not the central line of reasoning in *De Li Non Aliud* is consistent. Part of what Nicholas has in mind in calling God Not-other is the following: God transcends all creaturely distinctions—e.g., the distinction between sky and not-sky. So He is neither *other* than the sky nor *other* than not-sky, because he transcends these very categories.[44] He is absolutely and unqualifiedly Not-other. Yet, in a broader sweep, how can God be *absolutely* Not-other if He is, nonetheless, distinct from (i.e., in some respect other than) the universe? Indeed, even one of Nicholas's citations from Pseudo-Dionysius contains the following concession: "Theology itself says that, as something other than all things, He is unlike all things and is free from all things . . . . "[45] Nicholas attempts to resolve (not dissolve) this problem by distinguishing the true formula "In *x* God is not other than *x*" from the false assertion "God is *x*." If it is false that God is the sky (or the universe), it is nevertheless true that *in the sky* (or *in the universe*) He is none other than the sky (or none other than the universe). However, it still follows that God, or Not-other, is in some respect other; otherwise, He could not in any respect be other than anything, and hence it would not be false that He is the sky (or the universe). So Nicholas's philosophy is here beset by an incoherence. For unless Not-other is absolutely Not-other (i.e., is Not-other in every respect), then Not-other will be an other—even though it will be an other in a way different from that of everything else. To escape this incoherence, Nicholas would have to embrace pantheism—a doctrine he shuns.[46]

A corresponding incoherence is reflected in Nicholas's use of the expressions "*non aliud quam . . .*" and "*non aliud a . . . .*" The former is used to signify an identity; the latter is used to avoid signifying an identity. Thus, when in *De Li Non Aliud* 6 Nicholas identifies the sky with itself, he writes: "*Caelum non aliud quam caelum |est|*"; and when at the beginning of Chapter 14 he contrasts intelligible coldness with perceptible cold, he writes: "*Frigus . . . a frigido non est aliud.*" In order to display the distinctive uses of "*non aliud quam . . .*" and "*non aliud a . . . ,*" the present translation usually renders the former expression as "not other than" (though, occasionally, also as "no other than" or "none other than"), and always renders the latter expression as "not *other* than." Accordingly, the two preceding Latin sentences will read, respectively: "The sky is not other than the sky," and "|Intelligible| coldness is not *other* than |perceptible| cold." Now, when Nicholas maintains that in the sky God is not other than the sky, he uses "*non aliud quam*," thereby signifying that in the sky God is the sky— and thereby engendering an incoherence. For although it might be true that in the sky God is not *other* than the sky (i.e., is not different from the sky), it scarcely seems true that in the sky God is identical with the sky. For if in the sky God were identical with the sky, what would be the difference between affirming that *God* is present in the sky and affirming merely that the sky is the sky? That is, if God, *qua* Not-other, is present in the sky, and if to make such an assertion is not merely to utter a circumlocution for "the sky is (not other than) the sky," then in the sky God would have to be—in some respect, even if only conceivably—distinct from the sky. And, hence, in that respect He would be an other.

To be sure, Nicholas is striving to communicate intelligibly his metaphysical conviction that the self-identity of each finite being depends in an essential way upon the presence of God's sustaining power. But his playing upon the meanings of the words "*aliud*" and "*non-aliud*" seems, at times, to obscure his point rather than to illumine it.

So *De Li Non Aliud* is a curious blend of specious reasoning and innovative speculation. Talk about being, not-being, one-ness, temporality, goodness, participation, substance, essence, creation, causation, matter, form, universality, etc., is always prone to imprecision. Nicholas, it turns out, is even more care-less than many of his predecessors regarding discourse on meta-physical themes. Nevertheless, viewed historically rather than philosophically, he is clearer and more systematic than Pseudo-Dionysius, whom he emulates. Perhaps the most flattering trib-ute we can pay him is inherent in the following conviction: if he had chosen a different intellectual hero, he would have written better philosophy. For beneath the inconsistency, equivocation,

metaphor, etc., we catch glimpses of a highly original mind—
one ingenious enough to spin out a sophisticated metaphysics
but ingenuous enough to confess that it was only "ignorance."
Just as in his mathematics he tried to square the circle, so in his
metaphysics he also aimed to do the impossible: viz., to show
that Not-other and other are not opposed.[47]

In his quest of Not-other Nicholas is motivated by the words
of Scripture, which promise that invisible things can be seen[48]
and which tell us that God is all in all.[49] Yet, the God who is
omnia in omnibus is also said to be before all and above all—
even above every name which can be named, whether in this
world or in the world to come.[50] Such a God can be approached
only *per speculum in aenigmate*.[51] Through the symbolic expression "Not-other" Nicholas seeks enlightenment, for its signification befigures the unnameable name of God.[52]

In believing that God infinitely transcends our conception of
Him, Nicholas does not believe that we ought therefore to form
no conception of Him. Rather, he enjoins us to symbolize
Divine Being. *De Li Non Aliud* provides us with paradigmatic
instances of such symbolization. In the Cusan scheme the symbolic expression "*non-aliud*" no doubt serves the same envisioned end as the symbolic expression "*possest*"—of which he
says: "this name leads the one-who-is-speculating beyond all the
senses, all reason, and all intellect unto a mystical vision, where
there is an end to the ascent of all cognitive power and where
there is the beginning of the revelation of the unknown God."[53]
Since he believes that *speculatio* is propaedeutic to *revelatio*, he
cannot rightly be expected to accede to anyone who views his
speculation as simply *curiositas vana*.

4. Textual and Translation Problems

Although there is only one reliable manuscript of the text (viz.,
Codex Latinus Monacensis 24848), a number of editorial problems
occur.[54] In 1950 Paul Wilpert called the reader's attention to
some of these problems when he published a list of *addenda et*

corrigenda for the text as printed six years earlier by the Heidelberg Academy of Letters and edited by himself. But even Wilpert failed to detect all of the necessary *corrigenda*. The present edition of the Latin text builds upon Wilpert's earlier work. Consequently, it is able to introduce various improvements. For example, in Chapter 13, at 49:19, Wilpert's transcription *"inveniri"* should be corrected to *"nivem"*; and in Chapter 14, at 69:1, *"tertio decimo"* should be changed to *"duodecimo"*, the very word contained in the manuscript.[55] Similarly, in Chapter 6, at 20:2, there should be a note indicating that instead of *"Haec"* the manuscript incorrectly has *"Nec"*. In Chapter 8 (30:19-20) the manuscript's word *"cognoscibilis"* should be retained, rather than being amended to *"cognoscibilibus"*; likewise, in Chapter 10 (38:10) *"innumerabilis"* is preferable to the editorial emendation *"innumerabiliter"*. By contrast: at 51:18, in Chapter 13, the manuscript's word *"frigus"* should be amended to *"frigidum"*. In Chapter 14 (60:2-3) *"comprehendat"* should be retained, rather than amended to *"comprehenditur"*; and, in 60:3, Wilpert's *"antequam"* should be corrected to *"anteque"*—just as in Chapter 9 (35:9) Wilpert's transcription *"ascenditur"* should be corrected to *"accenditur"*. So, too, at 59:8 of Chapter 14 his *"ipsa"* should be changed to *"ipse"*; and in Chapter 20 (93:11) his *"omni"* is correctable to *"omnium"*. Moreover, the Latin manuscript has *"universaliter"*, and not Wilpert's *"ultra"* at 112:4 of Chapter 24. And in Chapter 23 (105:13-14) the actual manuscript reading is preferable to the modifications introduced by Wilpert—as is also true for 25:2-3 in Chapter 7.

Wilpert himself was painstaking in his attempt to provide us with an accurate and readable text. Yet, like all scholarly works, his text is one that admits of revision—revision not only in such ways as the foregoing but also in its very punctuation. The understandable difficulties that Wilpert had with the punctuation at 93:4-6 display how editorial interpretation always comes to be intrinsic to the printed Latin text itself. At first he made the following transcription: *"Ideo ipsum unum, quod dicit esse ante unum, quod est unum ab eo, non est aliud, cum eius sit causa* . . . ." In the list of *corrigenda*, however, he instructs us to change the commas: "*Ideo ipsum unum, quod dicit esse ante unum, quod est unum, ab eo non est aliud, cum eius sit causa* . . . ." The actual punctuation in the manuscript favors the first reading; but Wilpert feels that the sense of the passage requires the second. Given that the punctuation in the manuscript is so impulsive, the mere fact that the manuscript suggests placing the comma after "*eo*" scarcely counts as a weighty consideration. Thus, Wilpert is right to ignore it. Indeed, he wisely recognizes that an editor cannot punctuate a text except in accordance with a particular understanding of it. Given the ambiguity of many of Nicholas's sentences, an editor is often at a loss to know exactly what is being said—i.e., what the author means. Wilpert is not among those editors and translators who sometimes pretend that they are presenting us with only an uninterpreted *report* of what a writer wrote, leaving it to the exegete to decide what the writer meant.[56] Such a posture naively disregards the fact that oftentimes we cannot determine what is being said except by deciding what is meant.

Let us look at an even better example of how interpreting and translating are often inseparable. Proposition 4 of the list of propositions following *De Li Non Aliud* states: "*Qui videt ipsum non-aliud definire se et definitionem omnia definientem, is ipsum non-aliud videt non esse aliud ab omni definitione et ab omni definito.*" An isolated reading of this sentence might well lead a translator to give something like the following rendering: "If anyone sees that *Not-other* defines itself and the definition which defines all things, he sees that *Not-other* is not *other* than every definition and everything defined."[57] But immediately the talk about defining a definition which defines all things strikes us as unusual. For everywhere else—whether in Proposition 12 or in *De Li Non Aliud* 1 (3:7-11) or in *De Venatione Sapientiae* 14 (40:1-2) or in any other of his works—Nicholas speaks of Not-other as *defining itself and all |other| things*. Even in *De Li Non*

Aliud 5 (19:15-22), where the trinitarian implications of the formula "Not-other is not other than Not-other" are expounded, he does not speak otherwise. So it would be surprising if in Proposition 4 he expressed himself in a way completely different from his accustomed way.

Yet, someone might suppose that in Proposition 4 Nicholas had in mind the following tacit line of reasoning:

> (a) Not-other defines itself.
> (b) Not-other is the definition of all things.
> So (c) Not-other defines the definition of all things.

This reasoning is unsound, as we can see from a reformulation of the meaning of the second premise:

> (a) Not-other defines itself.
> (b) Not-other defines all things.
> So (c) Not-other defines the definition of all things.

There seems little reason to ascribe this unsound thinking to Nicholas in Proposition 4, since everywhere else he reasons only conjunctively:

> (a) Not-other is the definition of itself.
> (b) Not-other is the definition of all other[58] things (including definition).
> So (c) Not-other is the definition of itself and all other things (including definition).

For him to say that Not-other is the definition of definition, as he does in Propositions 2 and 3, is but for him to present an instantiation of his statement that Not-other is the definition of all other things. Of course, it is true that in defining itself Not-other defines that which defines all things. Nonetheless, it is *not* the case that Not-other defines itself *qua* being the Definer-of-all-things; for Not-other does not define itself at all in relation to the world. Moreover, I suspect that Nicholas would regard the expression "the definition of the definition of all other things (including definition)" as bizarre.

In this light, what are we to make of the Latin passage in

Proposition 4? At this point we may recall that, *as a matter of style*, Nicholas frequently omits the verb "*esse*" from statements in indirect discourse. Has this stylistic feature occurred in the present case? Well, when we assume that it has, we get the following reading: "If anyone sees that *Not-other* defines itself and is the definition which defines all things . . . . " And this reading accords with every other passage in which definition is discussed. It seems, then, to be not only the preferable construal but also the assuredly correct one. Now, any translator who claims to be avoiding all interpretation by *setting down what Nicholas said, not what he meant*,[59] will pay the price of making a mistake; for such a translator will fail to supply the verb "*esse*," which Nicholas intends but leaves unexpressed. Yet, even if the translation that failed to supply "*esse*" were not mistaken, it would still be just as much an interpretive translation as the alternative rendering that it excluded!

Looking at other aspects of Nicholas's style, we see that he sometimes uses "*ipsum*" as an intensive, sometimes merely as a case indicator, and sometimes as a substitute for the definite article, which Latin lacks. Similarly, "*hoc*" and "*illud*" may serve either as demonstratives or as substitutes for the definite article. An instance of such a substitution occurs at 47:16: "*Universum vero illud utique aliud video*": "I see that, assuredly, the universe is an other."[60] Similarly, at 113:1 ("*in una . . . mente*") we find "*una*" being used as a substitute for the indefinite article, which Latin also lacks.

In accordance with Codex Latinus Monacensis 24848 the title of the present work should be not simply "*De Non Aliud*" but "*De Li Non Aliud*." Since the word "*li*" is not commonly found, one immediately wonders how it functions in the title. R. E. Latham's *Revised Medieval Latin Word-List* (Oxford University Press, 1965) contains the following entry for "*li*": "article introducing word to be considered simply as such, not as object denoted . . . . " And, in fact, Nicholas does at times use the article in this way. For example, 95:15-17 reads: "*Nam cum non-aliud dico non aliud quam non-aliud, li quam in non-aliud visum simpliciter dirigit, uti ante aliud est*": "For when I say that Not-other is not other than Not-other, the word 'than' simply directs sight to Not-other insofar as it is prior to other." And 33:4-6 has "*Sed sine verbo visionem communicare non valentes, sine li esse, quod non est explicare non possumus . . .*": "But since we are unable to communicate the vision apart from words, we cannot without recourse to the verb 'to be' discourse about what is not . . . ."

But Nicholas does not uniformly use "*li*" to indicate that he is mentioning a word. That is, sometimes he mentions a word without prefacing it by "*li*," and sometimes he prefaces a word by "*li*" but is not mentioning it. Earlier[61] we saw an example of the former practice; 119:1 and 94:1-2 are instances of the latter.[62] Accordingly, the entry in Latham's word-list does not fully capture Nicholas's usage (nor, for that matter, does it purport to). For although "*li*" sometimes indicates that a word is being mentioned (e.g., in 95:2), its occurrence with "*non-aliud*" typically indicates that "*non-aliud*" is functioning not as a simple connective but as a noun. Accordingly, the title "*De Li Non Aliud*" is best translated with the help of a hyphen: "On Not-other." Within the Latin text itself, Wilpert often should have utilized the transcription "*non-aliud*" instead of " '*non aliud*,' " because the single quotes are suggestive of an expression which is being mentioned.

In last analysis, then, the word "*li*" in the phrase "*li non aliud*" has one of the same functions that the word "*ipsum*" usually has in the phrase "*ipsum non aliud*."[63] Moreover, both "*li*" and "*ipsum*" are employed sporadically rather than uniformly.

Just as there are difficulties of the foregoing sort, so there are difficulties with vocabulary. For example, "*comprehendo*" and "*apprehendo*" are not systematically distinguished. Moreover, phrases such as "*de quidditatis essentia*"[64] are utilized in spite of the fact that "*essentia*" and "*quidditas*" often are used synonymously. At 120:8 and 121:2 "*in quid*" and "*in quidditatem*" are used interchangeably, as are "*nominant*" and "*nuncupant*" at 19:5 and

8, and "*substantia*" and "*essentia*" at 41:19 and 22. "*Quasi*" is used with both the indicative and the subjunctive in the sense of "as," making it difficult to determine whether or not it should be translated by the expression "as if" at 101:6, where it governs the subjunctive (even though in the preceding two lines there was an occurrence of it which governed the indicative). "*Quando*" is used to mean "when," "since," and "if," whether or not it is accompanied by the subjunctive.[65] And "*dum*" is used in the sense of "when," "while," and "although," irrespective of the mood of the verb which follows.[66]

To be sure, examples of parallel difficulties are to be found in the texts of all medieval Latin writers. But in philosophical and theological writings they create more havoc than in, say, straight historical narrative.

5. Conclusion

Nicholas of Cusa's thoughts are not easy to determine, given the imprecisions of the language in which they are expressed. Having abandoned a technical, scholasticlike terminology, Cusa appears at times to use words as if to stimulate the imagination rather than to sharpen the understanding. This quasi-poetic use of language— rich as it is with metaphor—is intrinsic to the speculative Neoplatonic tradition. Such sentences as "*Deus est oppositio nihil mediatione entis*"[67] capture our fancy just as surely as does the refrain:

> *Li non aliud, quod est ipsius non-aliud non-aliud, relucet in aeterno, ubi est aeternae aeternitatis aeternitas, et in vero, ubi verae veritatis est veritas, et in bono, ubi bonae bonitatis est bonitas . . . . Unitrinum non-aliud in uno est unius unitatis unitas, et in ente entis entitatis entitas, et in magnitudine magnae magnitudinis magnitudo, et in quanto quantae quantitatis quantitas . . . .*[68]

Nicholas orchestrates his motif in order to enhance its suggestive power, for he seeks a Truth which he believes the intellect can never stand to gaze upon directly. In last analysis, we can approach it in this present lifetime only by way of conjecture and surmise and only insofar as these latter are "reasonable" rather than arbitrary. Upon occasion Nicholas slips into scholastic language and uses, with respect to his metaphysical claims, words such as "indubitable," "compelling," and "necessary." But, really, these adjectives are components of overstatements which spring (ironically) from an exuberant disregard of scholastic criteria of argumentation. In his more cautious moments he is content to say, more moderately: "*Optime et rationabiliter imprimis dicis*": "You speak very rightly and very reasonably."[69] Of course, he harbors the hope that God, breaking through all our conjecture and surmise, "will some day reveal Himself to us without a symbolism."[70] And this hope no doubt explains why Ferdinand can remark at the beginning of the dialogue: "You seem to grow young when, prodded, you discourse about the truth."

In recent years there has been some attempt to consider Nicholas as the existential hero of the fifteenth century. For he views the human being as unable to transcend the cognitive limitations of the human situation, as therefore doomed to the level of symbolism and of learned ignorance, and yet as constantly striving after a knowledge of the Infinite. In such a state—so Nicholas is said to have believed—the human being comes to feel strangely free. According to Van Velthoven, "*Wir stehen hier also vor der paradoxen Situation, dass die Erfahrung des Versagens seiner Kräfte den Menschen nicht entmutigt oder sein Streben lähmt, sondern im Gegenteil ihm ein Gefühl der Befreiung schenkt und ihn positiv anregt.*"[71] Similarly, Rose Finkenstaedt emphasizes a passage in *De Visione Dei* 7 which she deems to speak of God's "compelling," as it were, our freedom.[72] She goes on to remark:

> When Cusa resigned himself to the insolubility of the rational effort on earth, he was able to resign himself to the struggle of living, like Milton in the last part of *Paradise Lost*, or Goethe in the last part of *Faust*. It is a resignation which Hummel calls "obedience to oneself and to God." For by resigning himself to the voluntary exercise of his rational will, man gives up his expectation of reaching truth, and simply endures the continual dichotomy of his nature between his insatiable desire to know and the truth which remains unknowable.
>
> However, this resignation to God's will through the paradox of free will

is a heroic gesture, and, from this point of view, it is the dignity of rational man.[73]

Advocates of this interpretation find no better illustration of it than in the dialogue *De Li Non Aliud*. For throughout this entire piece Nicholas presents himself as groping toward truth by means of the enigmatic symbolism *Not-other*. It is not a readily graspable symbolism of the sort which provides the respective themes for *De Beryllo, De Visione Dei, De Possest,* and *De Ludo Globi*. Rather, by its very paradoxical character (e.g., "Not-other is not other; nor is it *other* than other; nor is it other in an other")[74] it is intended to remind us of the limitations of human cognition.

And yet, all things considered, the existential-heroic-romantic interpretation of Cusa's role at the dawn of Renaissance philosophy miscasts the emphasis of his thought. For Cusa is primarily a mystic and a Neoplatonist. As such, to be sure, he does teach that Reality itself—viz., God—is unknowable and that the human intellect can never overcome the disproportion between the finite and the Infinite. But his response to this unknowability and this disproportionality is found not in existential liberation, romantic longing, and heroic resignation but in his doctrine of *mystica visio*: the soul of the devout religious believer not only strives after, but indeed can really attain unto, mystical encounter with God. Surely, what Nicholas says about the name "*possest*" he also believes in regard to the name "*non-aliud*":

> This name leads the one-who-is-speculating beyond all the senses, all reason, and all intellect unto a mystical vision, where there is an end to the ascent of all cognitive power and where there is the beginning of the revelation of the unknown God. For, having left all things behind, the seeker-after-truth ascends beyond himself and discerns that he still does not have any greater access to the invisible God, who remains invisible to him. (For God is not seen by means of any light from the seeker's own reason.) At this point the seeker awaits, with the most devout longing, the Omnipotent Sun—expecting that when darkness is banished by its rising, he will be illumined, so that he will see the invisible |God| to the extent that God will manifest Himself.[75]

Thus, if anything, the limitations of the human intellect—

limitations which prevent our cognizing the Infinite—open the way for a noncognitive encounter which takes place mystically and Neoplatonically. For it is an encounter, somewhere beyond being and not-being, with the Being of being and the Not-being of not-being.

on not-other

de li non aliud

ı de li non aliud

ABBAS: Tu nosti nos tres, qui studio dediti tecum colloqui admittimur, in altis versari: ego enim in Parmenide Proculique
5 commentariis, Petrus vero in theologia Platonis eiusdem Proculi, quam de graeca latinam facit, Ferdinandus autem Aristotelis per- lustrat ingenium; tu vero, cum vacat, in Areopagita Dionysio theologo versaris. Gauderemus audire an ne ad illa quae per iam dictos tractantur, compendiosior tibi clariorque occurrat modus.
10   NICOLAUS: Undique circa profunda mysteria occupamur; ne- que, ut | credo, brevius quisquam faciliusque illa diceret, quam 2^v hii quos lectitamus, licet mihi aliquando visum sit illud per nos negligi, quod propinquius nos duceret ad quaesitum.

PETRUS: Hoc aperiri deposcimus.

2   FERDINANDUS: Ita omnes veritate afficimur quod, ipsam undi- que reperibilem scientes, illum habere magistrum optamus, qui ipsam nostrae mentis oculis anteponat. Tu autem te infatigabi- lem ostendis in eo etiam tuo declinante senio; et quando pulsa-
5 tus de ipsa loqueris, videris iuvenescere. Dicito igitur tu illud quod prae nobis ipse considerasti.

---

1 1 Tetralogus Cuse de li non aliud, cuius meminit in tractatu de Venacione sapiencie, campo tercio *habet S in folio 1*^r   Iesus Christus. Reverendissimi in Christo patris et domini Nicolai de Cusa cardinalis Sancti Petri ad vincula libellus incipit, qui inscribitur Directio speculantis. Interlocutores sunt cum cardinale Ioannes Andreas Vigevius Abbas, Petrus Balbus Pisanus, Ferdinandus Matim portugallensis nacione *habet S in folio 2*^r *ante* Capitulum primum

1 On not-otheR

ABBOT:[1] You know that we three, who are engaged in study and are permitted to converse with you, are occupied with deep matters. For I |am busy| with the *Parmenides* and with Proclus's commentary |thereon|; Peter |is occupied| with this same Proclus's *Theology of Plato*, which he is translating from Greek into Latin; Ferdinand is surveying the genius of Aristotle; and you, when you have time, are busy with the theologian Dionysius the Areopagite. We would like to hear whether or not there occurs to you a briefer and clearer route to the points which are dealt with by the aforenamed |individuals|.

NICHOLAS: In our respective directions we are busy with deep mysteries. And it seems to me that no one can speak of these matters more briefly and clearly than those whom we are reading. Nonetheless, I have sometimes thought that we have neglected a |point| which would lead us closer to what is sought.

PETER: We ask that this |point| be made known |to us|.

2   FERDINAND: We are all so influenced by the truth that, knowing it to be discoverable everywhere, we desire to have that teacher who will place it before the eyes of our mind. Now, you show yourself to be tireless in your declining years; and you seem to grow young when, prodded, you discourse about the truth. So speak of that which you have reflected upon more than have we.

2 1 veritate: veritati *SU*
2 5 Dicito: tu *post* Dicito *scribit, del., et post* igitur *rescribit* S

31

NICOLAUS: Dicam et tecum, Ferdinande, hoc pacto colloquar: quod omnia quae a me audies, nisi compellaris ratione, ut levia abicias.

10 FERDINANDUS: Sic philosophi, praeceptores mei, agendum esse docuerunt.

3 NICOLAUS: Abs te igitur imprimis quaero: quid est quod nos apprime facit scire?

FERDINANDUS: Definitio.

NICOLAUS: Recte respondes; nam oratio seu ratio est definitio.
5 Sed unde dicitur definitio?

FERDINANDUS: A definiendo, quia omnia definit.

NICOLAUS: Bene sane! Si igitur omnia definit definitio, et se ipsam igitur definit?

FERDINANDUS: Utique, cum nihil excludat. |

10 NICOLAUS: Vides igitur definitionem omnia definientem esse 3ʳ non aliud quam definitum?

FERDINANDUS: Video, cum sui ipsius sit definitio. Sed quaenam sit illa, non video.

NICOLAUS: Clarissime tibi ipsam expressi. Et hoc est id quod
15 dixi nos negligere in venationis cursu quaesitum praetereuntes.

FERDINANDUS: Quando expressisti?

NICOLAUS: Iam statim, quando dixi definitionem omnia definientem esse non aliud quam definitum.

FERDINANDUS: Nondum te capio.

4 NICOLAUS: Pauca quae dixi, facile rimantur, in quibus reperies non-aliud; quodsi toto nisu mentis aciem ad li non aliud convertis, mecum ipsum definitionem se et omnia definientem videbis.

FERDINANDUS: Instrue nos quonam modo id fiat; nam magnum est quod affirmas et nondum credibile.

NICHOLAS: I shall speak and converse with you, Ferdinand, |but only| on the following condition: viz., that unless you are compelled by reason, you will reject as unimportant everything you will hear from me.[2]

FERDINAND: My teachers, the philosophers, have taught that one ought to proceed in this way.

3   NICHOLAS: I ask you, then, first of all, what is it that most of all gives us knowledge?

FERDINAND: Definition.

NICHOLAS: You answer correctly, for the definition is the constituting ground (*oratio seu ratio*).[3] But on what basis is |definition| called definition?

FERDINAND: On the basis of defining, since it defines everything.

NICHOLAS: Perfectly correct. Hence, if definition defines everything, then does it define even itself?

FERDINAND: Certainly, since it excludes nothing.

NICHOLAS: Do you see, then, that the definition which defines everything is not other than what is defined?[4]

FERDINAND: I see |this|, since |this definition| is the definition of itself. But I do not see what this definition is.

NICHOLAS: I expressed it to you most plainly. (This is what I said we have neglected and passed over in the course of tracking down what is sought.)

FERDINAND: When did you express |it|?

NICHOLAS: Just now, when I said that the definition which defines everything is not other than what is defined.

FERDINAND: I do not yet understand you.

4   NICHOLAS: The few things which I have stated are easily investigated. Among them you will find *Not-other*. And if with all your might you turn the acute gaze of your mind toward *Not-other*, you will see with me the definition which defines itself and everything.

FERDINAND: Teach us how to do it; for what you assert is important, though not yet plausible.

NICOLAUS: Responde igitur mihi: quid est non-aliud? Estne aliud quam non-aliud?

FERDINANDUS: Nequaquam aliud.

NICOLAUS: Igitur non-aliud.

10 FERDINANDUS: Hoc certum est.

NICOLAUS: Definias igitur non-aliud.

FERDINANDUS: Video equidem bene, quomodo non-aliud est non aliud quam non-aliud. Et hoc negabit nemo.

NICOLAUS: Verum dicis. Nonne nunc certissime vides non-
15 aliud se ipsum definire, cum per | aliud definiri non possit?   *3ʳ*

FERDINANDUS: Video certe, sed nondum constat ipsum omnia definire.

5 NICOLAUS: Nihil cognitu facilius. Quid enim responderes si quis te "quid est aliud?" interrogaret? Nonne diceres: "non aliud quam aliud"? Sic, "quid caelum?", responderes: "non aliud quam caelum."

5 FERDINANDUS: Utique veraciter sic respondere possem de omnibus quae a me definiri expeterentur.

NICOLAUS: Cum igitur nihil maneat dubii, quin hic definiendi modus, quo non-aliud se et omnia definit, praecisissimus sit atque verissimus, non restat nisi circa ipsum attente immorari et
10 quae humanitus sciri possunt reperire.

FERDINANDUS: Mira dicis et promittis. Cuperem quidem imprimis audire, si quis palam hoc expresserit ex omnibus contemplativis.

NICOLAUS: Licet nullum legerim, prae ceteris tamen Dionysius
15 propinquius videtur accessisse. Nam in omnibus quae varie exprimit, non-aliud ipse dilucidat. Quando vero ad finem Mysticae pervenit theologiae, creatorem affirmat neque quidquam nominabile, neque aliud quid esse. Sic tamen hoc dicit, quod

4 15 definiri: definire *S* definiri *U*

NICHOLAS: Tell me, then, what is Not-other? Is it other than Not-other?

FERDINAND: Not at all other.

NICHOLAS: So |it is| Not-other.

FERDINAND: This is certain.

NICHOLAS: Then, define *Not-other.*

FERDINAND: Indeed, I see clearly how it is that Not-other is not other than Not-other. No one will deny this.

NICHOLAS: You speak the truth. Don't you now see most assuredly that *Not-other* defines itself, since it cannot be defined by means of |any| other?

FERDINAND: I see |this| assuredly. But it is not yet evident that *Not-other* defines everything.

5   NICHOLAS: Nothing is easier to recognize. For what would you answer if someone asked you, "What is *other?*" Would you not reply, "Not other than other"? Likewise, |if someone asked you| "What is the sky?" you would reply, "Not other than the sky."

FERDINAND: Assuredly, I could truthfully reply in this way regarding everything which I would be asked to define.

NICHOLAS: Therefore, since there is no remaining doubt that the mode of defining by which *Not-other* defines itself and every |other| 5 thing is most precise and most true, there remains |for us| only to dwell attentively upon it and to discover what can be humanly known about it.

FERDINAND: You state and promise wonderful things. I would like to learn, in the first place, whether anyone among all the speculative thinkers ever explicitly expressed the foregoing |point|.

NICHOLAS: Although I have read |it in| no one, nevertheless Dionysius (more than the others) seems to have come the closest |to it|. For, in all the things which he expresses in various ways, he elucidates *Not-other.* But when he comes to the end of his *Mystical Theology,* he maintains that the Creator is neither anything nameable nor any other thing whatever.6 Yet, he says this in such way that he there appears not to be setting forth any

non videatur ibi magni aliquid propalare, quamvis intendenti
20 non-aliud secretum | expresserit undique per ipsum aliter expli- *4ʳ*
catum.

6   CAPITULUM II

FERDINANDUS: Cum cuncti primum principium deum appellent, videris tu quidem ipsum per li non aliud velle significari.
Primum enim ipsum fateri oportet, quod et se ipsum et omnia
5 definit; nam cum primo non sit prius, sitque ab omnibus posteri-
oribus absolutum, utique non nisi per semetipsum definitur.
Principiatum vero cum a se nihil, sed, quidquid est, habeat a
principio, profecto principium est ratio essendi eius seu definitio.
NICOLAUS: Bene me capis, Ferdinande. Nam etsi primo prin-
10 cipio multa attribuantur nomina, quorum nullum ei adaequatum
esse potest, cum sit etiam nominum omnium sicut et rerum
principium, et nihil principiati omnia antecedat, per unum
tamen significandi modum mentis acie praecisius videtur quam
per alium. Neque hactenus equidem comperi quodcumque signi-
15 ficatum humanum visum rectius in primum dirigere. Nam omne
significatum quod in aliquid aliud sive in aliud ipsum termi-
natur, | quemadmodum alia omnia sunt ab ipso non-aliud, *4ᵛ*
utique non dirigunt in principium.
7   FERDINANDUS: Video quae dicis sane sic se habere. Nam
aliud, terminus visionis, principium videntis esse non potest.
Aliud enim cum sit non aliud quam aliud, utique non-aliud
praesupponit, sine quo non foret aliud. Omne igitur significatum
5 aliud a significato ipsius "non-aliud" in alio quam in principio
terminatur. Hoc certe verum perspicio.
NICHOLAS: Optime! Cum nos autem alter alteri suam non
possimus revelare visionem nisi per vocabulorum significatum,

---

6 7 Principiatum: Principatum *S* Principiatum *U*
6 12 antecedat: antecedit *SU*
7 8 possimus: possumus *S* possimus *U*

important point—although, for one who is attentive, he expressed the secret of Not-other, which secret he everywhere exhibited in one way or another.

6   CHAPTER 2

FERDINAND: Since all call the First Beginning *God*, you seem to intend for Him to be signified by the words "Not-other." For we must maintain that the First is that which defines both itself and all |others|. For since there is not anything prior to the First and since the First is independent of everything posterior, assuredly it is defined only through itself. But since what is originated has nothing from itself but has from the Beginning whatever it is, assuredly the Beginning is the ground of being, or the definition, of what is originated.

NICHOLAS: You understand me well, Ferdinand. For, to be sure, many names are attributed to the First Beginning, none of which can be adequate to it, since it is the Beginning of all names as well as of all things (and nothing that is originated precedes all things). Nevertheless, the mind's acute gaze sees the Beginning more precisely through one mode of signifying than through another.[7] Indeed, I have not previously found that any signification directs human sight unto the First more accurately |than does the signification of "Not-other"|. For |with regard to| any signification which terminates in something other or in other itself: just as all things[8] are *other* than Not-other, so, assuredly, they do not direct unto the Beginning.

7   FERDINAND: I see that what you say is surely so. For other, which is the terminal end of vision, cannot be the beginning of seeing. For since other is not other than other, surely it presupposes Not-other, without which it would not be other. Therefore, every signification that is *other* than the signification of "Not-other" terminates in something other than in the Beginning. I see that this |point| is certainly true.

NICHOLAS: Very good. Since each of us can disclose his own observation to the other only by means of the signification of

praecisius utique li non aliud non occurrit, licet non sit nomen
10 dei quod est ante omne nomen in caelo et terra nominabile,
sicut via peregrinantem ad civitatem dirigens non est nomen
civitatis.

FERDINANDUS: Sic est, ut dicis, et hoc clare conspicio, quando
deum esse non aliud quam deum video et aliquid non aliud
15 quam aliquid et nihil non aliud quam nihil et non-ens non aliud
quam non-ens et ita de omnibus quae qualitercumque dici possunt. Per hoc enim video non-aliud talia omnia antecedere, quia
ipsa definit, et ipsa alia esse, cum non-aliud antecedat.

NICOLAUS: Placet mihi mentis tuae promptitudo et vivacitas,
20 quia et bene | capis et cito quae volo. Ex his igitur nunc plane 5ʳ
vides de li non aliud significatum non solum ut viam nobis ser-
vire ad principium, sed innominabile nomen dei propinquius
figurare, ut in ipso tamquam in pretiosiori aenigmate relucescat
inquirentibus.

8   CAPITULUM III

FERDINANDUS: Quamvis appareat te per li non aliud videre
principium essendi et cognoscendi, tamen nisi idipsum mihi clarius ostendas, non percipio.
5   NICOLAUS: Dicunt theologi deum nobis in lucis aenigmate
clarius relucere, quia per sensibilia scandimus ad intelligibilia.
Lux profecto ipsa, quae deus, ante aliam est lucem qualitercumque nominabilem et ante aliud simpliciter. Id vero quod
ante aliud videtur, non est aliud. Lux igitur illa, cum sit ipsum
10 non-aliud et non lux nominabilis, in sensibili lucet lumine. Sed
sensibilis lux visui comparata sensibili ita sese habere aliqualiter

---

7 14 esse: qua *post* esse *scribit et del.* S
8 2 videre: videri S videre U

words, surely |this disclosure| occurs no more precisely than with the words "Not-other." Nevertheless, "Not-other" is not that name of God which is before every name nameable in Heaven and on earth.[9] (By comparison, the way which directs a pilgrim to a city is not the name of that city.)

FERDINAND: The matter is as you say. And I see it clearly when I see that God is not other than God, something is not other than something, nothing is not other than nothing, not-being is not other than not-being—and so on regarding all the things which can be spoken of in whatever way. For I see that *Not-other* precedes all such things by virtue of the fact that it defines these things,[10] and |I see that| these things are other since Not-other precedes |them|.

NICHOLAS: The quickness and alertness of your mind pleases me, for you grasp rightly and immediately what I mean. From these |considerations|, then, you now recognize clearly regarding the expression "Not-other" that its signification not only serves us as a way to the Beginning but also quite closely befigures the unnameable name of God, so that in this signification—just as in a quite precious symbolism—|God| shines forth to those who are searching.

8   CHAPTER 3

FERDINAND: Although it is evident that by means of the expression "Not-other" you see the Beginning of being and of knowing, still unless you disclose it more clearly to me, I shall not see it.

NICHOLAS: The theologians state that God shines forth to us more clearly in the symbolism of light, since we ascend to intelligible things by means of perceptible things. Surely, Light itself, which is God, is prior to |any| other light, howsoever nameable, and is prior to |any| other at all. Now, that which is seen prior to other is not other. Therefore, since that Light is Not-other and is not a nameable light, it shines forth in perceptual light. But perceptual light is in some way conceived to be related to

concipitur, sicut lux quae non-aliud, ad omnia quae mente videri queunt. Visum autem sensibilem absque luce sensibili nihil videre experimur, et visibilem colorem non esse nisi sensi-
15 bilis lucis terminationem sive | definitionem, ut iris ostendit; et 5ʳ ita sensibilis lux principium est essendi et visibile sensibile cognoscendi. Ita quidem conicimus principium essendi esse et principium cognoscendi.

9   FERDINANDUS: Clara manuductio et grata! Nam sic se habet in auditu sensibili. Sonus enim est principium essendi audibilis et cognoscendi. Deus igitur per "non-aliud" significatus essendi et cognoscendi omnibus principium est. Quem si quis subtrahit,
5 nihil manet neque in re neque in cognitione. Quemadmodum luce subtracta iris aut visibile nec est nec videtur, et sublato sono nec est audibile nec auditur, sic subtracto non-aliud neque est nec cognoscitur quidquam. Ista mihi sic se habere certissime teneo.

10   NICOLAUS: Utique bene tenes; sed advertas, quaeso: dum aliquid vides, puta lapidem quempiam, licet non consideres, non tamen nisi per lucem ipsum vides. Et ita dum aliquid audis, non nisi per sonum audis, quamvis non attendas. Prioriter igitur essendi cognoscendique principium sese offert tamquam sine
15 quo frustra ad videndum intenderes seu audiendum. Ceterum quia ad aliud, quod videre cupis audireve, est | intentio, in princi- 6ʳ pii consideratione non defigeris, quamquam id principium, medium, et finis est quaesiti.

10 Eodem modo in non-aliud adverte. Nam cum omne quod quidem est, sit non aliud quam idipsum, hoc utique non habet aliunde; a non-alio igitur habet. Non igitur aut est aut cognoscitur

9 3 et: *om. S* habet U

perceptual seeing as the Light which is Not-other |is related| to all the things which can be mentally seen. But we know from experience that perceptual sight sees nothing without perceptual light and that visible color is only the delimiting, or defining, of perceptual light—as |the example of| a rainbow shows. Thus, perceptual light is the beginning of both being and knowing what is visible and perceptible. Thus, we surmise that the Beginning of being is also the Beginning of knowing.

9   FERDINAND: Clear and gratifying guidance! Now, the same thing holds true of perceptual hearing. For sound is the beginning of both being and knowing what is audible. Therefore, God, who is signified by "Not-other" is, for all things, the Beginning of being and of knowing. If anyone were to remove God, nothing would remain either in reality or in knowledge. Just as when light is removed, no rainbow or visible thing either exists or is seen, and when sound is removed, no audible thing either exists or is heard, so when Not-other is removed, there is no thing which either exists or is known. For my part, I most surely regard these matters to be thus.

NICHOLAS: Assuredly, you understand well. But pay attention |to the following|, I request. When you see something—e.g., any stone—you see it only by means of light, even though you do not pay attention to |the light|. And similarly, when you hear something, you hear it only by means of sound, even though you do not attend to |the sound|. Hence, the beginning of being and of knowing presents itself antecedently |and| as |something| without which you would endeavor in vain to see and to hear. Nonetheless, the reason you are not intent upon a consideration of the beginning—even though it is the beginning, the middle, and the end of what is sought—is that your attention is directed toward some other thing which you wish to see or to hear.

10   In the same way, give heed to *Not-other*. Since everything which exists is not other than itself, assuredly it does not have this fact from any other. Therefore, it has it from Not-other.[11] Hence, |everything which exists| is that which it is, and is

esse id quod est, nisi per non-aliud, quae quidem est eius causa,
5 adaequatissima ratio scilicet sive definitio, quae sese prioriter
offert, quia principium, medium, et finis per mentem quaesiti;
sed nequaquam iuxta esse consideratur, quando quidem id quod
quaeritur, quaeratur ut aliud. Nam proprie non quaeritur principium, quod quaesitum semper antecedit, et sine quo quaesitum
10 minime quaeri potest. Quaerit autem omnis quaerens attrectare
principium, si id, ut Paulus ait, valeret. Quod quoniam fieri
nequit, veluti in sese est, ante aliud quaerens ipsum, cum ipse sit
aliud, ipsum sane quaerit in alio, sicut lux, quae in se est per
hominis visum invisibilis, ut in solaris lucis exprimitur puritate,
15 videri quaeritur in visibili. Neque enim opus est lucem quaeri,
quae se ipsam [prioriter offert, cum sit] alioquin incomprehensi-
bilis, oporteret enim lucem lu|ce quaeri. Lux igitur in visibili, *6ʳ*
ubi percipiatur, exquiritur, ut sic saltem attrectabiliter videatur.

11   CAPITULUM IV

FERDINANDUS: Circa non-aliud immorandum admonuisti; ob
maxima igitur tua promissa abire nequaquam festinabo; dic
ergo: quid tu per "non-aliud" intelligis?
5   NICOLAUS: Id quod ipsum intelligo, per alia aliter exprimi
nequit; nam omnis post ipsum foret alia expositio et minus ipso
profecto. Id enim quod per ipsum mens conatur videre, cum
omnia quae aut dici aut cogitari possunt antecedat, quonam
modo aliter dicetur? Omnes enim theologi deum viderunt quid
10 maius esse quam concipi posset, et idcirco "supersubstantialem,"
"supra omne nomen," et consimilia de ipso affirmarunt, neque
aliud per "super," aliud per "sine," aliud per "in," aliud per

10 16 prioriter offert, cum sit: *supplevi*

known to be that which it is, only through Not-other, which is its Cause, its most adequate Constituting Ground—or Definition—and which presents itself antecendently, because it is the Beginning, the Middle, and the End of what is sought by the mind. But when that which is sought is sought as an other, it is not at all considered as it is. For the Beginning—which always precedes what is sought and without which what is sought cannot at all be sought—is not a proper object of seeking. Now, everyone who seeks seeks to find the Beginning, if, as Paul says,[12] this is possible. But since it cannot be found as it is in itself, the one seeking it before any other thing rightly seeks it in another, since he himself is an other. Similarly, light—which in itself is invisible with respect to human sight (as is illustrated in the case of pure sunlight)—is looked for in what is visible. Indeed, it is not even necessary to look for light, which presents itself antecedently (for otherwise it would be inapprehensible, since we would have to look for it with light). Therefore, light is sought in what-is-visible, where it is perceived; thus, in this way it is seen at least gropingly.

11 CHAPTER 4

FERDINAND: You counseled that we ought to linger upon *Not-other.* So on account of the important points which you have promised, I shall not at all hasten to leave it. Tell me, then, what do you understand by "Not-other"?

NICHOLAS: That which I understand Not-other to be cannot be expressed in different ways by different |words|; for surely every exposition of it in other terms would be posterior and inferior to it. For since that which the mind tries to see with respect to Not-other precedes all the things which can be either stated or thought, how can we speak of it in other terms? All theologians have recognized that God is something greater than can be conceived;[13] and hence they affirmed that He is supersubstantial, and above every name, and the like. In the case of God they have not expressed to us one thing by "super,"

"non," et per "ante" nobis in deo expresserunt; nam idem est
ipsum esse substantiam supersubstantialem, et substantiam sine
15 substantia, et substantiam insubstantialem, et substantiam non-
substantialem, et substantiam ante substantiam. Qualitercumque
autem dixeris, cum id ipsum quod dicis, non aliud | sit quam   7ʳ
idem ipsum, patet non-aliud simplicius et prius esse per aliudque
ineloquibile atque inexpressibile.

12   FERDINANDUS: Visne dicere "non-aliud" affirmationem esse
vel negationem vel eius generis tale?

NICOLAUS: Nequaquam, sed ante omnia talia; et istud est
quod per oppositorum coincidentiam annis multis quaesivi, ut
5 libelli multi quos de hac speculatione conscripsi ostendunt.

FERDINANDUS: Ponitne non-aliud aliquid, aut aufert aliquid?

NICOLAUS: Videtur ante omnem positionem atque ablationem.

FERDINANDUS: Neque igitur est substantia neque ens neque
unum neque aliud quodcumque.

10   NICOLAUS: Sic equidem video.

FERDINANDUS: Eo pacto neque non-ens nec nihil.

NICOLAUS: Et hoc utique sic video.

FERDINANDUS: Sequor te, pater, quantum valeo, mihique videtur certissimum non-aliud nec affirmatione negationeve aut alio
15 quolibet modo comprehendi, sed mirum in modum ad aeternum ipsum videtur accedere.

NICOLAUS: Stabile, firmum, aeternum multum de non-aliud
videntur participare, cum alteritatem aut mutationem non-aliud
nequaquam possit accipere. Cum tamen aeternum sit non aliud
20 quam aeternum, erit sane aeternum aliud quidem quam non-
aliud; | et ideo ipsum ante aeternum et ante saecula perspicio   7ᵛ
supra omnem esse comprehensionem.

---

12 16 accedere: alias aspirare *in marg. explanat* S

another by "without," another by "in," another by "non," and |another| by "before"; for it is the same thing for God to be supersubstantial Substance, Substance without substance, insubstantial Substance, nonsubstantial Substance, and Substance before substance. Regardless of what words you use: since that of which you speak is not other than the self-same thing, it is evident that Not-other is simpler and prior and is inexpressible and unutterable in |any| other |terms|.

12   FERDINAND: Do you wish to say that *Not-other* is an affirmation or a negation or some such kind of thing?

NICHOLAS: Not at all. Rather, |I wish to say that it is| before all such things. It is that which for many years I sought by way of the coincidence of opposites—as the many books which I have written about this speculative matter bear witness.

FERDINAND: Does *Not-other* posit something, or does it remove something?

NICHOLAS: It is seen prior to all positing and removing.

FERDINAND: Therefore, it is not a substance or a being or one or any other thing whatsoever.

NICHOLAS: This is my view.

FERDINAND: By the same token, it is neither not-being nor nothing.

NICHOLAS: This too I regard as surely the case.

FERDINAND: I am following you, Father, as best I can. And it seems to me most certain that Not-other is not comprehended either by way of affirmation or by way of negation or in any other way.[14] But in a wonderful way it seems to approach the eternal itself.

NICHOLAS: The stable, the firm, and the eternal seem to participate a great deal in Not-other, since Not-other cannot at all receive otherness or change. Nevertheless, since the eternal is not other than the eternal, the eternal will indeed be something other than Not-other. And so, I see that Not-other, which is before the eternal and before the aeons, is beyond all comprehension.

13   FERDINANDUS: Ita quidem necesse est omnem quemcumque tecum perspicientem dicere, quando ad omnium quae dici possunt intendit antecedens. Verum equidem miror quomodo unum et ens et verum et bonum post ipsum existant.

5   NICOLAUS: Quamvis unum propinquum admodum ad non-aliud videatur, quando quidem omne aut unum dicatur aut aliud, ita quod unum quasi non-aliud appareat, nihilominus tamen unum, cum nihil aliud quam unum sit, aliud est ab ipso non-aliud. Igitur non-aliud est simplicius uno, cum ab ipso non-
10 aliud habeat quod sit unum; et non e converso. Enimvero quidam theologi unum pro non-aliud accipientes ipsum unum ante contradictionem perspexerunt, quemadmodum in Platonis Parmenide legitur atque [in] Areopagita Dionysio. Tamen, cum unum sit aliud a non uno, nequaquam dirigit in primum
15 omnium principium, quod sive ab alio sive a nihilo aliud esse non potest, quod item nulli est contrarium, ut inferius videbis.

14   Eodem modo de ente considera; nam etsi in ipso | non-aliud *8ʳ* clare videatur elucere, cum eorum quae sunt, aliud ab aliquo minime videatur: tamen ipsum non-aliud praecedit. Sic de vero, quod quidem similiter de nullo ente negatur, et bono, licet nihil
5 boni expers reperiatur. Sumunturque ob id omnia haec pro apertis dei nominibus, tametsi praecisionem non attingant. Non tamen proprie dicuntur illa post non-aliud esse; si enim forent post non-aliud, quomodo eorum quodlibet esset non aliud quam id quod est? Sic igitur non-aliud ante ista videtur et alia, quod
10 post ipsum non sunt, sed per ipsum. Recte igitur tu quidem miratus es de his quae non-aliud antecedit, si post ipsum sunt, et quonam modo id possibile.

FERDINANDUS: Si recte te capio, ita non-aliud videtur ante

13 FERDINAND: It is indeed necessary for whoever examines |the matter| with you to speak in the foregoing manner when he attends to what precedes all things which can be uttered. But, indeed, I wonder how it is that one and being and true and good exist subsequently to Not-other.

NICHOLAS: Since everything is said[15] to be either one thing or the other—so that one thing appears as not-the-other—one seems very near to Not-other. Nevertheless, since one is nothing other than one, it is *other* than Not-other. Therefore, Not-other is simpler than is one, since one has from Not-other the fact that it is one, whereas the converse is not true. But certain theologians who accept the One in place of Not-other have regarded it as prior to contradiction—as we read in Plato's *Parmenides* and in Dionysius the Areopagite. Nevertheless, since one is *other* than not-one, it does not at all direct |us| unto the First-beginning-of-all, which cannot be *other* than any other thing or than nothing (and which, as you will see later, is likewise not the opposite of anything).

14 In the same way, consider being. In it Not-other seems to shine forth clearly, since being does not seem to be *other* than any existing thing. Nevertheless, Not-other precedes it. The case is the same for the true (which also is not denied of any being) and for the good (in spite of its not being the case that anything is found to be deprived of the good). Hence, |the names of| all these things are taken as obvious names of God—even though they do not attain precision. Yet, they are not *properly* said to be subsequent to Not-other. For if they were subsequent to it, how would each of them be not other than what it is? Therefore, Not-other is seen to be before these (and other) things in such way that they are not subsequent to it but |exist| through it. Therefore, regarding these things which Not-other precedes, you were right in wondering whether they are subsequent to it and how this would be possible.

FERDINAND: If I understand you rightly, Not-other is seen before all things in such way that it cannot be absent from any

omnia, quod ex his quae post ipsum videntur, nullis abesse pos-
15 sit, si quidem etiam sint contradictoria.

NICOLAUS: Ita utique verum perspicio.

15 CAPITULUM V

FERDINANDUS: Oro te, pater, patere me loqui ea quae equidem sic in non-aliud ductus intueor ut, si me errantem senseris,
more corrigas tuo.

5 NICOLAUS: Eloquere, Ferdinande.

FERDINANDUS: Non-aliud seorsum ante om|ne aliud intuens, 8ʳ
ipsum sic video quod in eo quidquid videri potest intueor. Nam
neque esse nec cognosci extra ipsum quidquam possibile; aliud
etiam ipsum ab esse et cognosci id nequit effugere. Esse enim
10 intelligereve quippiam extra non-aliud sed ne fingere quidem
mihi est possibile—adeo ut, si ipsum quoque nihil et ignorare
videre absque non-aliud coner, videre frustra et incassum coner.
Quomodo enim nihil nihil visibile nisi per non-aliud, ut sit non
aliud quam nihil? Pari modo de ignorare et ceteris omnibus.
15 Omne enim quod est, in tantum est, in quantum non aliud est; et
omne quod intelligitur, in tantum intelligitur, in quantum non
aliud esse intelligitur; et omne quod videtur verum, usque adeo
videtur verum, in quantum non aliud cernitur. Et summatim
quidquid videtur aliud, in tantum aliud videtur, in quantum non
20 aliud. Sicut igitur sublato non-aliud nec manet nec cognoscitur quidquam: sic in ipso quidem omnia et sunt et cognoscuntur et
16 videntur. Ipsum enim non-aliud adaequatissima ratio est dis-
cretioque et mensura omnium, quae sunt, ut sint, et quae non |
sunt, ut non sint, et quae possunt esse, ut esse possint, et quae sic 9ʳ

---

14 14 his: iis *S*   hiis *U*
15 19 tantum: vide *post* tantum *scribit et del. S*

of the things which are seen after it, even if these things are contradictories.

NICHOLAS: Indeed, this is my view about the truth of the matter.

15 CHAPTER 5

FERDINAND: I ask you, Father, to permit me to discourse on the things which I, having been thus led, behold in Not-other, so that in your own manner you may correct me if you detect that I am erring.

NICHOLAS: Speak forth, Ferdinand.

FERDINAND: When I see Not-other by itself before every other thing, I see it in such way that I behold in it all that can be seen. For no thing can possibly either be or be known outside of it. Even what is *other* than being and than being known cannot escape it. But I am not able even to imagine any being or understanding outside of Not-other. |This fact is true| to such an extent that if I tried to view nothing itself and ignorance itself apart from Not-other, I would try altogether in vain. For how is nothing nothing-visible except through Not-other, so that nothing is not other than nothing? The case is the same with regard to ignorance and all other things. For everything which exists exists insofar as it is not other |than itself|. And everything which is understood is understood insofar as it is understood to be not other |than itself|. And everything which is seen to be true is seen to be true insofar as it is discerned as not other |than true|. And, in sum, whatever is seen to be an other is seen to be an other insofar as it is not other |than it is|. Therefore, just as were Not-other removed there would not be anything which continued to exist or to be known, so indeed all things exist and are **16** known and are seen in Not-other. For Not-other is the most adequate Constituting Ground (*ratio*), Standard, and Measure of the existence of all existing things, of the nonexistence of all nonexisting things, of the possibility of all possibilities, of the manner of existence of all things existing in any manner, of the

sunt, ut sic sint, et quae moventur, ut moveantur, et quae stant,
5 ut stent, et quae vivunt, ut vivant, et quae intelligunt, ut intel-
ligant, et eiusmodi omnia. Ita enim necessarium esse video in eo
quod video ipsum non-aliud se definire ideoque et omnia quae
nominari possunt.

17 NICOLAUS: Recte in deum aciem iecisti per "non-aliud" significatum, ut in principio, causa, seu ratione, quae non est alia nec
diversa, cuncta humaniter visibilia conspiceres, quantum tibi
nunc quidem conceditur. Tantum autem conceditur, quantum
5 ipsum non-aliud, scilicet rerum ratio, tuae se rationi seu menti
revelat sive visibilem exhibet; sed hoc nunc medio per "non-
aliud" quia sese definit, revelavit clarius quam antea. Nam quo
pacto mihi se visibilem praestiterit, in libellis pluribus legere
potuisti. Nunc autem in hoc aenigmate significati ipsius "non-
10 aliud" per rationem potissimum illam quia se definit, fecundius
et clarius, adeo ut sperare queam ipsum deum sese nobis aliquando sine aenigmate revelaturum.

FERDINANDUS: Licet in praemissis quaecumque videri | per 9ʳ
nos possunt, omnia complicentur, ut tamen acrius excitemur,
15 certa dubia tangamus, ut per illorum evacuationem pronior fiat
visio exercitata.

NICOLAUS: Placet ut ita facias.

18 FERDINANDUS: Imprimis quaerit scientiae avidus, ubi sumi
debeat ratio, quod deus trinus et unus est per li non aliud significatus, cum non-aliud numerum omnem antecedat.

NICOLAUS: Ex his quae dicta sunt, unica ratione omnia viden-
5 tur, quam tu quidem vidisti esse quia principium per "non-

18 4 his: iis *S* hiis *U*

motion of all moving things, of the rest of all nonmoving things, of the life of all living things, of the understanding of whatever is understood, and so on for all other things of this kind. I see this to be necessary, in that I see that *Not-other* defines itself and, hence, all nameable things.

17   NICHOLAS: You have rightly directed your acute |mental| gaze toward God (who is signified through "Not-other"), so that in this Beginning, Cause, or Constituting Ground, which is neither other nor diverse, you have seen—to the extent presently granted you—all the things which are humanly visible. You are granted |this vision| to the extent that Not-other—i.e., the Constituting Ground of things—reveals itself, or makes itself visible, to your reason [*ratio*] or mind. But through "Not-other"—by means of the fact that it defines itself—|God| now has revealed |Himself| more clearly than before. You have been able to read in |my| many treatises in what way |God| has |previously| made Himself visible to me. But in this symbolism of the signification of "Not-other"—chiefly by way of the consideration that it defines itself—|God has| now |revealed Himself| more richly and more clearly. |He has revealed Himself| to such an extent that I can hope that He will some day reveal Himself to us without a symbolism.

    FERDINAND: Whatever can be seen by us is enfolded in the foregoing statements. Nevertheless, so that we may be more keenly aroused, let us touch upon certain doubtful |points| in order that our already-trained vision may be sharpened by clearing up these |points|.

    NICHOLAS: It is agreeable that you do so.

18   FERDINAND: First of all, one who is desirous of knowledge asks where a rational consideration should be found |for maintaining| that the trine and one God is signified by "Not-other," since Not-other precedes all number.

    NICHOLAS: All things are seen from what has been said—seen on the basis of a single rational consideration. You have seen this to be |the consideration| that the Beginning, which is signi-

aliud" significatum se ipsum definit. In explicatam igitur eius definitionem intueamur, quod videlicet non-aliud est non aliud quam non-aliud. Idem triniter repetitum si est primi definitio, ut vides, ipsum profecto est unitrinum et non alia ratione quam
10 quia se ipsum definit. Non enim foret primum, si se ipsum minime definiret; se autem quando definit, trinum ostendit. Ex perfectione igitur vides resultare trinitatem, quam tamen, quoniam ante aliud vides, nec numerare potes nec numerum esse affirmare, cum haec trinitas non sit aliud quam unitas, et unitas
15 non sit aliud quam trinitas, quia tam trinitas quam unitas non sunt aliud quam simplex| principium per "non-aliud" significatum. *10ʳ*

FERDINANDUS: Optime perfectionis primi necessitatem video, quia se definit, exigere, ut sit unitrinum ante aliud tamen et numerum, cum ea quae ipsum primum praesupponunt, ad eius
20 nihil conferant perfectionem. Sed cum alias et saepe hanc divinam fecunditatem nisus sis aliquo modo, maxime quidem in Docta ignorantia, explanare per alios terminos, satis erit si istis nunc pauca addideris.

19 NICOLAUS: Trinitatis secretum, dei utique dono fide receptum, quamvis omnem sensum longe exsuperet atque antecedat, hoc medio quo in praesentia deum indagamus, non aliter nec praecisius quam superius audisti, declarari potest. Sed qui patrem et
5 filium et spiritum sanctum trinitatem nominant, minus praecise quidem appropinquant, congrue tamen nominibus illis utuntur propter scripturarum convenientiam. Qui vero unitatem, aequalitatem, et nexum trinitatem nuncupant propius accederent, si termini illi sacris in litteris reperirentur inserti. Sunt enim hi in
10 quibus non-aliud clare relucescit. Nam in unitate, quae indistinctionem a se dicit et ab alio distinctionem, profecto non-aliud cernitur. Ita et in| aequalitate sese manifestat et nexu consideranti *10ᵛ*

---

19 8 trinitatem: equalitatem *post* trinitatem *scribit et del. S*

fied by "Not-other," defines itself. Therefore, let us behold its unfolded definition: viz., that Not-other is not other than Not-other. If the same thing repeated three times is the definition of the First, as you recognize |it to be|, then assuredly the First is triune—and for no other reason than that it defines itself. If it did not define itself, it would not be the First; yet, since it defines itself, it shows itself to be trine. Therefore, you see that out of the perfection there results a trinity which, nevertheless, (since you view it prior to other) you can neither number nor assert to be a number. For this trinity is not other than oneness, and |this| oneness is not other than trinity. For the trinity and the oneness are not other than the simple Beginning which is signified by "Not-other."

FERDINAND: I see perfectly well that the necessity of the perfection of the First—viz., that it defines itself—demands that it be triune before other and before number. For those things which presuppose the First do not confer any perfection on it. But since you have elsewhere and often—especially in *Learned Ignorance*—attempted in some way to explicate this divine richness in other terms, it will suffice if you now add a few |points| to these others.

19   NICHOLAS: The mystery of the Trinity—a mystery which is received by faith and by the gift of God—by far exceeds and precedes all sensing. Nevertheless, by the means by which we investigate God in the present life, this mystery cannot be elucidated in any other way or any more precisely than you have just heard. Now, those who name the Trinity *Father* and *Son* and *Holy Spirit* approach |it| less precisely; nevertheless, they use these names suitably because of the conformity to Scripture. But those who call the Trinity *Oneness, Equality,* and *Union* would approach more closely |to it| if these terms were found to be inserted in Scripture.[16] For these are |the terms| in which Not-other shines forth clearly. For in *oneness*, which indicates indistinction from itself and distinction from another, assuredly Not-other is discerned. And, likewise, in *equality* and in *union* Not-other manifests itself to one who is attentive.

Adhuc simplicius hi termini "hoc," "id," et "idem" lucidius praecisiusque "non-aliud" imitantur, sed minus sunt in usu.

15 Sic itaque patet in "non-aliud et non-aliud atque non-aliud," licet minime usitatum sit, unitrinum principium clarissime revelari supra omnem tamen nostram apprehensionem atque capacitatem. Quando enim primum principium ipsum se definit per "non-aliud" significatum, in eo definitivo motu de non-alio non-20 aliud oritur atque de non-alio et non-alio exorto in non-alio concluditur definitio—quae contemplans, clarius quam dici possit intuebitur.

20   CAPITULUM VI

FERDINANDUS: Haec de hoc quidem sufficiant. Nunc ut in alio non-aliud ostendas, porro perge.

NICOLAUS: Non-aliud neque est aliud, nec ab alio aliud, nec 5 est in alio aliud—non alia aliqua ratione quam quia non-aliud, quod nullo modo esse aliud potest, quasi sibi desit aliquid, sicut alii. Aliud enim quia aliud est ab aliquo, eo caret a quo aliud. Non-aliud autem quia a nullo aliud est, non caret aliquo, nec extra ipsum quidquam | esse potest. Unde sicut non potest sine *11ʳ* 10 ipso neque dici quidquam nec cogitari, quod per ipsum non dicatur aut cogitetur, sine quo non esse, non discerni aliquid possibile est, cum talia omnia antecedat: tunc ipsum in se antecedenter et absolute non aliud quam ipsum videtur, et in alio cernitur non aliud quam ipsum aliud—puta si dixero deum 15 nihil visibilium esse, quoniam eorum causa est et creator, et dixero ipsum in caelo esse non aliud quam caelum. Quomodo enim caelum non aliud quam caelum foret, si non-aliud in ipso foret aliud quam caelum? Caelum autem cum a non-caelo aliud sit, idcirco aliud est. Deus vero, qui non-aliud est, non est cae-

Still more simply, the terms "this," "it," and "the same" imitate "Not-other" quite clearly and precisely, although they are less in use.[17]

So then, it is evident that in |the expression| "Not-other and Not-other and Not-other"—although |this expression| is not at all in use—the triune Beginning is revealed most clearly, though it is beyond all our apprehension and capability. For when the First Beginning—signified through "Not-other"—defines itself: in this movement of definition Not-other originates from Not-other; and from Not-other and the Not-other which has originated, the definition concludes in Not-other. One who contemplates these matters will behold them more clearly than can be expressed.

20   CHAPTER 6

FERDINAND: Let these |points| suffice regarding this |topic|. But proceed now to show Not-other in other.

NICHOLAS: Not-other is not other; nor is it *other* than other; nor is it other in an other. |These points are true| for no other reason than that |Not-other is| Not-other, which cannot in any way be an other—as if something were lacking to it, as to an other. Because other is *other* than something, it lacks that than which it is *other*. But because Not-other is not *other* than anything, it does not lack anything, nor can anything exist outside of it. Hence, without Not-other no thing can be spoken of or thought of, because it would not be spoken of or thought of through that without which, since it precedes all things, no thing can exist or be known. Accordingly, in itself Not-other is seen antecedently and as absolutely no other than itself; and in an other it is seen as not other than this other. For example, I might say that God is none of the visible things, since He is their cause and creator. And I might say that in the sky He is not other than the sky.[18] For how would the sky be not other than the sky if in it Not-other were other than the sky? Now, since the sky is *other* than not-sky, it is an other. But God, who is Not-other, is

20 lum, quod aliud, licet nec in ipso sit aliud, nec ab ipso aliud,
sicut lux non est color, quamvis nec in ipso nec ab ipso aliud sit.

21   Oportet te attentum esse, quomodo omnia quae dici aut cogitari possunt, ideo non sunt primum, per non-aliud significatum,
quia ea omnia a suis oppositis alia sunt. Deus autem quia non
aliud est ab alio, non est aliud, quamvis non-aliud et aliud
5 videantur opponi; sed non opponitur aliud ipsi a quo habet
quod est aliud, ut praediximus. Nunc vides quomodo recte theo-
logi affirmarunt deum in omnibus omnia, | licet omnium nihil.   *11*ᵛ

FERDINANDUS: Nemo est qui quidem, mentem applicans, haec
tecum non videat. Ex quo constat unicuique deum innominabi-
10 lem omnia nominare, infinitum omnia finire, interminum omnia
terminare, et de omnibus eodem modo.

22   NICOLAUS: Recte. Nam cum ipso non-aliud cessante omnia
quae sunt quaeque non sunt, necessario cessent, clare perspicitur
quomodo in ipso omnia anterioriter ipsum sunt et ipsum in
omnibus omnia. Cum igitur in alio ipsum intueor aliudque in
5 ipso ipsum prioriter: quomodo per ipsum sine alio aliquo omnia
id sunt quod quidem sunt, video. Non enim creat caelum ex
alio, sed per caelum quod in ipso ipsum est—sicut si ipsum
intellectualem spiritum diceremus seu lucem et in ipso intellectu
rationem omnium esse ipsum consideraremus. Tunc enim ratio
10 cur caelum caelum et non aliud prioriter in ipso est, per quam
constitutum est caelum sive quae in caelo est caelum. Sensibile

21 2 non-aliud: non non aliud *S*
21 9 videat: hec tecum *post* videat *scribit et del. S*
22 5 prioriter: peroritur *S*   preoritur *U*

not the sky, which is an other; nonetheless, in the sky God is not
an other; nor is He *other* than the sky. (Similarly, light is not
color, even though in color light is not an other and even
though light is not *other* than color.)

21   You ought to observe that the reason why all the things
which can be spoken of or thought of are not the First (which is
signified through "Not-other") is that all these things are *other*
than their respective opposites. But because God is not *other*
than |any| other, He is Not-other, although Not-other and other
seem to be opposed. But other is not opposed to that from
which it has the fact that it is other, as I said.[19] You see now
how it is that the theologians rightly affirmed that in all things
God is all things, even though |He is| none of these things.

FERDINAND: There is no one who, if he applies his mind, fails
to recognize these |points| with you. Hence, it is evident to
anyone that God, though unnameable, names all things; though
infinite, defines all things; though limitless, delimits all things;
and likewise for everything else.

22   NICHOLAS: Correct. For since if Not-other ceased existing,
then necessarily all existing and nonexisting things would cease,
we see clearly how it is that in Not-other all things are Not-
other antecedently |to being themselves| and how it is that in all
things Not-other is all things. Therefore, when I behold Not-
other in an other and behold the other antecedently in Not-
other as Not-other, I see how it is that through Not-other, and
without any other, all things are that which they are. For Not-
other creates the sky not from an other but through the sky
which in Not-other is Not-other. (By comparison, we might
speak of Not-other as intellectual spirit—or as intellectual light—
and might consider that, in the intellect, it is the Constituting
Ground [*ratio*] of all things |intellectual|.) For the Constituting
Ground (*ratio*)[20] of the sky's being the sky and not any other
thing is antecedently in Not-other. Through this Constituting
Ground |the sky| is constituted as the sky; and in the sky this
Constituting Ground is the sky. Therefore, it is not the case that

igitur caelum non est id quod est ab alio aut quid aliud a caelo,
sed ab ipso non-aliud, ab aliquo quod vides ante nomen, quia
omnia in omnibus est nominibus et omnium nullum. Nam
15 eadem ratione qua rationem illam | caelum nominarem, eadem   *12ʳ*
ratione ipsam terram nominarem atque aquam et pari de singulis modo. Et si rationem caeli non video caelum nominandam,
quasi causa causati non habeat nomen, sic ipsum eadem ratione
nullo nomine video nominabilem. Non video igitur innomina-
20 bilem quasi nomine privatum, verum ante nomen.

23   CAPITULUM VII

FERDINANDUS: Intelligo et ita etiam verum cerno. Si enim cessaret causa, cessaret effectus; et ideo cessante ipso non-aliud cessaret omne aliud et omne nominabile et ita etiam ipsum nihil,
5 cum nihil nominetur. Ostende mihi, quaeso, ut idipsum perspiciam.
NICOLAUS: Certum est quod si cessaret frigus, cessaret et glacies, quae iam Romae videtur multiplicata. Verum propterea
aqua prior glacie non cessaret; cessante vero ente cessaret et
glacies et aqua, ita quod actu non esset; et tamen materia seu
10 possibilitas essendi aquam non cessaret. Quae quidem possibilitas essendi aquam una dici possibilitas potest. Cessante vero uno
et glacies et aqua et essendi aquam cessaret possibilitas. At non
cessaret om| ne intelligibile, quod posset ad essendi aquam possi-   *12ᵛ*
bilitatem necessitari per omnipotentiam—puta ipsum intelligi-
15 bile nihil vel chaos non cessaret, quod quidem ab aqua distan-
tius est quam ipsa essendi aquam possibilitas, quae, quamvis
remotissima confusissimaque, omnipotentiae tamen necessitatur
oboedire. Vigor autem omnipotentiae in ipsum non cessaret per

the perceptible sky (1) is from an other that which it is or (2) is anything *other* than the sky. Rather, |that which the sky is| it is from Not-other—i.e., from something which you see before |any| name, because it is all things in all names and yet is none of all |these names|. For the same reason that I would call this Constituting Ground sky,[21] I would call it earth, and water, and so on in like manner regarding each thing. And if I see that the Constituting Ground of the sky ought not to be named sky—as the cause does not have the name of the caused—so, for the same reason, I see that Not-other is not nameable by any name. Therefore, I view the Unnameable not as deprived of |every| name but as prior to |every| name.

23   CHAPTER 7

FERDINAND: I understand; and I also discern that it is true. For if the cause were to cease, the effect would cease. And so, if Not-other ceased, everything other and everything nameable would cease. Hence, even nothing itself, since it is named *nothing*, would cease. Make this clear to me, I ask, so that I may understand it.

NICHOLAS: It is certain that if coldness were to cease, then ice (which is already seen extensively here in Rome) |would| also |cease|. But it is not the case that for this reason water, which is prior to ice, would cease. However, if the being ceased, then so too would the ice and the water, so that they would not actually exist. Nevertheless, the matter, or the possibility-of-being-water,[22] would not cease. This possibility-of-being-water can be said to be one possibility. Now, if the one ceased, then the ice, the water, and the possibility of being water would cease. Yet, not every intelligible-thing-which-Omnipotence-can-necessitate-with-respect-to-the-possibility-of-being-water would cease. For example, intelligible nothing, or chaos, would not cease. To be sure, nothing, or chaos, is more distant from water than is the possibility-of-being-water. Although this possibility is very remote and very disordered, it must obey Omnipotence. But it is not the case that by virtue of the

unius cessationem. Verum si ipsum non-aliud cessaret, statim
20 omnia cessarent quae ipsum non-aliud antecedit. Atque ita non
entium solummodo actus cessaret ac potentia, sed et non-ens et
nihil entium, quae non-aliud antecedit.
24 FERDINANDUS: Satis dubio fecisti. Nunc nihil video, quod est
non aliud quam nihil, non-aliud ante se, habere, a quo distat
ultra actu esse et esse potentia. Videtur enim mente quam confusissimum chaos, quod infinita dumtaxat virtute, quae non-aliud
5 est, ut determinetur, potest astringi.
NICOLAUS: Dixisti virtutem actu infinitam esse non-aliud. Quomodo id vides?
FERDINANDUS: Virtutem unitam et minus aliam video fortiorem;
quae igitur penitus non-aliud, illa erit infinita.
10 NICOLAUS: Optime et rationabiliter imprimis dicis—rati|onabiliter *13ʳ*
inquam. Sicut enim sensibilis visio quantumcumque acuta absque
omni sensatione seu sensibili motu esse nequit, ita et mentalis
non est absque omni ratione seu motu rationali. Et quamvis recto
intuitu te videam uti, scire tamen opto, an ipsum non-aliud sic per
15 mentem videatur in omnibus, quod non possit non videri.
25 FERDINANDUS: Ad principium se et quae dici queunt omnia
definiens recurro, videoque quomodo videre est non aliud quam
non-videre; et video equidem quod ipsum non-aliud tam per
videre quam non videre conspicio. Si igitur mens sine ipso non-
5 aliud nec videre potest nec non videre, non igitur ipsum non-
aliud potest non videri, sicut non potest non sciri, quod per
scientiam scitur atque ignorantiam.
In alio ipsum non-aliud cernitur, quia, cum aliud videtur,
aliud videtur et non-aliud.
10 NICOLAUS: Bene ais. Sed quomodo vides aliud, si in alio non
vides aut in non-alio?

cessation of the one, the strength of Omnipotence with respect to chaos would cease. However, if Not-other ceased, all the things it precedes would immediately cease. And so, not only would the actuality and the possibility of the beings which Not-other precedes cease, but so also would the not-being and the nothing of these beings.[23]

24 FERDINAND: You have dealt successfully with my puzzlement. I now see that nothing, which is not other than nothing, has Not-other as prior to itself. It is more distant from Not-other than are actual being and possible being. For the mind sees how utterly disordered is the chaos which, to be sure, Infinite Power (which is Not-other) can constrain to be ordered.

NICHOLAS: You said that Not-other is actually infinite power. What is your reason for this view?

FERDINAND: I see that the power which is unified and less-other is the stronger. Hence, the power which in every respect is Not-other will be infinite.

NICHOLAS: You speak very rightly and very reasonably—very reasonably, indeed. For just as perceptual seeing—no matter how acute—cannot exist without any sensation or perceptual stimulus,[24] so also mental |seeing| does not exist without any reasoning or rational stimulus. Although I see that you have a correct viewpoint, I wish to know whether the mind so beholds Not-other in all things that Not-other cannot fail to be seen.

25 FERDINAND: I return to the *Beginning*, which defines itself and all things that can be spoken of. And I see how it is that seeing is not other than not-seeing; and I see that I behold Not-other both with respect to seeing and with respect to not-seeing. Therefore, if without Not-other the mind cannot either see or not see, then Not-other cannot fail to be seen—just as what is known through knowledge and through ignorance cannot fail to be known.

Not-other is seen in an other because when the other is seen, both other and Not-other are seen.

NICHOLAS: Your statement is correct. But how is it that you see other unless you see it either in an other or in Not-other?

26 FERDINANDUS: Quoniam positio ipsius non-aliud omnium est
positio et eius sublatio omnium sublatio, ideo aliud nec extra
non-aliud est nec videtur.

NICOLAUS: Si in non-alio aliud vides, utique non vides ipsum
5 ibi esse aliud, sed non-aliud, cum in non-alio esse aliud sit
impossibile.

FERDINANDUS: Aliud in non-alio videre me idcirco aio, quia
extra | ipsum nequit videri. Sed si me quid sit aliud in non-alio *13ʳ*
interrogares, dicerem esse non-aliud.

10 NICOLAUS: Recte.

27   CAPITULUM VIII

FERDINANDUS: De quidditate aliquid attingere expedit.

NICOLAUS: Attingam. Non haesitas, ut opinor, ipsius non-
aliud quidditatem non-aliud ipsum esse. Ideo dei sive ipsius
5 non-aliud quidditas ab aliqua quidditate non est alia, sed in
omni alia quidditate ipsum non-aliud est ipsa non alia. Alia
igitur a quidditate ipsius aliud idcirco accidunt ei quia aliud—
quod sine alio non-aliud foret. Alia igitur illa ad ipsius aliud
quidditatem consequenter se habentia quidditatis ipsius aliud
10 splendores sunt, qui in nihil umbra occumbunt. Quidditas igitur
quae non-aliud, quidditatis ipsius aliud quidditas est, quae quidem quidditatis est prioris relucentia. Suntque alia quae illi
accidunt, in quibus quidditas illa, cui accidunt, lucet.

28   Quidditas quam mente ante quantitatem video, cum sine
quanto imaginari non possit, in imaginatione varias recipit
imagines quae sine varia quantitate esse non queunt. Et licet de
quidditatis essentia quantitas non sit, quam mens quidem supra
5 imaginationem | contemplatur, cumque quidditas illa quam *14ʳ*
mens videt, non alia a quidditate sit, quam imaginatio imagi-
natur: quantitas tamen sic est consequenter ad imaginis quidditatem, quod sine ipsa esse nequit imago.

---

26 5 esse¹: *bis S   semel U*

26   FERDINAND: Since the positing of Not-other is the positing of all things and its removal is the removal of all things, other neither exists nor is seen apart from Not-other.

NICHOLAS: If it is in Not-other that you see other, surely you do not see it *there* to be other but |you see it to be| Not-other, since it is impossible for other to be in Not-other.

FERDINAND: The reason I say that I see other in Not-other is that other cannot be seen apart from Not-other. But if you should ask me what other in Not-other is, I would say that it is Not-other.

NICHOLAS: Correct.

27   CHAPTER 8

FERDINAND: It is expedient to say something about quiddity.

NICHOLAS: I shall take up |this topic|. You do not doubt, I believe, that the quiddity of Not-other is Not-other. And so, the quiddity of God, or of Not-other, is not *other* than any quiddity; rather, in every other quiddity Not-other is no other quiddity. Therefore, |accidents, which are| *other* than the quiddity of the other, happen to the other because it is other. (If the other were without anything other, it would be Not-other.) Therefore, these accidents which follow upon the quiddity of the other are elucidations of the quiddity of the other—elucidations which sink into the shadow of nothing. Hence, the quiddity which is Not-other is the Quiddity of the quiddity of the other; the quiddity of the other is the shining forth of the First Quiddity. And the accidents are what happen to the quiddity; in them the quiddity to which they happen, shines forth.

28   Since the quiddity which I mentally view before quantity[25] cannot be imagined as nonquantitative, it admits (in imagination) of various images which are not able to be devoid of some measure of quantity. And although quantity does not belong to the essence of the quiddity which the mind contemplates above imagination, and although that quiddity-which-the-mind-sees is not *other* than the quiddity-which-imagination-imagines, nevertheless quantity follows upon the image's quiddity in such way that in the absence of quantity there can be no image.

29   Sic de magnitudine dico quae mente supra imaginationem videtur ante imaginariam quantitatem. Sed in imaginatione cernitur quantitas. Quanto est autem absolutior eius imaginatio a grossa et umbrosa quantitate subtiliorque atque simplicior, tanto
5 in ea magnitudinis quidditas simplicius et certius et imaginaria verior relucescit. Non enim quantitas aliquid est ad magnitudinis quidditatem, quasi ex eo constituatur, necessarium, cum maxima simplicitas sive indivisibilitas magna sit absque quantitate. Sed si debet imaginari magnitudo sive imaginabiliter apparere,
10 statim quantitas est necessaria, tamquam sine qua hoc non sit possibile. Quantitas igitur est relucentia magnitudinis in sua imagine imaginabiliter.

30   Verum in intelligentia certius relucet. Magnum enim intellectum et scientiam magnam dicimus; ibi autem intellectualiter relucet magnitudo, separatim scilicet et absolute ante corpoream qua|ntitatem; sed supra omnem intellectum verissime cernitur, *14ᵛ*
5 scilicet supra et ante omnem modum cognitivum. Et ita incomprehensibiliter comprehenditur, incognoscibiliterque cognoscitur, sicut invisibiliter videtur. Quae quoniam supra hominis cognitionem est cognitio, non nisi negative in humaniter cognitis attrectatur. Nam non dubitamus quin imaginabilis magnitudo non
10 aliud quam imaginabilis sit, et sic intelligibilis non aliud quam intelligibilis. Et ita magnitudinem illam videmus, quae in imaginabili imaginabilis et intelligibilis est in intelligibili—non illam quae non-aliud ipsum est et ante aliud, qua non existente neque intelligibilis foret. Imaginabilis enim magnitudo magnitudinem
15 praesupponit, quae est ante imaginabilem contractionem, et intelligibilis eam quae ante contractionem intelligibilem. Quae sic et sic relucet in speculo et aenigmate, ut quae est ante aliud

---

29 9 imaginabiliter: *bis S*
30 11-12 imaginabili: imagibili *S*
30 13 est: esse *SU*

29 Thus, I am talking about the magnitude which is mentally viewed beyond imagination and before imagined quantity. However, quantity is seen in the imagination. But the freer the imagination-of-quantity is from coarse and shadowy quantity and the subtler and simpler it is, the more simply and certainly there shines forth in the imagination the quiddity of magnitude and the truer is the image |of quantity|. For quantity is not something necessary to the quiddity of magnitude, as if magnitude were constituted by quantity; for Maximal Simplicity, or Maximal Indivisibility, is great without quantity. But if magnitude is to be imagined or is to appear imaginatively, then quantity is immediately necessary; for quantity is that without which this |imagining| is not possible. Therefore, quantity is the shining-forth-of-magnitude, imaginatively, in the image of quantity.

30 But magnitude shines forth more certainly in the understanding. For we speak of the understanding as great, and we speak of knowledge as great. But in the understanding magnitude shines forth intellectually—i.e., abstractly and absolutely, before corporeal quantity. Yet, it is seen most truly above all understanding—i.e., above and before every cognitive mode. And so, it is comprehended incomprehensibly and is known unknowably, even as it is seen invisibly. Since this knowledge is above human knowledge, it is descried only negatively in the things which are known to humans. We do not doubt that imaginable magnitude is not other than imaginable and, likewise, that intelligible |magnitude| is not other than intelligible. And so, we behold the magnitude which in imaginable |magnitude| is imaginable and in intelligible |magnitude| is intelligible; |we do| not |behold| the Magnitude which is Not-other and is before other and in whose absence not even intelligible |magnitude| would be present. For imaginable magnitude presupposes a magnitude which is prior to the contraction |of magnitude| in the imagination; and intelligible |magnitude presupposes| a Magnitude which is prior to the contraction |of magnitude| in the understanding. This presupposed Magnitude shines forth in one way or another in a mirror and a symbolism,[26] so that that which is before *other* and *mode* and before everything effable and knowable

et modum et omne effabile et cognoscibile, cognoscatur, qualis
est illa dei cuius non est ullus finis magnitudo, quae nullis cog-
20 noscibilis terminis comprehenditur.

31   Ita universaliter | quidditas quae est ipsum non-aliud, sese et *15ʳ*
rerum omnes definit quidditates, sicut est dictum de magnitudinis quidditate. Quemadmodum igitur non-aliud non est multiplicabile, quia est ante numerum, eodem modo et quidditas
5 quae non-aliud, licet aliis in rebus aliisque in modis alia sit.

   FERDINANDUS: Aperuisti mihi oculos, ut videre incipiam, quomodo se habeat veritas quidditatis. Et in aenigmate quidditatis
magnitudinis me ad gratissimam utique visionem perduxisti.

   NICOLAUS: Bene nunc quidem clareque mente vides ipsum
10 non-aliud in omni cognitione praesupponi et cognosci, neque
quod cognoscitur ab ipso aliud esse, sed esse ipsum incognitum,
quod in cognito cognite relucescit, sicut solis claritas sensibiliter
invisibilis in iridis coloribus visibilibus visibiliter relucet varie in
varia nube.

32   CAPITULUM IX

   FERDINANDUS: Dic, rogo te, aliqua de universo, ut te sequens
ad dei melius subintrem visionem.

   NICOLAUS: Dicam. Dum corporeis caelum oculis video ter-
5 ramque et quae in his sunt, et illa quae vidi, ut universum |
imaginer, colligo, intellectualiter conspicio quodlibet universi *15ᵛ*
suo in loco et congruenti ordine ac pace; pulchrum contemplor
mundum et cum ratione omnia fabrefacta, quam in omnibus
comperio relucere tam in his quae tantum sunt, quam in his
10 quae sunt simul et vivunt, in hisque quae pariter sunt, vivunt, et
intelligunt—in primis quidem obscurius, vivacius in secundis et

---

31 1 non-aliud: non aliter aliud (aliter *deletum*) S
32 5 his: iis S hiis U
32 10 hisque: iis que S hiis U

is known. This is the kind of Magnitude which belongs to God, whose Magnitude is without end—i.e., a Magnitude which is comprehended as knowable-by-no-bounds.

31   Just as has been stated about the quiddity of magnitude, so in general the Quiddity which is Not-other defines itself and all the respective quiddities of things. Therefore, just as Not-other is not multiple, since it is prior to number, so also the Quiddity which is Not-other |is not multiple|, even though in other things and in other modes it is these others.

FERDINAND: You have opened my eyes, so that I begin to see what the truth about quiddity is. And through the symbolism of the quiddity-of-magnitude you have led me to a very pleasing sight.

NICHOLAS: Your mind now sees accurately and clearly (1) that Not-other is presupposed and known in every cognition and (2) that what is known is not *other* than Not-other but is Not-other-qua-unknown, which shines forth knowably in what is known. (By comparison, in the visible colors of the rainbow, the clarity of perceptibly invisible sunlight shines forth visibly in various ways in various clouds.)

32   CHAPTER 9

FERDINAND: Say something about the universe, I ask, in order that as I follow you, I may better come upon a vision of God.

NICHOLAS: I shall do so. When with my bodily eyes I see the sky and the earth and the objects which are in the sky and on the earth, and when in order to imagine the universe I gather together what I have seen, I behold intellectually each object of the universe in its own place and in suitable order and in tranquillity; and I contemplate the beautiful world and everything produced with reason [*ratio*]. And I find that reason shines forth in all things—as much in (1) things which merely exist as in (2) things which both exist and live and in (3) things which exist, live, and understand. In the case of the first |-mentioned| things |it shines forth| dimly; in the case of the second things, more

clarius, in tertiis vero lucidissime, et in singulis modis varie in variis. Deinde ad ipsam me rerum rationem converto, quae mundum praecedit et per quam mundum video constitutum, et
15 illam incomprehensibilem invenio. Non enim haesito ipsam mundi rationem, per quam omnia rationabiliter facta sunt, omnem cognitionem praesupponere et in creatis ipsam omnibus elucere, cum nihil sit factum absque ratione; ipsam tamen minime comprehendo. Nam si ipsam comprehenderem, profecto
20 cur mundus sic est et non aliter scirem, cur sol sol, luna luna, terra terra, et quodvis id quod est et nec aliud, nec maius, nec minus. Quippe si statim haec scirem, non ego essem creatura et portio universi, | quia ratio mea esset ars universi creativa ita et *16ᵣ* sui ipsius creatrix. Quare ipsum non-aliud comprehendo, quando
25 quidem universi rationem non esse comprehensibilem video, cum antecedat omne comprehensibile. Ipsam igitur incomprehensibilem, quod in comprehensibilibus comprehensibiliter relucet, perspicio.

FERDINANDUS: Difficile comprehenditur, quod esse praecedit.
33   NICOLAUS: Forma dat esse et cognosci; ideo quod non est formatum, quia praecedit aut sequitur, non comprehenditur, sicut deus et hyle et nihil et talia. Quando illa visu mentis attingimus, supra vel citra comprehensionem attingimus. Sed sine
5 verbo visionem communicare non valentes, sine li esse, quod non est explicare non possumus, quia aliter audientes non comprehenderent. Unde hae mentis visiones, sicut sunt supra comprehensionem, sic etiam supra expressionem. Et locutiones de

brightly and clearly; but in the case of the third things, most clearly; and in each of these |three| different modes |reason shines forth| in different ways in different things. Next, I turn myself toward the Constituting Ground [*ratio*] of things—a Ground which precedes the world and through which the world is constituted, as I recognize; and I find this Ground to be incomprehensible. I do not doubt that all knowledge presupposes the Constituting Ground of the world, through which all things have been reasonably created, and that this Ground shines forth in all created things; for it is not the case that anything is created unreasonably. Nevertheless, I do not at all comprehend this Constituting Ground. For were I to comprehend it, surely I would know why the world is the way it is and not otherwise, why the sun is the sun, the moon the moon, the earth the earth, why any given thing is what it is and not another or greater or lesser. Indeed, if I once knew all of this, I would no longer be a creature and a part of the universe, since my reason would be the Creative Principle (*ars creativa*) of the universe and the creator of itself. Therefore, I comprehend Not-other when I see that the Constituting Ground of the universe is not comprehensible since it precedes everything comprehensible. Hence, I see this incomprehensible Ground because it shines forth comprehensibly in comprehensible things.

FERDINAND: That which precedes being is difficult to comprehend.

33   NICHOLAS: The form bestows being and being-known. And so, what is not formed (whether because it precedes or succeeds |form|) is not comprehended—e.g., God, matter (*hyle*), nothing, and the like. When we attain to these things by mental vision, we attain to them either beyond or short of comprehension. But since we are unable to communicate the vision apart from words, we cannot without recourse to the verb "to be" discourse about what is not, because otherwise those who hear us would not understand. Hence, just as these mental visions are beyond comprehension, so too they are beyond expression. Moreover,

ipsis sunt impropriae, praecisione carentes, sicut cum dicimus
10 materiam esse materiam, hyle esse hyle, nihil esse nihil, et huiusmodi. Oportet igitur speculantem facere; uti facit videns per
vitrum rubeum nivem, qui nivem videt et apparentiam rubedinis
non nivi sed | vitro attribuit, ita facit mens per formam videns *16ʳ*
informatum.

34   FERDINANDUS: Quo pacto hoc verum videbo quod theologi
dicunt?: omnia dei creata voluntate.

NICOLAUS: Voluntas dei est non-aliud, nam velle determinat;
quo autem voluntas perfectior, eo rationabilior atque ordinatior.
5 Voluntas igitur quae ante aliud non-aliud cernitur, non est alia a
ratione neque sapientia nec alio quolibet nominabili. Si voluntatem igitur esse ipsum non-aliud vides, ipsam esse rationem
sapientiam, ordinem vides, a quibus non est aliud. Et sic illa
vides voluntate omnia determinari, causari, ordinari, firmari, sta-
10 biliri, et conservari, et in universo relucere, sicut Traiani in sua
columna, voluntatem, in qua sapientia est atque potentia. Nam
cum posteris gloriam suam ostendere Traianus vellet, quae non
nisi in aenigmate ostendi sensibili potuit sensibilibus, quibus gloriae
suae praesentiam exhibere fuit impossibile: hoc fecit in columna,
15 quae sua dicitur, quia sua voluntate id est columna quod est, et
non est ipsa columna aliud ab eius voluntate, licet columna
nequaquam sit voluntas. Sed quidquid est columna, hoc habet
ab ipsa voluntate, quae ipsam definit et terminat. Sed in | volun- *17ʳ*
tate sapientia cernitur ordoque, quae relucet in sculpturis rerum
20 bellicarum peractis cum felicitate; in pretiositate quoque operis,
quod ab impotente perfici non potuisset, Traiani potentia relucet.

35   Eo te iuvabis aenigmate, ut videas regem regum, qui per
"non-aliud" significatur, ad gloriae suae ostensionem, voluntate,

since the locutions about them are devoid of precision, they are improper—as when we say "matter is matter," "*hyle* is *hyle*," "nothing is nothing," and so on. Therefore, it is necessary to speculate. For example, when someone sees snow through a red glass, he sees the snow and attributes the appearance of redness not to the snow but to the glass. The mind does something similar when it views the unformed through a form.[27]

34   FERDINAND: But how will I see to be true what the theologians say?: viz., that all things are created by the will of God.

NICHOLAS: The will of God is Not-other, for |the will of God| determines willing. A will is rational and orderly in proportion to its perfection. Therefore, the will which is seen to be Not-other and to be prior to any other is not *other* than reason or wisdom or any other nameable thing. Hence, if you see that the will is Not-other, you see that it is reason, wisdom, and order—none of which it is *other* than. And so, you see (1) that all things are determined, caused, ordered, established, stabilized, and conserved by this will and (2) that |this| will, in which there is wisdom and power, shines forth in the universe, just as Trajan's |will shines forth| in his column. For when Trajan wanted to show his glory (which could only be manifested in a perceptible symbol by perceptible things) to his posterity, to whom it was impossible to exhibit the |actual| presence of his glory, he did this by means of a column. This column is called Trajan's column because by his will the column is what it is and because the column is not *other* than his will, even though it is not at all his will. Rather, whatever the column is, this it has from his will, which defines and delimits the column. Now, wisdom and order are discerned in the will; the wisdom shines forth in the carvings of warfare, completed with skill. And Trajan's power shines forth in the preciousness of the work, which could not have been completed by someone powerless.

35   By means of the foregoing symbolism you will be helped to see that in order to show His glory the King of kings, who is signified by "Not-other," created by His own will (in which is

in qua est sapientia et potentia, universum et quamlibet eius
partem creasse. Quae etiam triniter relucet in omnibus: essential-
5 iter scilicet, intelligibiliter, et desiderabiliter—ut in anima nostra
experimur. Nam ibi relucet ut principium essendi, a quo anima
habet esse, et ut principium cognoscendi, a quo cognoscere, et ut
principium desiderandi, a quo habet et velle; et suum unitrinum
in his principium speculando ad eius accenditur gloriam.
10 FERDINANDUS: Optime ista sic esse contemplor, et video voluntatem, quae non-aliud, creatricem ab omnibus desiderari et
nominari bonitatem. Nam quid desiderant omnia quae sunt?
Non aliud utique quam esse. Quid quae vivunt? Non aliud
quam vivere. Et quae intelligunt? Non aliud quam intelligere.
15 Hoc igitur quodlibet desiderat quod ab ipso est non aliud. Non-
| aliud vero cum ab aliquo non sit aliud, ab omnibus summopere *17ᵛ*
desideratur tamquam principium essendi, medium conservandi,
et quiescendi finis.
    NICOLAUS: Recte in ipsum non-aliud intendis, in quo omnia
20 elucescunt.

36   CAPITULUM X

    FERDINANDUS: Quidam theologorum creaturam aiebant non
aliud quam dei participationem. Circa hoc te audire percupio.
    NICOLAUS: Primum tu vides quidem ipsum non-aliud innomin-
5 abile, quia nullum nomen ad ipsum attingit, cum omnia praecedat. Omne nomen tamen id est quod est, ipsius participatione;
nominatur igitur minime nominabile. Sic in omnibus imparticipa-
bile participatur. Sunt sane quae obscure non-aliud participant,
quia confuse atque generaliter; sunt quae magis specifice; sunt

---

36 4-5 innominabile: nominabile *S*   innominabile *U*

wisdom and power) the universe and each part of it. His will shines forth in all things in a threefold way: viz., through being, through understanding, and through desire—as we experience in our soul. For in our soul His will shines forth (1) as the beginning-of-being, from which the soul has being, and (2) as the beginning-of-knowing, from which the soul has knowing, and (3) as the beginning-of-desiring, from which the soul has willing. And by speculating upon its own beginning, which is triune in the foregoing respects, the soul is illumined for the glory of God.

FERDINAND: I consider these matters to be exactly so; and I see that the Creative Will, which is Not-other, is desired by all things and is called Goodness. For what do all existing things desire? Nothing other than to be. What |do all| living things |desire|? Nothing other than to live. What |do all| intelligent things |desire|? Nothing other than to understand. Therefore, each thing desires that which is not *other* than itself. But since Not-other is not *other* than anything, all things supremely desire it as the beginning of being, the conserving means, and the rest-giving terminal goal.

NICHOLAS: You are striving aright toward Not-other, in which all things shine forth.

36   CHAPTER 10

FERDINAND: Certain of the theologians maintained that the creation is none other than a participation in God.[28] I would very much like to hear you |speak| about this matter.

NICHOLAS: You see, first of all, that Not-other is unnameable; for no name attains to Not-other, since it precedes all things. Nevertheless, every name is-what-it-is by participation in Not-other; therefore, Not-other is named the Unnameable. Thus, |Not-other|, which cannot be participated in, is participated in by all things.[29] Indeed, there are things which participate in Not-other dimly, because |they participate| disorderedly and generally; there are things which |participate| in a more special way;

10 quae specialissime, sicut animae vitam aliqua membra obscure,
aliqua clarius, aliqua vero specialissime participant; potentiae
item animae aliae clarius, aliae obscurius participant intelligentiam. Creaturae quoque quae minus ab aliis aliae sunt, veluti
purae intelligentiae, de ipso plus participant. At quae magis ab
15 aliis aliae sunt, ut puta corporales, quae sese uno non compati-
untur loco, | de natura eius quae non aliud est ab aliquo, minus *18ʳ*
participant.

37   FERDINANDUS: Video ita se habere quae dixisti. Sed adhuc,
quaeso, adicere ne pigriteris, quonam id modo verum videtur
quod rerum essentiae incorruptibiles sunt.

NICOLAUS: Primum non haesitas tu quidem ipsum non-aliud
5 esse incorruptible; si enim corrumperetur, in aliud corrumperetur. Posito autem aliud et non-aliud ponitur. Non est igitur
corruptibile. Deinde certum est ipsum non-aliud se et omnia
definire. Omnes igitur rerum essentiae nisi ipsius non-aliud non
sunt. Ex quo ipsum non-aliud igitur in ipsis est, ipsae essentiae
10 quomodo non-aliud perdurante corrumperentur? Sicut enim
ipsum non-aliud essentias praecedit et omne nominabile, ita
mutabilitatem ac fluxibilitatem, quae in alterabili materia radicatur, praecedunt essentiae. Non-aliud quidem non est essentia,
sed quia in essentiis essentia, essentia dicitur essentiarum. Dice-
15 bat Apostolus: "Quae videntur, temporalia sunt; quae non
videntur, aeterna." Materialia enim sunt quae sensu quocumque
sentiuntur, et secundum materiae naturam fluxibilia atque insta-
bilia. Quae vero | non videntur sensibiliter et tamen sunt, tem- *18ᵛ*
poraliter quidem esse non videntur, verum sunt aeterna. Dum
20 essentiam in alio, ut in Socrate vides humanitatem, ipsam in alio
aliam vides, ideoque propter hoc in Socrate corruptibili per

---

37 9-10 igitur . . . non-aliud: *bis S*
37 14 essentiarum: essenciatum *S* essentiarum *U*
37 15 non: *om. S habet U*
37 16 quae: non videntur eterna *post* que *scribit et del. S*

and there are things which participate in a most special way. By comparison, some members |of the body| participate in the life of the soul dimly, others more clearly, and others in a most special way; likewise, some powers of the soul participate more clearly, and others more dimly, in intelligence. So too, those creatures which are less *other* than others—e.g., pure intelligences—participate the more in Not-other. But those which are more *other* than others—e.g., corporeal creatures, which cannot occupy one and the same place—participate less in the nature of that which is not *other* than anything.

37   FERDINAND: I see that what you have said holds true. But still, I ask, do not be hesitant to say something about how we see it to be true that the essences of things are indestructible.

    NICHOLAS: First, you do not doubt that Not-other is indestructible. For if it were destroyed, it would become other. But as soon as other is posited, Not-other is posited. Hence, Not-other is not destructible. Next, it is certain that *Not-other* defines itself and all |other| things. Therefore, all the essences of things are |essences| only of Not-other. Accordingly, given the fact that Not-other is in them, how could these essences be destroyed while Not-other continued to exist? For just as Not-other precedes the essences and everything nameable, so the essences precede the mutability and fluxibility which is rooted in alterable matter. Indeed, Not-other is not an essence; but because in the essences it is the essence, it is called the Essence of essences. The Apostle said: "The things which are seen are temporal; the things which are not seen are eternal."[30] For material things are those which are perceived by any one of the senses; and, in accordance with the nature of matter, they are fluxible and unstable. However, things which are not seen perceptibly but which, nonetheless, exist are not seen to exist temporally; rather, they are eternal. When |you see| an essence in something other—as |when| you see humanity in Socrates—you see it as other in this other; and so for this reason |you see the essence| to be destructible *per accidens* in Socrates, who is destructible. But

accidens esse corruptibilem. Sin eam ab alio videas separatam et
in non-alio, nempe secundum ipsius naturam in quo illam vides,
ipsam vides incorruptibilem.

38   FERDINANDUS: Videris essentiam illam quam non-aliud praecedit et aliud sequitur, ideam sive speciem dicere.

NICOLAUS: Sic rerum exemplaria ante res et post deum vidit
Plato; namque rem ratio rei antecedit, cum per ipsam fiat. Varie-
5 tas autem rerum varias dicit rationes, quas oportet post fontem
esse a quo, secundum ipsum, emanant. Sed quia non-aliud ante
res est, quod adaequatissima causa est cur quodlibet id est quod
est, non-aliud autem multiplicabile non est: idcirco rerum ratio,
quae aliud praecedit, et numerum praecedit et pluralitatem, et
10 innumerabilis secundum res ipsam participantes numeratur.

39   FERDINANDUS: Videris dicere rerum essentias non esse, verum
unam esse, quam rationem asseveras.

NICOLAUS: Nosti | tu quidem "unum," "essentiam," "ideam,"   *19ʳ*
"formam," "exemplar," sive "speciem" non-aliud ista non attin-
5 gere. Quando igitur in res intueor ipsarum essentias videns: cum
res quidem per ipsas sint, per intellectum eas ipsas prioriter con-
templando alias et alias assevero. Quando ipsas vero supra intellectum ante aliud video, non video alias aliasque essentias, sed
non aliud quam essentiarum quas in rebus contemplabar simpli-
10 cem rationem. Et ipsam non-aliud aut essentiarum essentiam
appello, cum sit quidquid omnibus in essentiis cernitur.

40   FERDINANDUS: Essentiae igitur esse essentiam dicis, quod [eam]
ob rem Aristoteles non admisit, ne in infinitum transitus fieret
numquamque deveniretur ad primum et scientia omnis interiret.

---

39 9 quam: nominis *SU Sequor Paulum Wilpert, qui confusionem textus
feliciter corrigit*   quas: quam *S*   quas *U*
40 1 eam: *addidi cum Wilpert*

if you see the essence as free from other and in Not-other, surely in accordance with the nature of that in which you see it |viz., in Not-other|, you see it to be indestructible.[31]

38 FERDINAND: You seem to mean the essence (or Idea or species), which Not-other precedes and other succeeds.

NICHOLAS: This is the way Plato viewed the exemplars-of-things, which are prior to things but posterior to God. For the form (*ratio*) of a thing precedes the thing, since the thing is made in accordance with the form. But the variety of things bespeaks a variety of forms, which must exist posterior to the fount from which they emanate, according to Plato. But because Not-other is prior to things (since it is the most adequate reason (*causa*) why each thing is what it is) but is not multiple, it is the Constituting-Ground-of-things, which precedes other and number and plurality but which, though innumerable, is numbered in accordance with the things which participate in it.

39 FERDINAND: You seem to mean that the essences of things are not plural but are one essence, which you call the Constituting Ground.[32]

NICHOLAS: You know that "one," "essence," "Idea," "form," "exemplar," and "species" are not applicable to Not-other. Therefore, when I look at things, beholding their essences: since things exist in accordance with their essences, then when I behold these essences through the understanding prior to |the things' existence|, I maintain that they are different from one another. But when I view them above the understanding and prior to other, I do not see different essences but see no other than the simple Constituting Ground of the essences that I was contemplating in these things. And I call this Ground *Not-other* or the *Essence of essences*, since it is whatever is observed in all the essences.

40 FERDINAND: You claim, then, that there is an Essence of an essence. Aristotle did not concede this |point| lest there be a continuation unto infinity and we never come to a first term and all knowledge perish.

NICOLAUS: Recte dicebat Aristoteles in infinitum non posse
5 pertransiri, prout quantitas mente concipitur, ideoque ipsum
excludit. Sed uti est ante quantitatem atque omne aliud et in
omnibus omnia, eiusmodi non refutavit infinitum, sed ad ipsum
cuncta deduxit ut de primo motore, quem virtutis repperit infini-
tae. Et hanc participari in omnibus virtutem vidit, quod equi-
10 dem infinitum non-aliud dico. Unde non-aliud formarum est
forma sive for|mae forma et speciei species et termini terminus *19ʳ*
et de omnibus eodem modo—sine eo quod sic ulterius in infinitum sit progressus, cum iam ad infinitum omnia definiens sit
perventum.

41   CAPITULUM XI

FERDINANDUS: Velis, optime pater, aliquo aenigmate me ducere
ad dictorum visionem, ut melius quid velis intuear?
NICOLAUS: Perlibenter. Videsne hunc lapillum carbunculum,
5 quem rustici rubinum nuncupant, hac ipsa tertia noctis hora,
tempore et loco obscurissimo, nec opus candela esse, quia in eo
lux est? Quae dum se ipsam vult exserere, medio lapilli hoc
facit, quia in se esset sensui invisibilis. Non enim occurreret sensui ideoque nequaquam sentiretur, cum nisi obvium sibi sensus
10 non cognoscat. Illa igitur lux quae fulgescit in lapillo, ad lucem
quae in oculo est, id defert quod de lapillo illo visibile est. Considero autem quomodo carbunculorum alius plus, alius minus
fulget, et perfectior is est qui fulgidior et maior quantitate, minor
autem fulgore ille quidem ignobilior. Fulgoris igitur intensitatem
15 eius pretiositatis mensuram perspicio—non autem corporis |
molem, nisi secundum ipsam fulgoris etiam intensitas sit mican- *20ʳ*
tior. Non ergo molis quantitatem de carbunculi essentia video,

40 11 forma²: forme *S* forma *U*
41 7 exserere: exerere *S* (id est manifestare *in marg. explanat S*) exercere *U*

NICHOLAS: Aristotle rightly said that with respect to the mind's conceiving of quantity there cannot be a continuation unto infinity, and hence he rules out this infinity. But Aristotle did not refute an infinity which is such that it is prior to quantity and is prior to everything other and is all in all. Rather, he traced all things back to it—as being things from the First Mover, which he found to be of infinite power. He regarded all things as participating in this power—to which infinity I give the name "Not-other." Hence, Not-other is the Form of forms (or the Form of form), the Species of species, the Boundary of boundary, and likewise for all things. There is no further progression unto infinity, since we have already reached an Infinity which defines all things.

41   CHAPTER 11

FERDINAND: In order that I may better discern what you mean, would you like to lead me, Excellent Father, by way of a symbolism, toward understanding what has been said?

NICHOLAS: Gladly. You see this carbuncle stone, which the peasants call a ruby. Do you see that at this third hour of the night—at a very dark time and in a very dark place—a candle is not needed because there is light in the stone? When this light wants to manifest itself, it does so by means of the stone. For in itself the light would be invisible to the sense |of sight|; for it would not be present to the sense and so would not at all be sensed, because the sense perceives only what is presented to it. Therefore, the light which glows in the stone conveys to the light which is in the eye what is visible regarding the stone.[33] I am aware that, among carbuncles, the one glows more, the other less. Now, *that* one is the more perfect which is the more glowing and is the larger. But the one which glows the less is the less valuable. Hence, I recognize that the intensity of the glow is the measure of the stone's preciousness. |The measure is| not the |stone's| physical size—unless the intensity of the glow is greater in accordance with the physical size. Therefore, I see that physi-

quia et parvus lapillus carbunculus est, sicut et magnus. Ante
magnum igitur corpus et parvum carbunculi substantiam cerno.
20 Ita de colore, figura et ceteris eius accidentiis. Unde omnia quae
visu, tactu, imaginatione de carbunculo attingo, carbunculi non
sunt essentia, sed quae ei accidunt cetera, in quibus, ut sensibilis
sit, ipsa enitescit, quia sine illis nequit esse sensibilis.

42   Illa igitur, quae accidens praecedit, substantia ab accidentibus
nihil habet. Sed accidentia habent ab ipsa omnia, quoniam eius
sunt accidentia seu substantialis lucis eius umbra vel imago. Lux
igitur illa substantialis carbunculi in clarioris fulgore splenden-
5 tiae se clarius ostendit ut in similitudine propinquiori. Carbunculi autem, hoc est rubini, color, rubeus scilicet, non nisi lucis
terminus est substantialis—non autem substantia, sed est similitudo substantiae, quia extrinsecum est sive sensibilis. Lux igitur
substantialis, quae praecedit colorem et omne accidens quod
10 quidem sensu et imaginatione potest apprehendi, intimior et
penitior carbunculo | est et sensui ipsi invisibilis. Per intellectum   *20ʳ*
autem, qui ipsam anterioriter separat, cernitur. Ipse sane illam
carbunculi substantiam videt non aliud quam carbunculi esse
substantiam. Et ideo ipsam etiam ab omni substantia non car-
15 bunculi aliam videt. Et hoc in aliis atque aliis operationibus
experitur, quae substantiae carbunculi virtutem sequuntur et non
alterius rei cuiuscumque. Quia igitur sic aliam substantialem
invisibilem carbunculi lucem videt, aliam substantialem invisibilem magnetis substantiam, solis aliam, aliam leonis, et ita de
20 omnibus: substantialem lucem in visibilibus omnibus aliam et
aliam videt, et ante omne sensibile intelligibilem, cum substan-

---

41 18 parvụs: parvulus *scribit, et* lus *del., S*
42 10 intimior: intimor *S*
42 12 ipsam: ipsum *SU*
42 16 sequuntur: *habet S (abbreviationem in marg. explicat S)*

cal size does not belong to the essence of the carbuncle, since a carbuncle may be a small stone as well as a large one. Hence, I see the substance of a carbuncle prior to the largeness or the smallness of the physical object. The same thing holds true regarding the stone's color, its shape, and its other accidents. Thus, none of all the things which my sight, my touch, and my imagination attain regarding the carbuncle are its essence. Instead, they are other things which happen to the essence. In these other things the essence shines forth, so that it is perceptible; for without these it cannot be perceptible.

42 Therefore, the substance, which precedes accident, has nothing from the accidents. But the accidents have everything from the substance, since they are its accidents—i.e., the shadow, or image, of its substantial light. Hence, the substantial light of the carbuncle shows itself more clearly—as in a closer likeness—in the glow of brighter splendor. But the color of a carbuncle, i.e., of a ruby (viz., the color red), is only an endpoint of the substantial light. It is not the substance but a likeness of the substance, for it is exterior and perceptible. Therefore, the substantial light, which precedes color and every accident that can be apprehended by the senses and the imagination, is more internal to and more intrinsic to the carbuncle and is invisible to the senses. However, this light is discerned by the intellect, which distinguishes it antecedently. Surely, the intellect sees that the substance of the carbuncle is not other than the substance of the carbuncle. And so, it sees that the substance is *other* than every substance of what is not a carbuncle. |The intellect| witnesses this fact in different operations which follow from the power of the carbuncle's substance but not from |the power| of any other thing's |substance|. Therefore, because |the intellect| in this way sees that the substantial, invisible light of a carbuncle is one thing, the substantial, invisible substance of a magnet another thing, that of the sun another thing, that of a lion another, and so on for all things, it sees that the substantial light is distinct in all visible things. And |it sees| the intelligible prior to all that is

tia, quae prior accidente videtur, non nisi intellectu videatur, qui solum videt intelligibile.

43   Acutius deinde mente introspiciens in universum ipsum et eius singulas partes, is videt quod sicut carbunculi substantia a sua quantitate non est alia colore, duritie, et reliquis, quando quidem eius sunt accidentia et ipsa in ipsis est omnia quae-
5   cumque illa sunt (quamquam non est ipsa nec quantitas illa nec qualitas nec accidentium aliud, sed in ipsis ipsa quae alia sunt atque alia, quoniam aliud accidens quantitas est, aliud | qualitas,   *21ʳ* et pari de omnibus modo): ita necessarium video quod, cum alia carbunculi substantia sit, alia magnetis, alia hominis, alia solis,
10   tunc in ipsis omnibus aliis aliisque substantiis non-aliud ipsum antecedere necesse est, quod quidem ab omnibus quae sunt, non sit aliud, sed omnia in omnibus sit—omne id scilicet quod in quocumque subsistit. Quemadmodum Ioannes Evangelista deum lucem dicit ante aliud, scilicet tenebras, quia ipsum asserit lucem
15   in qua ullae non sunt tenebrae. Si lucem igitur id quod ipsum est non-aliud dixeris, erunt creaturae tenebrae aliud. Sic mens cernit ultra intelligibilem substantialem lucem singulorum lucis principium non-aliud, quia non aliud a singulis est substantiis.

44   CAPITULUM XII

FERDINANDUS: Intelligere te equidem videor mihi. Ut tamen experiar, dicito: nonne tu admittis parvum hunc carbunculum esse alium ab illo grandiori?
5   NICOLAUS: Cur non admittam?

FERDINANDUS: At cum ambo sint carbunculi, substantia utique unius ab alterius substantia alia non videtur. Unde sunt ergo ab invicem alia?

---

43 12 omnia: omnibus *S* omnia *U*
43 14 lucem¹: dedit *post* lucem¹ *scribit et del. S*
44 7 unius: minus *S* unius *U*

perceptible; for the substance, which is seen prior to the accident, is seen only by the intellect, which sees only the intelligible.

43 If someone next mentally takes a closer look at the universe and its individual parts, he will see the following: The substance of a carbuncle is not *other* than its quantity, its color, its hardness, etc., since they are accidents of it and since in them it is whatever they are. (Nonetheless, the substance is neither the quantity nor the quality nor any of the accidents. But in the accidents |the substance is| these things which differ from one another since the quantity is one accident, the quality another, and likewise for all the other |accidents|.) By comparison, I see it to be necessary that since the substance of a carbuncle is one thing, the substance of a magnet another thing, the substance of a man another thing, the substance of the sun another thing, |etc.|, Not-other necessarily precedes all these different substances because it is not *other* than all existing things but is all in all—i.e., |it is| everything which exists in anything. Similarly, John the Evangelist states[34] that God is light prior to an other, viz., darkness; for he states that God is a light in which there is no darkness. Therefore, if you call that-which-is-Not-other *light*, then *qua* what is other, creatures will be darkness. Thus, the mind discerns—beyond intelligible, substantial light—Not-other as the Beginning of the light of individual things, because |Not-other| is not *other* than |these| individual substances.

44   CHAPTER 12

FERDINAND: It seems to me that I understand you. Nevertheless, so that I may test |my understanding|, answer the following: you admit, do you not, that this small carbuncle is *other* than that larger one?

NICHOLAS: Why shouldn't I admit it?

FERDINAND: Well, since both are carbuncles, assuredly the substance of the one is not seen to be *other* than the substance of the other. For what reason, then, are the carbuncles *other* than each other?

45 NICOLAUS: Tu quidem in substantiam absolutam intueris, quae
in | aliis alia esse non potest per ipsam substantificatis, at quae, *21ʳ*
ut sensibilis fiat substantia, materiam requirit substantificabilem,
sine qua non posset substantificari. Quomodo enim substantifi-
5 cari posset absque sensibiliter essendi possibilitate? Idcirco cum
ab illo alius sit iste carbunculus, ex essendi possibilitate, in uno
alia quam in altero, hoc evenire necesse est. Cum igitur materia
sensibilis ad sensibilem substantiam necessaria sit, erit substantialis materia in sensibilibus, ex quo secundum substantialem
10 hanc materiam, quae alia in alio est carbunculo, substantialiter
duo carbunculi differunt. At vero secundum intelligibilem substantiam, quae essendi forma possibilis sensibilisque substantiae
intelligitur, alii et alii duo non sunt carbunculi.

46 FERDINANDUS: Erit igitur carbuncularis, id est rubinalis, substantia non alia a qualibet cuiusvis carbunculi substantia, cuius
quidem extrema ei accidentia, ut sensibilis et materialis est,
ipsam consequuntur.

5 NICOLAUS: Optime intelligis. Nam in diversis carbunculis est
substantia, quae non est alia a quacumque cuiuslibet carbunculi
substantia, licet neutrius substantia sit ob substantialis possibilitatis ipsorum et accidentium consequenter advenientium varieta-
|tem. Prima igitur substantia, quam intellectus videt separatam, *22ʳ*
10 est substantia seu forma specifica. Alia vero, quae sensibilis dicitur, est per primam et materiam specificabilem specificata.

47 FERDINANDUS: Clarissima haec sunt. Sed nonne sic ipsum
non-aliud se habere ad alias et alias intelligibiles substantias
vides?

NICOLAUS: Praecise.

5 FERDINANDUS: Non erit igitur unum universum quasi unus
iste carbunculus.

---

45 2 in: *bis S (semel in folio 21ʳ et semel in folio 21ᵛ)*

45 NICHOLAS: You are looking at the absolute substance, which in the different things substantified by it cannot be other. Rather, in order for the absolute substance to be made perceptible substance, it requires substantifiable matter, without which there cannot be substantification. For how could there be substantification if there were no possibility of existing perceptibly?[35] Therefore, since this carbuncle is *other* than that one, it is necessary that this difference be due to the possibility-of-being, which in the one carbuncle is other than in the other carbuncle. Therefore, since perceptible matter is necessary for perceptible substance, substantial matter will be present in perceptible things. Therefore, the two carbuncles differ substantially in accordance with this substantial matter, which in the one carbuncle is *other* |than| in the other carbuncle. But in accordance with the intelligible substance, which is understood to be the form-of-being for the possible and perceptible substance, the two carbuncles are not distinct.

46 FERDINAND: Therefore, the carbuncular—i.e., the rubyesque—substance will not be *other* than any substance of any carbuncle. This substance's ultimate accidents—viz., that it is perceptible and that it is material—follow from it.

NICHOLAS: You understand very well. For in the |two| different carbuncles there is a substance which is not *other* than any substance of any carbuncle. And, yet, it is not the substance of either carbuncle. The reason for this fact is the diversity both in the substantial possibility of the carbuncles and in the ensuing accidents. Therefore, first substance, which the intellect sees as abstract, is the specific substance or the specific form. But the other |substance|, which is called the perceptible |substance|, is specified through first |substance| and through specifiable matter.

47 FERDINAND: These points are very clear. But isn't it your view that this is how Not-other is related to the different intelligible substances?[36]

NICHOLAS: Yes, precisely.

FERDINAND: Then, the one universe will not be like this one carbuncle.

NICOLAUS: Quam ob rem hoc?

FERDINANDUS: Quia eius substantia a qualibet ipsius partis
substantia alia non foret; puta eius substantia non foret alia a
10 carbunculi vel hominis substantia, sicut nec hominis substantia a
substantia manus eius, licet non sit manus, quae alia est substantia.

NICOLAUS: Quid tum?

FERDINANDUS: Absurdum profecto! Nam ipsum non-aliud substantia foret universi, et ita ipsum universum foret. Quod tamen
15 video impossibile, quando ipsum ante universum et aliud conspicio. Universum vero illud utique aliud video.

NICOLAUS: Non aberras nec devias, Ferdinande. Nam cum
omnia ad deum seu non-aliud ordinentur et nequaquam ad
aliud post ipsum, non est considerandum universum quasi finis
20 universorum; tunc enim deus esset universum. | Sed cum ad 22ʳ
suum sint principium ordinata universa—per ordinem enim a
deo universa esse se ostendunt—ad ipsum igitur ut ordinis in
omnibus ordinem sunt ordinata. Omnia enim ordinat, ut ipsum
non-aliud sive ordinis ordo in ordinatorum ad ipsum perfectione
25 perfectius relucescat.

48   CAPITULUM XIII

FERDINANDUS: Colligendo quae iam intellexi, ita in pluribus
carbunculis aliquid cernit intellectus quod eiusdem ipsos speciei
efficit. Et licet ipsis hoc insit omnibus ut specificans, anterioriter
5 tamen ipsum tale ante pluralitatem illam carbunculorum intuetur ipsius non-aliud similitudinem, quia carbunculum quemlibet esse carbunculum facit; et carbunculi cuiuslibet est inter-
num substantiale principium, quo subtracto carbunculus non

---

47 24 perfectione: *bis S*
48 6 carbunculum: carbunculi *S* carbunculum *U*

NICHOLAS: Why is that?

FERDINAND: Because the substance of the universe would not be *other* than the substance of any part of the universe. (For example, the substance of the universe would not be *other* than the substance of a carbuncle or of a man—just as the substance of a man is not |*other*| than the substance of the man's hand, although it is not the hand, which is another substance.)

NICHOLAS: What of it?

FERDINAND: This would surely be absurd! For the substance of the universe would be Not-other; and so, the universe would be Not-other. But I see that this is impossible, since I see Not-other prior to the universe and prior to other. And I see that, assuredly, the universe is an other.

NICHOLAS: You neither err nor deviate, Ferdinand. Since all things are ordered toward God, or Not-other, and are not at all ordered toward other, which is subsequent to God, the universe must not be considered as the goal of all things; for were it the goal of all things, it would be God. But since all things are ordered toward their Beginning (for through their order all things show themselves to be from God), they are ordered toward Him who is the Order of the order in all things. For He orders all things, so that Not-other, or the Order of order, shines forth the more perfectly in the perfection of the things ordered toward God.

48   CHAPTER 13

FERDINAND: To bring together the things which I have now understood: The intellect discerns in the many carbuncles something which causes them to be of the same species. Although this |something| is present in all these |carbuncles|, constituting them a species, nevertheless |the intellect| sees this thing antecedently to the plurality of the carbuncles—|sees it| as a likeness of Not-other. For it causes every carbuncle to be a carbuncle; and it is the internal, substantial principle (*principium*) of every carbuncle. If this principle is removed, the carbuncle will not

49 manebit. Hoc igitur specificum principium specificat carbunculi
possibilitatem essendi specificabilem ipsique possibilitati esse tri-
buit actuale, quando quidem posse esse carbunculi facit actu suo
actu esse carbunculum, quando confusam essendi possibilitatem
5 per specificum actum determinatam et specificatam experimur.
Et tunc | illud quod prius intellectualiter absolutum vidisti, in   *23ʳ*
singulo carbunculo possibilitatis actum vides, quoniam actu est
carbunculus—veluti si quis glaciem respiciens consideret fuisse
prius fluidum rivulum, quem nunc concretam et stabilitam gla-
10 ciem videt. Ille causam inspiciens reperiet quomodo frigus, quod
intellectualiter separatum videt, essendi quaedam species est,
quae in concretam et stabilem glaciem omnium rivulorum materiam crustavit et perstrinxit congelabilem, ut quilibet rivulus,
ob ipsius causae suae actualis praesentiam, actu glacies sit,
15 quamdiu per ipsam, quominus effluat, continetur. Et licet a frigidis non reperiatur frigus separatum, intuetur tamen intellectus
ut frigidorum causam ipsum ante frigida, et frigefactum actu per
frigus frigidabile cernit in frigidis, indeque ita glaciem ortam aut
nivem aut pruinam aut grandinem aut secundum frigidabilium
20 varietatem eius generis reliqua.

   Sed quoniam materia frigidabilis calefactibilis quoque est,
ideo in sese frigus alioquin incorruptibile, propter materiam, sine
qua nequaquam actu reperitur, | dum ipsa per caliditatem utpote   *23ᵛ*
calefactibilis alteratur, per accidens in corruptionem cadit. Sic
25 mihi videris ipse dixisse.

50   Quomodo etiam consequenter se habent ad specificas substantias accidentia intelligo. Sicut alia sunt quae unam quam
aliam glaciem consequuntur, alia item quae nivem, pruinam,
grandinem, cristallum, et alium quemvis lapidem. Satis, ex his

49 19 nivem: *ex ? corr. S*   nivem *U*
49 25 ipse: *supra lin. S*

49 remain. Therefore, this specific principle specifies the carbuncle's specifiable possibility-of-being and bestows actual being upon this possibility. For by its own actuality it causes the carbuncle's possible being to be actually a carbuncle; for we experience the indistinct possibility-of-being—experience it as it is determined and specified by the actuality of the species. And that which at first you intellectually beheld as abstract you now behold in a given carbuncle as the actuality of possibility, since it is actually a carbuncle.

The case is similar to someone who looks at ice and considers it to have first been a flowing rivulet which he now sees as solid and rigid ice. As he investigates the cause, he will discover that the coldness which he beholds intellectually as something abstract is a species of being—a species which hardens and contracts the freezable matter of all the rivulets into solid and rigid ice. Thus, each rivulet—as a result of the presence of its cause, which is actual—will actually be ice as long as it is kept, by its cause, from flowing. And although coldness is not found as separate from cold things, nevertheless the intellect beholds it prior to the cold things as their cause. In the cold things |the intellect| discerns what-is-able-to-become-cold actually made cold by coldness. |The intellect discerns| that from this cause there has arisen ice or snow or frost or hail or other things of this kind in accordance with the variety of things which can become cold.

But since matter which can become cold can also become hot, coldness—which in itself is indestructible—falls into destruction *per accidens* on account of matter (without which it is not at all actually found to be) when this matter is altered by heat, since it is capable of receiving heat. (You yourself seem to me to have been saying these things.)

50 I also understand how it is that accidents are consequentially related to specific substances. Just as there are some |accidents| which accompany one |piece of| ice as well as another, so there are other |accidents| which |accompany| snow, frost, hail, crystal, and any other "stone." On the basis of these open and

5 naturae operibus apertis et patulis, profundiora quoque reperio
non aliter se habere quam ipse breviter perstrinxisti: formas videlicet specificas et substantificas separatas per intellectum conspici
ac in specificatis rebus substantificatisque modo praemisso attingi.
De sensibilibus autem substantiis ad intelligibiles me per simili-
10 tudinem erigo.

51   NICOLAUS: Video te meum quidem conceptum in exemplo
naturae aptissimo dilucide explanasse, et gaudeo; omnia enim eo
pacto considerando perspicies. Nam quod parvo calore cristallum non dissolvatur, ut glacies, propter congelantis victoriam
5 frigoris super aquae congelatae fluxibilitatem, plane ostendit, ubi
materiae fluxibilitatem omnem forma in actu ponit, veluti in
caelo, illius corruptionem non sequi. | Ex quo impossibilem esse   24ʳ
intelligentiis corruptionem, quae in sensibilibus est, patet, quod
sunt a materia separatae, quae apta est alterari. Unde cum in
10 intelligente intellectum calor, ut calefiat, non immutet, sicut in
sentiente, ubi sensum immutat, facit, evidens est intellectum
materialem non esse aut alterabilem, quia sensibilia, quorum
propria immutatio est, non sensibiliter in eo, sed intellectualiter
sunt. Dumque acriter attente intellectum ante sensum esse con-
15 sideras et idcirco nullo attingibilem sensu, omnia quaecumque
in sensu sunt anterioriter in intellectu reperies. (Anterioriter
autem, hoc est insensibiliter, dico.) Sicut in intellectu frigus est ac
frigidum in sensu, frigus in intellectu ad sensibile frigidum anterioriter est. Non enim sentitur, sed intelligitur frigus, cum frigidum
20 ipsum sentiatur. Sicut nec calor sentitur sed calidum, ita nec
aqua sed aqueum, neque ignis sed igneum, in sensibilium regione
52 reperitur. Quod similiter de compositis omnibus est dicendum,

51 18 frigidum²: frigus *SU*

obvious works of nature I also sufficiently recognize that the more impenetrable matters are exactly as you yourself have briefly mentioned: viz., (1) that specific and substantial forms are seen by the intellect as abstract and (2) that in specified and substantified things they are apprehended in the aforesaid way. Now, from perceptible substances I raise myself up to intelligible |substances| by means of a likeness.

51   NICHOLAS: I see that you have lucidly explicated my concept by means of a most suitable example from nature; and I rejoice, for by this manner of consideration you will understand all |my points|. For instance, because of the triumph of the coldness-which-congeals over the fluxibility of the water-which-is-congealed, a crystal (e.g., ice) is not dissolved by a small amount of heat. This fact shows plainly that where a form makes actual the entire fluxibility of matter (as in the case of the heavens) the destruction of that material does not occur. Accordingly, it is evident that destruction, which occurs in perceptible things, is impossible for intelligible things—since they are free of matter, which is suited to being changed. Now, in the case of someone who understands |heat|, heat does not modify his understanding so that it becomes hot—as heat does do in the case of someone who perceives, when it modifies his sense. Therefore, it is evident that the intellect is neither material nor changeable. For perceptible things—for which change is a proper characteristic— are in the intellect intelligibly, not perceptibly. And when you consider keenly and carefully that the intellect is prior to the senses and so is not within reach of any of the senses, you will find that whatever is in the senses is antecedently in the intellect. (I say "antecedently"—that is, imperceptibly.) Just as coldness is in the intellect and cold is in the sense, |so| the coldness in the intellect is antecedent to the perceptible cold. For coldness is not perceived but is understood, since |it is| cold |that| is perceived. |Moreover,| just as we perceive not hotness but what is hot, so in the realm of perceptible things we experience not water but

52 what is watery, not fire but what is fiery.[37] This |point| must be

quoniam omne sensibilis mundi tale, simplex (quod est de regione
intelligibilium) antecedit. Aliaque et alia intelligibilia non-aliud
ipsum, simplicium intelligibilium simplicitas, | praecurrit, quam *24ᵛ*
5 ob rem non-aliud nequaquam in se, sed in simplici simpliciter,
composite vero intelligitur in composito. Quae quidem sunt, ut
sic dixerim, non aliata eius, et a quibus scilicet ipsum non-aliud
aliud non est. Video igitur quoniam eorum quae in regione sensibilium reperiuntur, quidquam sentitur, simplex eius, quod qui-
10 dem intelligitur, antecedit. Nec minus omnia quae in intelligibilium reperiuntur regione, principium, quod non-aliud nominamus,
antecurrit. Intellectuale quippe frigus eius praevenit causa, quae
ipsum non aliud quam frigus esse definit. Sicut ergo intellectus
per intellectuale frigus omnia sensibiliter frigida intelligit sine
15 mutatione sui sive frigefactione, ita ipsum non-aliud per se
ipsum sive non-aliud omnia intellectualiter existentia facit non
alia quam id esse quod sunt, sine sui vel mutatione vel alteritate.
Et sicut frigidum sensibile intellectuale non est frigus, licet aliud
ab ipso frigus nequaquam sit, sic frigus intellectuale principium
20 non est primum, etsi primum principium, quod est non-aliud, ab
ipso non sit aliud.

53   CAPITULUM XIV

| FERDINANDUS: Prime equidem et clarissime ita haec esse *25ʳ*
perspicio, quemadmodum ais; elicioque in intellectualibus non-
aliud valde relucere principium, quoniam, etsi ipsa non sunt sen-
5 sibilia, tamen a sensibilibus non sunt alia. Frigus enim a frigido
non est aliud, ut dixisti, quoniam summoto frigore nec frigidum
erit, neque esse intelligetur. Sic intellectus se habet ad sensum.

---

52 6 intelligitur: intelligiter *S*   intelligitur *U*
52 20 non-aliud: non aaliud *S*

asserted in similar fashion regarding all composite things, since the simple, which is of the realm of intelligible things, precedes every such thing |i.e., every composite thing| of the perceptible world. And Not-other, which is the Simplicity of simple intelligibles, precedes the different intelligible things. Hence, Not-other is not at all understood in itself; but in the simple it is understood simply and in the composite, compositely. The simple and the composite are, so to speak, its *non aliata*—i.e., things than which it is not *other*. Therefore, regarding the things found in the realm of perceptible objects: I see that whichever-of-them-we-perceive is preceded by its simple, which is understood. And it is no less true that the Beginning, which we call Not-other, precedes all that is found in the realm of intelligible things. Indeed, the Cause which determines coldness to be no other than coldness precedes intelligible coldness. Therefore, just as the intellect (without any change in itself and without becoming cold) understands by means of intelligible coldness all things which are perceptibly cold, so Not-other (without any change or otherness of its own) causes through itself (i.e., through Not-other) all things existing intelligibly to be no other than what they are. And just as perceptible cold is not intelligible coldness (even though intelligible coldness is not at all *other* than perceptible cold), so intelligible coldness is not the First Beginning (even though the First Beginning, which is Not-other, is not *other* than intelligible coldness).

53   CHAPTER 14

FERDINAND: I see readily and most clearly that these |matters| are as you say. And I ascertain that in intelligible things Not-other clearly shines forth as the Beginning. For although intelligible things are not perceptible things, nevertheless they are not *other* than perceptible things. For example, coldness is not *other* than cold, as you stated; for when coldness is removed, there will neither be, nor be understood to be, cold. This is the way in

Similiter ideo agens omne simile producere video, quia omne id
quod est, ab ipso non-aliud habet. Quapropter calor calefacere
10 et frigefacere frigus nititur, et de omnibus eodem modo.

Sed haec nunc ita sufficiant. Quaeso vero ut iuxta tua promissa ab hoc me principio in magnum illum theologum Dionysium aliosque quam brevissime introducas.

54   NICOLAUS: Obsequar tibi, quam fieri poterit brevissime, ut
poscis. Dionysius, theologorum maximus, impossibile esse praesupponit ad spiritualium intelligentiam praeterquam sensibilium
formarum ductu hominem ascendere, ut visibilem scilicet pulch-
5 ritudinem invisibilis decoris imaginem putet. Hinc sensibilia
intelligibilium | similitudines seu imagines dicit. Deum autem *25ᵛ*
principium asserit intelligibilia omnia praecedere, quem scire se
dicit nihil omnium esse, quae sciri possunt aut concipi. Ideo hoc
solum de ipso credit posse sciri, quem esse inquit omnium esse,
10 quod scilicet omnem intellectum antecedit.

FERDINANDUS: Dic eius, nisi tibi grave est, verba.

NICOLAUS: Alii aliter eius verba latine reddiderunt. Ceterum
ego ex fratris Ambrosii Camaldulensium generalis, novissimi
interpretis, translatione, quae mihi proposito videbuntur inser-
15 vire, ex ordine subiungam.

55   Ex capitulo primo Caelestis Hierarchiae: "Impossibile est
hominem ad intelligentiam spiritualium ascendere, nisi formis et
similitudinibus sensibilium ducatur, ut scilicet visibilem pulchritudinem invisibilis decoris imaginem putet."

5   Ex capitulo secundo: "Cum simplex divinarum rerum substantia in se ipsa et incognita sit nobis et intelligentiam fugiat
nostram . . . . "

---

53 8 omne¹: sibi *add. U*
54 12 latine: latitine *S*   latine *U*
54 13 Camaldulensium: Camaldunensium *SU*

which the intellect is related to the sense. Likewise, I see that the reason every cause produces something similar |to itself| is that it has from Not-other whatever it is. Therefore, heat endeavors to cause-to-be-hot, and coldness endeavors to cause-to-be-cold, and likewise for all |other| things.

But let these statements now suffice. I ask that in accordance with your promises at the beginning[38] you introduce me, very briefly, to that great theologian Dionysius and to the others.

54 NICHOLAS: I will comply with your request and will be as brief as possible. Dionysius, the greatest of the theologians, assumes the following: that it is impossible for a human being to ascend unto an understanding of spiritual matters except by the guidance of perceptible forms, so that, for example, he regards visible beauty as an image of invisible beauty. Hence, Dionysius maintains that perceptible things are likenesses or images of intelligible things. However, he asserts that God, as the Beginning, precedes all intelligible things; and he purports to know that God is not among any of the things which can be either known or conceived. Hence, he believes that the only thing which can be known about God (whom he affirms to be the *being* of all things) is that He precedes all understanding.[39]

FERDINAND: Cite his words—unless |to do so| is burdensome to you.

NICHOLAS: Different |individuals| have translated his words into Latin in different ways.[40] Nevertheless, I shall append in succession—from the translation of Brother Ambrose,[41] general of the Camaldolese and very recent translator |of Dionysius|— some |quotations| which will be seen to serve my purpose.

55 From Chapter 1 of *The Celestial Hierarchy*: "It is impossible for a human being to ascend unto an understanding of spiritual |matters| unless he is led by forms and likenesses of perceptible things, so that, for example, he regards visible beauty as an image of invisible beauty."[42]

From Chapter 2: "Since in itself the simple substance of divine things is unknown to us and escapes our understanding . . . ."[43]

Ex eodem: "Dum ipsam esse aliquid negamus ex his quae
sunt, verum profecto loquimur, etsi modum, quo illa indefinita
10 est, qui|ppe supersubstantialem et incomprehensibilem atque *26ʳ*
ineffabilem prorsus ignoramus."

Caelestis hierarchiae capitulo quarto: "Igitur omnia quaeque
subsistunt providentiae ratione reguntur ex summa illa omnium
auctore deitate manantis. Alioquin essent profecto nulla, nisi
15 substantiae rerum atque principio communicarent. Itaque in-
animata omnia hoc ipsum quod sunt ab ipso suscipiunt. Quippe
esse omnium est ipsa divinitas, quae modum totius essentiae
superat."

Eodem capitulo: "Secretum ipsum dei, quodcumque tandem
20 illud est, nemo umquam vidit neque videbit."

Eiusdem capitulo tertio decimo: "Admonebatur ergo theologus, ex his quae cernebat, ut secundum omnem substantialem
eminentiam cunctis visibilibus invisibilibusque virtutibus absque
ulla comparatione deus excelsior sit."

56   De ecclesiastica hierarchia capitulo primo: "Ut vere et proprie
dixerim: unum quidem est quod appetunt omnes qui unius speciem praeferunt. Sed non uno modo eius quod idem atque
unum est, participes fiunt, verum ut cuique pro merito sortem
5 divina et aequissima libra distrib|uit."   *26ᵛ*

Eodem capitulo: "Initium est fons vitae, bonitatis essentia,
unica rerum omnium causa, beatissima trinitas, ex qua sola
bonitatis causa, quae sunt omnia, ut et essent et bene essent,
acceperunt. Hinc transcendenti omnia divinae beatitudini trinae
10 atque uni, cui soli vere esse inest (modo nobis quidem incognito,
sed sibi plane perspecto et noto), voluntas quidem est rationalis
salus humanae omnis caelestisque substantiae."

55 8 ipsam: ipsum *S* ipse *U*

From the same |chapter|: "When we say that this |Substance| is not any of the things which exist, we surely speak the truth—even though we do not at all know its supersubstantial, incomprehensible, and ineffable measure, since this |Substance| is undefined."[44]

In Chapter 4 of *The Celestial Hierarchy*: "Therefore, all existing things are governed by virtue of the providence which flows from the Supreme Deity, who is the Author of all things. Assuredly, none of these things would exist unless they participated in the Beginning, and Substance, of things. And so, all inanimate things receive from this Beginning that which they are. Indeed, this Divinity, which transcends the measure of every being, is the being of all things."[45]

In the same chapter: "Whatever the mystery of God ultimately is, no one ever has seen it or ever will see it."[46]

In Chapter 13 of the same work: "Therefore, from the things which he discerned, the theologian was admonished that with respect to all substantial excellence God is incomparably loftier than all visible and invisible powers."[47]

56 In Chapter 1 of *The Ecclesiastical Hierarchy*: "To speak truly and properly: what is desired by all those who display the image [*species*] of the One is one thing. But they do not participate in one manner in that which is one and the same; rather, |they participate in such way| that the divine and most equal scales distribute a destiny to each according to his merit."[48]

In the same chapter: "The Beginning is the Fount of life, the Essence of goodness, the singular Cause of all things, the most blessed Trinity. From this sole Cause-of-goodness all existing things have received the fact of their existing and faring well. Hence, the will that is possessed by the Divine Beatitude—|a Beatitude| which is trine and one, which transcends all things, and in which, alone, being is truly present (in a manner unknown to us but clearly known and manifest to itself)—is |a will for| the rational well-being of every human and celestial substance."[49]

57   De divinis nominibus capitulo primo: "Sicut enim spiritalia
carnales percipere et inspicere nequeunt, et qui figmentis et figuris inhaerent ad simplicia figurisque vacua non aspirant, quique
secundum corporum lineamenta formantur incorporearum rerum
5 informitatem nec tactui nec figuris obnoxiam nequaquam attingunt: eadem ratione veritatis supereminet substantiis omnibus
supersubstantialis infinitas, sensusque excellit omnes unitas sensu
eminentior, ac mentibus omnibus inexcogitabile est unum illud
mente superius, ineffabileque est verbis omnibus bonum, quod
10 superat verbum."

   Eodem: "Ipsa de se in sacris tradit litteris, quod sit omnium
causa, initium et sub|stantia, et vita."   *27ʳ*

58   Eodem: "Invenies omnem, ferme dixerim, theologorum lau-
dationem ad beneficos divinitatis progressus exponendos atque
laudandos divina effingere nomina. Quocirca in omnibus ferme
sanctis libris advertimus divinitatem sancte praedicari ut singu-
5 larem quidem atque unicam ob simplicitatem atque unitatem
excellentis illius individui, ex quo veluti unifica virtute in unum
evadimus. Dividuisque nostris alteritatibus supra mundanum
modum conglobatis, in divinam monadem atque unionem deum
imitantem colligimur," etc.

59   Eodem: "In quo termini omnes omnium scientiarum plus
quam ineffabiliter praesubsistunt; neque intelligere neque eloqui
possumus neque omnino quomodolibet intueri, quod sit excep-
tus omnibus et excellenter ignotus."

5 Eodem: "Si enim scientiae omnes rerum substantium sunt
atque in substantiis desinunt, quae substantiam excedit omnem,
scientia quoque omni superior sit necesse est. Cum percipiat et
comprehendat atque anticipet omnia, ipse tamen omnino incomprehensibilis manet."

10 Eodem: "Ipsaque iuxta scripturae fidem sit omnia in omni-

---

58 3 Quocirca: qua circa *S*   quo circa *U*

57   In Chapter 1 of *The Divine Names*: "Those who are carnal cannot perceive and inspect spiritual things; those who cling to images and figures do not aspire unto simple things and things devoid of figures; and those who are formed according to corporeal lines do not at all attain unto the formlessness of incorporeal things—a formlessness which is not susceptible to touch or to figures. Similarly, on this same basis of truth, Supersubstantial Infinity excels all substances; Oneness, which is loftier than the senses, excels all the senses; the One, which is higher than mind, is inconceivable for every mind; and the Good, which excels |every| word, is not effable in any words."⁵⁰

In the same |chapter|: "In sacred Scripture this |Deity| teaches about itself that it is the Cause, the Beginning, the Substance, and the Life of all things."⁵¹

58   In the same |chapter|: "You will find that all—I should have said nearly all—the praise of the theologians forms divine names for exhibiting and praising the beneficent progressions of the Divinity. Accordingly, in nearly all of the sacred books we find that the Divinity is sacredly spoken of as singular, and one, on account of the simplicity and the oneness of that excellent Indivisibility through which, as a unifying power, we mount up unto the One; and after our distinct differences have been heaped together in a supramundane way, we are collected into the Divine Oneness, into a union which imitates God . . . . "⁵²

59   In the same |chapter|: "In this |Supreme Ray| all the limits of all the sciences more than ineffably preexist; and we cannot understand, articulate, or in any way at all behold it, because it is unlike all |other| things and is perfectly unknown."⁵³

In the same |chapter|: "If all the sciences of things pertain to substances and terminate in substances, then, necessarily, |the Supreme Ray,| which exceeds every substance, is also superior to every science. Although |this Divine Ray| perceives and comprehends and anticipates all things, it remains altogether incomprehensible."⁵⁴

In the same |chapter|: "According to the assurance of Scrip-

bus; verissime laudatur ut substantiae indultrix et consummatrix
continensque | custodia et domicilium et ad se ipsam convertens 27ʳ
atque ista coniuncte, incircumscripte, excellenter."
   Eodem libro, capitulo secundo: "Ineffabile quoque multis
15 vocibus praedicatur: 'ignoratio,' 'quod per cuncta intelligitur,'
'omnium positio,' 'omnium ablatio,' 'quod positionem omnem
ablationemque transcendit.' Divina sola participatione noscuntur."
60 In epistola Hierothei: "Neque pars neque totum est, et pars
est et totum, ut quae omne et partem et totum in se ipsa comprehendat, et excellenter habeat, anteque habeat. Perfecta est
quidem in imperfectis utpote perfectionis princeps; porro inter
5 perfectos imperfecta est quippe perfectionem excellentia temporeque transcendens."
   In eadem: "Mensura est rerum et saeculum et supra saeculum
et ante saeculum."
   In eadem: "Nec unum est, neque unius particeps; longeque ab
10 his unum est super unum illud quod in substantiis est."
61 Eodem libro de divinis nominibus, | capitulo quarto: "Theo- 29ʳ
logi peculiariter bonitatem summae deitati ex omnibus appli-
cant, ipsam (ut reor) substantiam divinam appellantes."
   Eodem: "Cum neque augeri neque minui possit substantia
5 quae bonum," et ita.
   Eodem: "Ex illo namque bono lux est et imago bonitatis;
idcirco lucis appellatione laudatur bonum, veluti in imagine | ex- 29ʳ
pressa primitiva forma."
   Eodem: "Illuminat quae lucem admittunt omnia; et creat
10 atque vivificat continetque et perficit; mensuraque substantium

---

60 2-3 comprehendat: comprehenditur S   comprehendent U
60 4 utpote: *ex* utputa *corr.* (pote *in marg.*) S   utputa U
61 1 Eodem . . . quarto: Eodem libro de divinis nominibus capitulo tercio S
*Ordinem impositum a Paulo Wilpert hic sequor, quia S confusionem in foliis
perpetuat. Transitum facit Wilpert ex folio 27ʳ, lineis 22-23, ad folium 29ʳ,
lineas 18-19*

ture this |Cause of all things| is all in all; it is most truly lauded as the Bestower and Completer of substance, the containing Repository and Abode, the Converter to itself—|being all of| these conjointly, uncircumscribedly, and excellently."[55]

In the same book, Chapter 2: "The Ineffable is spoken of by many words: 'Ignorance,' 'What is understood through all things,' 'the Positing of all things,' 'the Negating of all things,' 'What transcends all positing and negating.' The divine things are known only by participation."[56]

60   In the *Letter of Hierotheus*: "|The divinity of Jesus| is neither part nor whole, and it is both part and whole, so that it is what includes in itself everything—both part and whole—and has it in an excellent way and has it antecedently. In things imperfect, it is perfect because it is the Principle of perfection; on the other hand, among things perfect it is imperfect, transcending in duration [*tempus*] and in excellence what is perfect."[57]

In the same |letter|: "|The divinity of Jesus| is the measure and the duration of things; and it is above duration and before duration."[58]

In the same |letter|: "|God| is not one, nor does He participate in one; and yet, in a far different sense, He is One above the one which is present in the case of substances."[59]

61   In Chapter 4 of the same book of *The Divine Names*: "From among all things the theologians ascribe especially goodness to the Supreme Deity—calling, I believe, the Divine Substance *Goodness*."[60]

In the same |chapter|: "Since the Substance which is the Good can neither be increased nor decreased . . . . "[61]

In the same |chapter|: "Light is from that Good and is the image of Goodness; therefore, just as an original form is expressed in an image, so the Good is praised in speaking of it as light."[62]

In the same |chapter|: "|The Divine Goodness| illumines all things that admit of light; and it creates, enlivens, contains, and perfects them. It is the measure, the duration, the number, the

est et saeculum et numerus et ordo," etc. Nota exemplum de
sole.

62   Eodem: "Ut intelligibilis lux bonus ipse dicitur, qui omnem
supercaelestem spiritum spiritali impleat luce, omnemque ignorantiam pellat erroremque abigat ex animabus quibus sese insinu-
averit omnibus," etc.

5   Eodem: "Lux igitur intelligibilis dicitur bonum illud omnem
superans lucem ut principalis radius et exuberans effusio luminis."

Eodem: "Bonum istud ut pulchrum quoque a theologis sanctis praedicatur."

Eodem: "Ut pulchri omnis principalem pulchritudinem excel-
10 lentissime in se ipso ante tempora habens . . . . "

Eodem: "Idem pulchrum esse quod bonum perspicuum est."

Eodem: "Neque est aliquid in substantiis rerum, quod pulchri
et boni non sit aliquatenus particeps. Et istud item dicere disser-
endo praesumimus: id quoque quod non est, pulchri et boni
15 particeps esse. Tunc enim . . . ," etc.

Eodem: "Ut perstringam breviter: omnia | quae sunt, ex *30ʳ*
pulchro et bono sunt; et quae non sunt omnia, supersubstantialiter in pulchro sunt et bono, estque ipsum initium omnium et
finis," etc.

63   Eodem, capitulo octavo: "Neque est, sed his quae sunt, esse
ipse est. Neque ea quae sunt solum, verum ipsum quoque eorum
esse ex eo est, qui est ante saecula. Ipse enim est saeculum saeculorum, qui ante saecula est."

5   Eodem, capitulo octavo: "Resumentes itaque dicamus: ut iis
quae sunt omnibus et saeculis esse ab eo est, qui ante est; et
omne quidem saeculum et tempus ab eo est."

Eodem: "Omnia ipsi participant et a nullo existente discedit."

Eodem: "Si quid quomodolibet est: in ipso, qui ante est, et est

63 1 his: iis *S*   hiis *U*

order, etc., of substantive things." (Note the example of the sun.)[63]

62   In the same |chapter|: "This Good is spoken of as intelligible light, for it fills every supercelestial spirit with spiritual light; it dispels all ignorance, and drives out all error, from all the souls into which it has introduced itself," etc.[64]

In the same |chapter|: "Therefore, that Good, which (as a primordial ray and an abundant discharge of light) transcends all light, is said to be intelligible light."[65]

In the same |chapter|: "This Good is also spoken of as the Beautiful by the holy theologians."[66]

In the same |chapter|: "As having in itself most excellently, before time, the original Beauty of everything beautiful . . . . "[67]

In the same |chapter|: "The Beautiful is seen to be the same thing as the Good."[68]

In the same |chapter|: "Among substances there is not anything which does not to some extent participate in the Beautiful and Good. And we presume to say in our discussion even this: that even what-is-not participates in the Beautiful and Good. For then . . . ," etc.[69]

In the same |chapter|: "To summarize briefly: all existing things are from the Beautiful and Good; and all nonexisting things are supersubstantially in the Beautiful and Good, which is the Beginning and the End of all things," etc.[70]

63   In the same |book|, Chapter 8: "He does not exist; but He is the being of the things which exist. And not only those things which exist but also the being of that which exists is from Him who precedes the aeons. For He who is before the aeons is the Aeon of aeons."[71]

In the same |book|, Chapter 8: "And so, let us say by way of summary: all existing things and all aeons have being from Him who preexists; indeed, every aeon and all time come from Him."[72]

In the same |chapter|: "All things participate in Him, and He is absent from no existing thing."[73]

In the same |chapter|: "If something in any way exists, then it exists and is conceived and is preserved in Him who preexists.

10 et cogitatur atque servatur. Ceterisque ipsius participationibus
praefertur."

64   Eodem: "Deus ante habet, ut ante sit et eminentissime sit
excellenterque ipsum esse habeat. Omnia ipsum in se ipso esse
praestituit; atque ipso esse omne quod quomodolibet est, ut sub-
sisteret fecit. Denique et rerum principia omnia esse ipsius parti-
5 cipatione et sunt et principia sunt; et prius sunt, postea principia
sunt. Et si velis vitam ipsam viventium ut viventium initium
dicere et similium ut similium similitudinem . . . , " etc.

| Eodem: "Haec esse ipsius invenies participare primum, *30ᵛ*
atque esse ipso primo manere, deinde huius aut illius esse prin-
10 cipia, essentiaeque participando et esse et participari. Si autem
ista participatione essentiae sunt, multo magis quae ipsorum participia sunt."

Eodem: "Bonitas prima participationum celebratur."

| [Eodem:] "Neque in aliquo subsistentium est, neque aliquid *27ᵛ*
15 est horum."

65   Eodem, capitulo nono: "Ipsi nihil contrarium."

Eodem, capitulo decimo: "Qui invenitur ex omnibus, incom-
prehensibilem et investigabilem theologi | dicunt."   *28ᵛ*

Eodem capitulo: "Divina oportet non intelligamus humano
5 more, sed toti integre a nobis ipsis excedentes atque prorsus in
deum transeuntes."

Eodem capitulo: "Non habet deus peculiarem scientiam sui,
aliam vero communem omnia comprehendentem. Ipsa enim se
omnium causa cognoscens, qua tandem ratione quae ab se sunt
10 et quorum est causa, ignorabit?"

Eodem capitulo: "In omnibus deus cognoscitur, et seorsum ab

---

64 14 *Transitum recte facit Wilpert, quem sequor, ex folio 30ᵛ, linea 8, ad*
folium 27ᵛ, lineam 23   14 Eodem: *addidi cum Wilpert*
    65 10 ignorabit: ignorabat *S* ignorabit *U*
    65 11 seorsum: seorsam *S* seorsum *U*

Moreover, |this existential participation| takes precedence over the other participations in Him."[74]

64   In the same |chapter|: "God prepossesses, so that He preexists and exists most eminently and exists excellently.[75] He has determined beforehand that in Himself all things are being itself; and by His own being He has caused to exist everything-which-in-any-way-exists. Finally, by participating in His being, all the beginnings of things exist and are beginnings; first they exist, and then they are beginnings. And if you want to call life itself the beginning of living things *qua* living things and call likeness |the beginning| of like things *qua* like things . . . " etc.[76]

In the same |chapter|: "You will find that (1) first these |beginnings| participate in being and by means of being remain in being and (2) then they are beginnings of this or that and (3) by participating in being, they both exist and are participated in. But if they exist by participation in being, this is all the more true of the things which participate in them."[77]

In the same |chapter|: "Goodness is honored as the first of the participations."[78]

In the same |chapter|: "He is not in any existing things; nor is He any of these things."[79]

65   In the same |book|, Chapter 9: "Nothing |is| opposite to |the Divine Life|."[80]

In the same |book|, Chapter 10: "He who is discovered from all things is called by the theologians incomprehensible and undiscoverable."[81]

In the same chapter: "We ought not to understand divine things in a human manner; rather, we all |ought| wholly |to| take leave of ourselves and cross over straightway unto God."[82]

In the same chapter: "God does not have one knowledge which is exclusively of Himself and a distinct |knowledge which is| common and which comprehends all things. For, if the Cause of all things knows itself, how will it fail to know the things which exist from it and of which it is the cause?"[83]

In the same chapter: "God is known in all things and apart

omnibus. Et per scientiam et ignorationem cognoscitur deus."

Eodem capitulo: "In omnibus omnia est, et in nihilo nihil."

66 Eodem, capitulo undecimo: "Virtus est deus et omnis virtutis auctor."

Eodem capitulo: "Infinite potens divina distributio in omnia quae sunt, se intendit; et nihil est in rebus quod non sit virtuti 5 alicui percipiendae idoneum."

Eodem capitulo: "Quod enim omnino nulla virtute ṣubnititur, neque est; neque aliquid est; neque est penitus ipsius ulla positio."

Eodem capitulo: " . . . quique quae sunt omnia excellenter et ante tempora habeat supersubstantiali virtute sua, qui his quae 10 sunt omnibus, ut esse possint et hoc sint, excellentis virtutis copia et exuberanti profusione largitur."

67 Eodem libro, capitulo duodecimo: | "Magnus quidem appel- 28ᵛ latur deus iuxta propriam ipsius magnitudinem, quae magnis omnibus suimet consortium tradit et extrinsecus super omnem magnitudinem funditur et supra expanditur, omnem continens 5 locum, omnem transcendens numerum, omnem transiliens infinitatem."

Eodem: "Magnitudo haec et infinita est et quantitate caret et numero."

Eodem: "Parvum vero sive tenue dicitur, quod molem omnem 10 excedit atque distantiam, quod absque impedimento ad omnia pergit, quamquam certe omnium causa pusillum est: nusquam enim invenies pusilli speciem incommunicabilem."

Eodem: "Hoc pusillum quantitate caret, et qualitate tenetur nulla; infinitum est et indeterminatum, comprehendens omnia et 15 ipsum comprehensibile nulli."

66 1 virtutis: virtus *S* virtutis *U*
66 5 percipiendae: percipiendi *SU*

from all things. And God is known through knowledge and ignorance."[84]

In the same chapter: "In all things He is all things, and in nothing He is nothing."[85]

66   In the same |book|, Chapter 11: "God is Power; and He is the Author of all power."[86]

In the same chapter: "The infinitely powerful Divine Distribution stretches forth into all existing things; and among |these| things there is nothing which is not suitable for receiving power."[87]

In the same chapter: "For what is not at all supported by any power does not exist; nor is it anything; nor is there any positing of it at all."[88]

In the same chapter: " . . . who by His own supersubstantial power contains all existing things excellently and before |all| times and who from the fulness and the abundant outpouring of His excellent power bestows upon all existing things their ability to exist and the fact that they are this |or that thing|."[89]

67   In the same book, Chapter 12: "Indeed, God is called great in accordance with His own greatness, which bestows on all great things communion with itself, and which is shed from without upon every magnitude, and which is extended above, containing every place, transcending every number, surpassing every infinity."[90]

In the same |chapter|: "This greatness is both infinite and free of quantity and of number."[91]

In the same |chapter|: "That which transcends all size and distance and which passes unimpeded to all things is called small or tiny. And yet, this small thing is assuredly the Cause of all things; for you will never discover the form of |this| small thing to be incommunicable."[92]

In the same |chapter|: "This small thing is free of quantity and is possessed of no quality; it is infinite and undetermined, encompassing all things and yet able to be encompassed by none."[93]

Eodem: " . . . quod augeri minuique non possit."

68   Eodem: "Porro alterum dicitur, quia omnibus providentiae ratione deus adest et omnia in omnibus pro omnium salute fit, in se ipso et sua identitate manens."

Eodem: " . . . divinae similitudinis virtus, per quam quae
5 producuntur omnia ad auctorem convertuntur. Haec quidem deo similia dicenda sunt | et ad divinam imaginem et similitudi- *29ʳ* nem ficta. Non autem illis similis dicendus est deus, quia neque homo est suae imagini similis."

Eodem: "Ipsa theologia ipsum dissimilem praedicat et omni-
10 bus incompactum, ut ab omnibus alterum; et quod est profecto mirabilius, nihil simile esse ait. Et certe non adversatur hoc divinae similitudini. Quippe eadem deo et similia et dissimilia sunt— similia quia ipsum pro viribus imitantur, quem ad liquidum imitari possibile non est."

15 Eodem: "Hoc autem quia causalia auctore suo multum inferiora sunt, et infinitis inconfusisque mensuris ab eo absunt."

69   Eodem, capitulo duodecimo: " . . . ex se velut ex omnipotente radice cuncta producens."

Eodem: " . . . neque sinens ea ab se cadere."

|Eodem, capitulo duodecimo: "Ipse omnium et saeculum et *30ᵛ*
5 tempus, et ante dies et ante saeculum ac tempus—quamvis et tempus et diem et momentum et saeculum eum convenientissime appellare possimus et qui per omnem motum incommutabilis atque immobilis sit. Cumque semper moveatur, in se ipso manet ut saeculi et temporis et dierum auctor."

10 Eodem, capitulo tertio decimo: "Vitam omnium quae vivunt

69 3 sinens: siniens *S*   sinens *U*
69 4 *Transitum recte facit Wilpert, quem sequor, ex folio 29ʳ, linea 18, ad folium 30ᵛ, lineam 8*

In the same |chapter|: " . . . which cannot be increased or decreased."⁹⁴

68   In the same |chapter|: "But God is called Other because He is present to all things by virtue of Providence and because for the well-being of all He becomes all in all, while remaining in Himself and |retaining| His own identity."⁹⁵

In the same |chapter|: " . . . the power of their likeness to God, through which all created things are turned toward their Creator. Created things must be said to be like unto God and formed according to the image and likeness of God. However, God must not be said to be like unto created things; for not even a man is similar to his own image."⁹⁶

In the same |chapter|: "Theology itself says that, as something other than all things, He is unlike all things and is free from all things; and—what is surely more marvelous—it denies that anything is like unto |Him|. And, assuredly, this point is not opposed to the |doctrine of the| likeness-to-God. Indeed, the same things are both similar and dissimilar to God—similar because, as much as they can, they imitate Him who cannot possibly be imitated clearly."⁹⁷

In the same |chapter|: "But this |is true| because created things are much lower than their Creator and are infinitely and distinctly distant from Him."⁹⁸

69   In the same |book|, Chapter 12: " . . . producing all things from Himself, as from an omnipotent Source."⁹⁹

In the same |chapter|: " . . . and not allowing them to fall away from Himself."¹⁰⁰

In the same |book|, Chapter 12: "He is the duration and the time of all things, and He is before the days and before duration and before time—although we can very suitably call Him time and day and moment and duration and Him who is unchangeable and immovable by any motion. And although He is always moved, he remains in Himself as the Creator of duration and of time and of the days."¹⁰¹

In the same |book|, Chapter 13: "The One, which principally

et ipsius vitae causam, ipsum esse ipsamque vitam et ipsam dei-
tatem diximus principaliter quidem et divine et secundum causam unum principia cuncta excellens."

70   Eodem, capitulo quinto decimo: "Omnem terminat infinitatem, et supra omnem expanditur finem, atque a nullo capitur
seu comprehenditur; sed pertingit ad omnia | simul."   *31ʳ*

Eodem: "Neque est unum illud, omnium causa, unum ex
5 pluribus, sed ante unum," etc.

Eodem: " . . . uniusque omnis ac multitudinis definitivum."

Eodem: "Si omnibus omnia coniuncta quis ponat, erunt
omnia toto unum."

Eodem: "Est unum omnium veluti elementum."

10   Eodem: "Si unum tollas, neque totum erit neque pars aliqua
neque aliud quidquam in rebus. Omnia enim in se ipso unum
uniformiter antea cepit atque complectitur."

Eodem: "Unum ante finem atque infinitatem," etc.

Eodem: "Omnia quae sunt ipsumque esse determinat."

15   Eodem: "Quod supra ipsum unum est, ipsum quod unum est
determinat."

Eodem: "Unum quod est, inter ea quae sunt connumeratur.
Porro numerus substantiae particeps est. Unum vero illud supersubstantiale, et unum quod est et omnem numerum determinat."

71   Circa finem Mysticae theologiae: "Neque aliud aliquid ex his
quae nobis aut alteri cuiquam in mundo est cognitum, neque
aliquid eorum quae non sunt, neque eorum quae sunt, est."

In eadem: "Neque est ulla eius positio, neque ablatio."

---

70 14 determinat: determinant *SU*
71 3 aliquid: aliquod *S*   aliud *U*

and divinely and causally excels all beginnings, we have called the Life of all living things, and the Cause-of-life-itself, and Being itself, and Life itself, and Deity itself."[102]

70   In the same |book|, Chapter 15: "|The Perfect| is the End of every infinity and is extended beyond every end and is not contained or encompassed by anything; rather, it stretches forth to all things at once."[103]

In the same |chapter|: "And that One, the Cause of all, is not a one composed of many, but is before one," etc.[104]

In the same |chapter|: " . . . the limitation both of everything one and of everything many."[105]

In the same |chapter|: "If someone were to suppose that everything is conjoined with everything, then everything would be wholly one."[106]

In the same |chapter|: "The One is the 'elemental principle' (so to speak) of all things."[107]

In the same |chapter|: "If you remove the One, then there will remain neither the whole nor any part nor any other thing at all. For the One uniformly and antecedently contains and includes all things in itself."[108]

In the same |chapter|: "The One is prior to the finite and the infinite," etc.[109]

In the same |chapter|: "|The One| determines both all existing things and being itself."[110]

In the same |chapter|: "What is above the one determines that which exists as one."[111]

In the same |chapter|: "The one which exists is numbered among existing things, and number participates in substance. But that Supersubstantial One determines both the existing one and every number."[112]

71   Toward the end of *The Mystical Theology*: "He is not any other of the things which are known to us or to anyone else in the world; nor is He any existing or nonexisting thing."[113]

In the same |*Theology*|: "There is no positing of Him and no negating of Him."[114]

5 In epistola ad Gaium: "Si aliquis videns deum intellexerit
quod vidit, non ipsum vidit, sed aliquid . . . . Non | cognosci *31ᵛ*
neque esse, est supersubstantialiter et super mentem cognoscitur.
Perfecta ignorantia cognitio est eius, qui est super omnia quae
cognoscuntur."

72   CAPITULUM XV

FERDINANDUS: Haec theologi ponderosa et profunda esse dicta
perspicio et talia quae in ineffabilem divinitatem, modo quo
quidem homini conceditur, visum dirigunt.
5 NICOLAUS: Advertistine quomodo de ipso non-aliud loquitur?
FERDINANDUS: Non adhuc clare percepi.
NICOLAUS: Tu saltem ipsum de prima causa loqui considerasti,
quam in omnibus omnia nunc sic, nunc alio modo ostendit.
FERDINANDUS: Sic videtur. Sed duc me, quaeso, ut idipsum
10 clarius tecum inspiciam.
73 NICOLAUS: Nonne, ubi ipsum principium unum nominat, considerasti quomodo post hoc dicit unum supersubstantiale unum
quod est et omnem numerum determinare?
FERDINANDUS: Consideravi et placuit.
5 NICOLAUS: Quare placuit?
FERDINANDUS: Quia licet ipsum unum propinque ad ipsum
non-aliud accedat, adhuc tamen fatetur ante unum esse supersub-
stantiale unum; | et hoc utique est unum ante ipsum unum quod *32ʳ*
est unum. Et hoc tu quidem ipsum non-aliud vides.
10 NICOLAUS: Optime cepisti! Unde si A foret significatum de li
non aliud, tunc A id de quo loquitur foret. Si autem, ut ait,
unum est ante finem et infinitatem omnem terminans infinitatem, ad omnia simul pertingens et ab omnibus incomprehensi-
bile manens uniusque et omnis multitudinis definitivum: utique
15 A ipsum unum definiens, ipsum unum sane, quod est aliud,

71 5 Gaium: Caium *SU*
71 9 - **72** 1 cognoscuntur. Capitulum XV: cognoscuntur. Expliciunt allegaciones.
Sequitur Capitulum quintum decimum *S*

In the *Letter to Gaius*. "If anyone who has seen God understands what he has seen, then he has not seen God but some-
thing |else| . . . . Not being known and not existing, He exists
supersubstantially and is known supermentally. Our knowledge
of Him who is above all known things is perfect ignorance."[115]

72   CHAPTER 15

FERDINAND: I see that these statements of the Theologian[116]
are weighty and deep and such that, in the manner granted unto
man, they direct our sight unto the Ineffable Divinity.

NICHOLAS: Did you notice the way in which he speaks of
Not-other?

FERDINAND: I have not yet clearly discerned |this point|.

NICHOLAS: You at least noted that he is speaking about the
First Cause, which he shows—now in this way, now in that
way—to be all in all.

FERDINAND: So it seems. But guide me, I ask, so that with
you I may view this |point| more clearly.

73   NICHOLAS: When he gives to the Beginning the name "One,"
did you not note how thereafter he says that the Supersubstantial One determines the existing one and every number?

FERDINAND: I noted it; and it pleased me.

NICHOLAS: Why did it please you?

FERDINAND: Because, although the one approaches closely to
Not-other, nevertheless |Dionysius| states that before the one
there is the Supersubstantial One; and assuredly this One is
prior to the one which exists as one.[117] And you see that this
|Supersubstantial One| is Not-other.

NICHOLAS: You have understood perfectly! Hence, if A were
what is signified by "Not-other," then A would be that of which
he speaks.[118] But if, as he says, the One is prior to the finite and
the infinite and is the End of every infinity and stretches forth
unto all things at once and remains unencompassable by all
things and is the limitation both of everything one and of everything many, then, surely, since A defines the one, A precedes the

antecedit. Nam cum unum sit non aliud quam unum, tunc A subtracto unum desineret.

FERDINANDUS: Recte! Nam cum dicat quomodo unum quod supra unum est, ipsum quod unum est determinat, hoc utique
20 unum supra unum prius dixit unum ante unum. Determinat igitur A unum et omnia, cum, ut dicit, ipsum unum omnis unius et multitudinis sit definitivum.

74   NICOLAUS: Potuisti etiam videre quomodo theologus, ad ipsum ante, mentem convertit, dicens deum habere ante, ut ante sit et sit eminentissime. Tamen A ante ante conspicitur, cum ante sit non aliud quam ante. Unde cum ante non nisi ante aliquid quod
5 praecedit, intelligatur, utique A est emi|nentissime ipsum ante, *32ᵛ* cum aliud omne praecedat. Ante autem dici de alio potest, ut aliud quod praecedit et aliud quod sequitur, sit. Igitur si, ut theologus vult, in anteriori omnia eminenter sunt seu anterioriter quae reperiuntur in posteriori, in A utique eminentissime omnia
10 cernimus, cum ante ipsum ante sit.

75   FERDINANDUS: Optime rememoras. Adverti enim quomodo dicit theologus ipsum, qui est ante saecula, esse saeculorum saeculum; et ita ipsum de omnibus velle arbitror dicere. Per hoc igitur quod deum anterioriter ipsum A video, omnia in ipso
5 ipsum video; per hoc vero quod deum posterioriter cerno in alio, ipsum in omnibus omnia esse cerno. Si ipsum ante saecula perspicio, in ipso saeculum deum esse perspicio; nempe ante saeculum videtur saeculum in suo principio seu ratione. Si video ipsum in saeculo, ipsum saeculum video. Quod enim ante vidi
10 deum, post video saeculum; nam saeculum quod in deo deum vidi, in saeculo saeculum intueor. Quod quidem non est aliud quam cum in ipso priori posterius ipsum videtur, tunc enim est ipsum prius; quodsi in ipso posteriori prius ipsum cernitur, tunc ipsum poste|rius est.   *33ʳ*

one, which is an other. For since the one is not other than the one, the one would cease to be if A were removed.

FERDINAND: Right! For since he speaks of how the One-which-is-above-the-one determines that which exists as one, assuredly he previously spoke of this One-above-one as One-before-one. Therefore, A determines the one and all things, since (as he says) the One itself is the limitation both of everything one and of everything many.

74   NICHOLAS: You were able to see how it was that the Theologian turned his attention to *before* (*ante*)—saying that God prepossesses, so that He preexists and exists most eminently. Nevertheless, A is seen before *before*, since *before* is not other than *before*. Hence, since *before* is understood only before something which it precedes, assuredly A is most eminently *before*, since A precedes every other thing. But *before* can be predicated of an other—so that what precedes and what succeeds are distinct. Therefore, if, as the Theologian proposes, all things which exist in something posterior exist eminently and antecedently in something antecedent, then assuredly we discern all things most eminently in A, since A is before *before*.

75   FERDINAND: You recollect perfectly. For I noticed the Theologian's saying that God, who is before the aeons, is the Aeon of aeons; and I think he wants to speak in a similar way about all things. Therefore, by virtue of the fact that I see God antecedently as A itself, I see that in Him all things are Him; but by virtue of the fact that I see God subsequently in an other, I see that in all things He is all things. If I see God before the aeons (*saecula*), then I see that in God duration (*saeculum*) is God; assuredly, in its own Beginning or Constituting Ground, duration is seen before duration. If I see God in duration, I see Him as duration. For what I saw antecedently as God, I see subsequently as duration. For the duration that I saw in God as God, I view in duration as duration. This |point| is no different from the following |point|: viz., that when the later is seen in the earlier, it is the earlier; but if the earlier is seen in the later, it is the later.

15   NICOLAUS: Omnia penetras per ea quae de ipso non-aliud
concepisti; et quantum tibi lucis ipsum A principium praestitit,
intueris ad ea quae tibi alioquin erant abscondita. Sed mihi
adhuc unum dicito: quomodo apprehendis theologum asserere
deum convenientissime saeculum et tempus et diem et momen-
20 tum posse nuncupari?

76   CAPITULUM XVI

FERDINANDUS: Intelligo iuxta theologi visionem. Vidit enim in
tempore omnia temporalia temporaliter moveri, tempus tamen
ipsum manere semper immutabile. Unde in tempore ipsum non-
5 aliud valde intelligere elucescit. In hora enim est hora, dies in
die, mensis in mense, in anno annus. Et ut ante haec omnia
cernitur, in ipso ipsum sunt, sicut ipsum in omnibus omnia. Et
quamvis ipsum in omnibus quae tempore participant, omnia sit
et ad omnia pergat et maneat cum omnibus inseparabiliter
10 eaque definiat et terminet, non minus tamen apud se ipsum stabile manet et immobile neque augetur neque minuitur, licet
maius esse tempus maiori in duratione videatur, ut in mense
maius quam die, qu|od non nisi ex alio venit, quod de ipso plus *33ᵛ*
minusve participat. Aliter igitur et aliter eo manente imparticipa-
15 bili varie participatur.
77 NICOLAUS: Ut equidem video, nihil te latet. Sed ut ad cuncta
theologi verba mentem applices opus est, nihil enim frustra dicit.
Momentum enim ipsum deum convenientissime dici posse ait.
FERDINANDUS: Utique sic dicit. Sed cur hoc attendendum
5 acriter mones?
NICOLAUS: Momentum est temporis substantia. Nam eo sub-

NICHOLAS: You grasp all these |points| by means of the things you have understood about Not-other; and insofar as A, the Beginning, has accorded to you light, you will see those things which otherwise would have been hidden from you.

But tell me one more thing. In what way do you construe the Theologian's statement that God can most suitably be called duration and time and day and moment?

76 CHAPTER 16

FERDINAND: I understand |the foregoing| in accordance with the view of the Theologian. For he saw all things temporal as moved temporally in time but, nonetheless, saw time itself as always remaining immutable. (Hence, in time an understanding of Not-other is especially manifest.) For example, in an hour |time| is the hour; in a day it is the day; in a month, the month; in a year, the year. And as |time| is seen before all these things, |so| in time they are time—just as in all things time is all things. And although in all the things which partake of time time is all things, and although time proceeds to all things and remains with them inseparably and defines them and delimits them, nonetheless within itself it remains fixed and immovable, and is neither increased nor decreased, although it seems to be greater in a greater duration. For example, in a month |time seems to be| greater than in a day. This |impression| comes about only because of the thing other |than time| which participates more or less in time. Therefore, time is participated in in different ways, while remaining unable to be participated in in different ways.

77 NICHOLAS: It seems to me that nothing is hidden from you. But you need to pay attention to all the words of the Theologian, for he says nothing in vain. For example, he says that God can very suitably be called the Moment.

FERDINAND: Yes, he says this. But why do you caution that this |statement| ought to be carefully noted?

NICHOLAS: The moment is the substance of time. For if it

lato nihil temporis manet. Momentum igitur valde admodum de
A participat ob suam simplicissimam indivisibilitatem et inaltera-
bilitatem; videtur enim ipsa substantialitas, quae si duratio
10 nominaretur, tunc facillime cerneretur quomodo in aeternitate
aeternitas est, in tempore tempus, mensis in mense, in die dies,
in hora hora, momentum in momento, et de omnibus durationem participantibus eodem modo. Et non est aliud ab omnibus
quae durant, ipsa duratio, et maxime quidem a momento sive
15 nunc, quod stabiliter durat. Igitur duratio in omnibus est omnia,
licet ante omnia, quae ipsam participant. Unde quia alia sunt
quae ipsam participant, et a participantibus ipsa non est aliud:
patet quomodo ipsum | non-aliud per aeternitatem seu verius 34ʳ
durationem et momentum participatur.

78 FERDINANDUS: Puto te per momentum velle praesentiam dicere.

NICOLAUS: Idem esse nunc, momentum, et praesentiam volo.

FERDINANDUS: Clare iam video quoniam praesentia est cognoscendi principium et essendi omnes temporum differentias
5 atque varietates. Per praesentiam enim praeterita cognosco et
futura, et quidquam sunt per ipsam sunt. Quippe praesentia in
praeterito est praeterita, in futuro autem est futura, in mense
mensis, in die dies, et ita de omnibus. Et quamquam est omnia
in omnibus et ad omnia pergens, est tamen ab omnibus incom-
10 prehensibilis stabiliter manens absque alteritate.

NICOLAUS: Perfecte subintrasti, atque ideo etiam nequaquam
te latet A praesentiam esse praesentiae. Nam ipsam antecedit
praesentiam, cum praesentia, quae non aliud est quam praesentia, ipsum non-aliud, quod in ipso est ipsum, praesupponat. Et
15 quia praesentia est temporis substantia, recte quidem ipsum A

77 11 aeternitas: ernitas *S* eternitas *U*

77 16 sunt: *ut* funt *scribit S*

78 6 quidquam: quitquam *(?) S (confuse abbreviat S; partem maiorem
ipsius 6-7 om. U)*

were removed, nothing would remain of time. Therefore, because of its most simple indivisibility and unchangeableness, the moment participates to a very great degree in A; for |the moment| seems to be substantiality. If this |substantiality| were called duration, then we would discern very easily how it is that in eternity duration is eternity; in time it is time; in a month, the month; in a day, the day; in an hour, the hour; in a moment, the moment; and |so on| in the same way for all things which partake of duration. Moreover, duration is not *other* than all the things which endure; and especially it is |not *other*| than the moment or the now, which endures in a fixed way. Therefore, in all things duration is all things, even though it precedes all things, which participate in it. Hence, from the fact that the things which participate in it are *other* |than it| but it is not *other* than the things which participate |in it|, we see clearly how Not-other is participated in by eternity or, more truly, by duration and the moment.

78   FERDINAND: I think that by "moment" you mean "the present."

NICHOLAS: I intend for *now, moment,* and *present* to be the same thing.

FERDINAND: I now see clearly that the present is the beginning of being and being known for all the differences and varieties of time. For by means of the present I know past and future things. And whatever they are they are through the present. Indeed, in what is past the present is the past; in what is future the present is the future; in a month it is the month; in a day, the day; and so on for all things. And although |the present| is all things in all things and although it proceeds to all things, it is not encompassable by anything, and it remains fixedly without otherness.

NICHOLAS: You have explored |the matter| perfectly; and so, it is also not at all hidden from you that A is the Present of the present. For |A| precedes the present, since the present (which is not other than the present) presupposes Not-other (because in Not-other the present is Not-other). And because the present is the substance of time, you rightly see that A is the Substance of

substantiae vides esse substantiam. Sublata enim praesentia non
permanent tempora; sed sublato A nec praesentiam nec tempora
nec aliud quidquam possibile est manere.

79 FERDINANDUS: Bene admonuisti, pater, et iam equidem clare
|video cuncta ipsius theologi dicta per ipsum A illuminari. Pla- *34ᵛ*
cetque plurimum quod Dionysius ipse affirmat theologos bonitatem ipsius dei primam celebrare participationem. Ex quo
5 video quod omnia nomina divina imparticipabilis participationem significant. Sed cum omnia talia ipso A sublato cessent a
significatione et participatione, quod A ipsum in omnibus participatur, habere me gaudeo et prioriter quidem secundum theologos in bonitate. Nam cum id quod ab omnibus appetitur, sub
10 boni ratione appetatur, recte A ipsum, sine quo omnia cessant,
bonitas nominatur. Moyses creatorem ad omnia creandum motum
inquit, quia ipsa vidit bona. Si igitur rerum principium bonum
est, omnia profecto in tantum sunt, in quantum bona sunt.
Bonum sicut non est aliud a pulchro, ut ait Dionysius, sic nec ab
15 omni existenti. Hoc autem habet ab ipso A. Idcirco in ipso
optime relucescit. Si enim A ipsum optime splendescit in aliquo,
id ipsum utique et est et dicitur bonum.

NICOLAUS: Perspicue cernis, quia medio ipsius A recte cuncta
per|lustras. Numquid et id etiam considerasti, quomodo unum *35ʳ*
20 esse veluti omnium elementum theologus dicit, deum tamen in
Mystica theologia unum negat?

80   CAPITULUM XVII

FERDINANDUS: Consideravi, inquam, ipsum dixisse veluti ais;
sed, quaeso, quid per hoc expresserit, dissere.

NICOLAUS: Dicere ipsum voluisse arbitror: sicut uno sublato
5 cessant singula, et quemadmodum elemento sublato desinunt

---

78 18 quidquam: quiiquam *S* quicquam *U*

substance. For if the present were removed, no time would remain; but if A were removed, neither the present nor time nor anything else could possibly remain.

79 FERDINAND: You have cautioned well, Father; and now I see clearly that all the statements of the Theologian are elucidated through A. And I am very much pleased by Dionysius's statement that the theologians esteem the first participation in God to be goodness. Herefrom I see that all the names of God signify a participation in Him who cannot be participated in. But since if A were removed, all such things would cease signifying and participating (because A is participated in by all things), I rejoice to be situated in goodness—indeed, |situated there| first of all, according to the theologians. For, since that which is desired by all is desired under the form of the good, then A—without which all things would cease to be—is rightly called goodness. Moses says that the Creator was moved to create all things because He saw that they were good. Therefore, if the Beginning of things is good, assuredly all things exist insofar as they are good. Just as the good is not *other* than the beautiful (as Dionysius says), so |it is| not |other| than any existing thing. But the good has this |fact about itself| from A. Hence, the good shines forth perfectly in A. For if A shines forth perfectly in something |else|, then assuredly this other thing both is, and is said to be, good.

NICHOLAS: You discern clearly, because you rightly behold all things by means of A. But have you also considered the Theologians's affirming that the One is the "elemental principle" (so to speak) of all things, whereas in *The Mystical Theology* he denies that God is one?

80   CHAPTER 17

FERDINAND: I indeed observed that Donysius spoke as you say; but explain, I ask, what he meant by this.

NICHOLAS: I think he meant |the following|: just as, if the one were removed, single things would cease to be, and just as, if the

elementata, ita ipso A summoto omnia pariter cessant. Habet
enim se modo ad cuncta intimiore penitioreque quam elementum ad elementata.

81   FERDINANDUS: David igitur de Dynanto et philosophi illi quos
secutus is est, minime errarunt, qui quidem deum hylen et noyn
et physin, et mundum visibilem deum visibilem nuncuparunt.

NICOLAUS: David hylen corporum principium vocat, noyn seu
5 mentem principium animarum, physin vero seu naturam principium motuum. Et illa non vidit differre inter se ut in principio;
quocirca sic dixit. Tu autem iam ipsum A haec ipsa vidisti defi|-
nire ipsaque in ipsis esse, etsi ipsorum sit nullum. Ideo haec et *35ʳ*
huiusmodi nihil te moveant, quod scilicet theologus unum veluti
10 elementum dicat. Sed semper ad ipsum A et praemissa recurrens
non errabis.

FERDINANDUS: Sancte me instruis informasque, idque etiam
mihi admodum est gratum, quod ad Gaium theologus scripsit.
Est enim lucidum, et ad ea quae dixisti, conforme atque
15 consentaneum.

NICOLAUS: Quidnam illud?

FERDINANDUS: Quando aiebat theologus: "Si quis deum videns intellexerit quod vidit, non ipsum vidit, sed aliquid." Unde si
David de Dynanto deum vidisset esse hylen aut noyn aut physin,
20 utique aliquid et non deum vidisset.

82   NICOLAUS: Mirabilis es, Ferdinande; et mirabilior sane, si id in
dictis etiam verbis, quod est altius, considerasti.

FERDINANDUS: Quid istuc est? rogo.

NICOLAUS: Quando scilicet inquit: "Cum omnia quae intelli-

---

80 7 intimiore: in timore *S*   in timore *(?) U (ex* in amore *corr. U)*
81 6 illa: illi *S*   illa *U*
81 13 Gaium: Caium *S*   Cayum *U*

elemental principle were removed, things composed of elemental principles would cease to be, so likewise, if A were
removed, all things would cease to be. For |A| is more inti-
mately and inwardly related to all things than the elemental
principle is related to things composed of elemental principles.

81 FERDINAND: Therefore, David of Dinant and the philosophers
whom he followed did not at all err when they called God
matter [*hyle*] and thought [*nous*] and nature [*physis*] and when
they called the visible world the visible God.

NICHOLAS: David calls *hyle* the beginning of physical objects,
calls *nous* or *mens* the beginning of souls, and calls *physis* or
natura the beginning of motions. But he did not see that they
differ among themselves as beginnings. Hence, he spoke as he
did. However, you now have seen that A defines these things
and that in these things A is these things, even though it is none
of them. And so, let not these |statements| and |statements| of
this kind—e.g., the Theologians's saying that the One is the
"elemental principle," as it were—at all disturb you. And you
will not err if you have recourse always to A and to the afore-
mentioned |points|.

FERDINAND: You instruct and teach me faultlessly. Moreover,
that which the Theologian wrote to Gaius is also very agreeable
to me. (For it is clear; and it is conformable to, and harmonious
with, what you have said.)

NICHOLAS: What was that?

FERDINAND: When the Theologian said: "If anyone who has
seen God understands what he has seen, then he has not seen
God but something else." Hence, if David of Dinant saw that
God is matter or thought or nature, assuredly he saw not God
but something |else|.

82 NICHOLAS: You are remarkable, Ferdinand. And you are truly
the more remarkable if in these cited words you have noted |the
point| which is deeper.

FERDINAND: What |point| is that, pray tell?

NICHOLAS: When he says: "since all things which are under-

5 guntur, sint aliquid, ideo non sunt deus." Aliquid autem quid
aliud est. Deus igitur si intelligeretur, utique non esse aliud intelligeretur. Unde si non potest intelligi esse id quod per aliud et
aliquid significatur, nec aliquid intelligi potest, quod per aliquid
non signi|ficetur: ideo deus si videretur, necesse est quod supra *36ʳ*
10 et ante quid aliud et supra intellectum videatur. Ast ante aliud
nil nisi non-aliud videri potest. Habes igitur quod non-aliud in
principium nos dirigit, intellectum et aliud et aliquid et omne
excellens et antecedens intelligibile. Haec ibidem theologus declarat, atque etiam quomodo ipsius non-aliud cognitio, perfecta
15 dici potest ignorantia, quando quidem eius qui est super omnia
quae cognoscuntur, est cognitio.

Haec nunc de nostro admirabili theologo sic dicta sint; suffi-
ciunt enim proposito ad quaeque alia per ipsum taliter dicta.

83   CAPITULUM XVIII

FERDINANDUS: Nunc si otium tibi est, maximi illius Peripatetici
et argutissimi Aristotelis quaedam hoc nostro principio scripta
forte non indigna subintremus. Et quoniam ignotus penitus
5 nequaquam tibi est, dic, quaeso, quid nobis voluit ostendere tan-
tae sollicitudinis philosophus?
NICOLAUS: Ea sane arbitror, quae circa veri notitiam adinvenit.
FERDINANDUS: Quid igitur invenit?
NICOLAUS: Equidem, ut ingenue fatear, nescio. Sed quiddita-
10 tem, obiectum intellectus, | semper quaesitam, numquam reper- *36ᵛ*
tam dicit. Sic enim ait in prima philosophia: "Omnibus difficilli-
mum est maximamque ambiguitatem habet, utrum unum et ens,
ut Pythagorici et Plato dicebat, non est aliud quidquam sed
entium substantia, an non; an aliud quidem subiectum, ut Emped-
15 ocles amicitiam ait, alius ignem, alius aquam, alius aërem." Et

stood are something, they are not God." Now, "something" |here| means "something other." If God were understood, then He would be understood not to be an other. Hence, if |God| cannot be understood to be what is signified by "other" and "something," and if whatever is not signified by "something" cannot be understood, then if God were seen, He would have to be seen above and before any other thing and above the intellect. But nothing except Not-other can be seen before other. Therefore, you see that Not-other directs us unto the Beginning, which excels and precedes the intellect and other and something and everything intelligible. The Theologian here shows these things; and he also shows how it is that our knowledge of Not-other can be called perfect ignorance, since it is knowledge of Him who is beyond all known things.

Let these statements concerning our admirable theologian be enough for now,[119] since for present purposes they avail for whatever else he said along similar lines.

83   CHAPTER 18

FERDINAND: Let us now, if you have the time, explore various written statements (statements perhaps not unworthy of this beginning of ours) of the greatest and most acute Peripatetic, viz., Aristotle. Since he is not altogether unknown to you, tell |me|, I ask, what the Philosopher was so concerned to show us.

NICHOLAS: I surely think |he wanted to show us| what he had found out regarding knowledge of the truth.

FERDINAND: What, then, had he found out?

NICHOLAS: Indeed, to be candid, I do not know. But he says that quiddity, which is the object of the intellect and which is always sought, has never been found. For in *First Philosophy* he says: "It is |a question| very difficult for all and very much in doubt: namely, whether or not one and being are not something other but are the substance of beings, as the Pythagoreans and Plato said, or whether there is some other substance (*subjectum*); for example, Empedocles speaks of friendship; another

alibi idem in eodem libro: "Tam olim quam nunc et semper
quaeritur semperque dubitatur, quidnam ipsum ens sit, hoc est
quaenam substantia est. Hoc enim quidam unum aiunt esse, quidam plura."

84   FERDINANDUS: Verba haec magni philosophi utique sunt aestimanda. Fac igitur ut acuto visu hos philosophi sermones
subintremus.

NICOLAUS: Tentabo pro virili. Equidem considero quomodo
5 quaerit utrum unum et ens non est aliud quidquam, sed entium
substantia, qualiter per ipsum non-aliud rerum substantiam quaesivit. Vidit enim rerum substantiam non esse aliud quidquam, et
ideo de ente et de uno et de amicitia [et] de aëre et aqua et omnibus dubitavit an aliquid horum foret rerum substantia, quoniam
10 illa omnia aliud aliquid esse perspiciebat. Esse igitur rerum sub-
stantiam praesupposuit | et plures tales non esse. Dubitavit autem,   *37ʳ*
sicut alii omnes, quaenam haec esset. Et cum omnibus quaerens
concurrit, qui ipsam varie nominabant, sciscitans an per aliquem
esset bene nominata. Et demum illi visum est quod illam bene
15 nemo nominavit, quia quicumque eam nominarunt, aliquid aliud
sive quid aliud, non ipsam simplicissimam rerum nominarunt
quidditatem, quam utique vidit non posse esse aliud aliquid. Et in
hoc quidem non erravit, sed ibi, sicut alii homines, cessavit. Vidit
enim quod omnis rationalis venandi modus ad capiendum ipsam
20 tantopere desideratam et sapidam scientiam minime sufficit.

FERDINANDUS: Video philosopho id accidisse quod praedixisti.
NICOLAUS: Quid illud?

85   FERDINANDUS: Quia qui quaerit videre quaenam visibilium sit
substantia, cum visu illam inter visibilia quaerat, lucem se anterioriter percipere non attendit, sine qua nec posset quaerere nec

---

84 8 et³: *supplevi*
84 13 nominabant: nominabat *S*   nominabant *U*

speaks of fire; another, of water; and another, of air."[120] And elsewhere in the same book the same |philosopher says|: "In time past, as now and always, it is asked, and is ever in doubt, what being is—i.e., what substance is. Some say that it is one thing, others that it is many things."[121]

84 FERDINAND: These words of the great Philosopher are surely worthy of esteem. See to it, then, that we examine with acute vision these words of the Philosopher.

NICHOLAS: I will do my best. I will consider his inquiring whether one and being are not something other but are the substance of beings—his having sought, through Not-other, the substance of things. For he saw that the substance of things is not anything other; and so, with regard to being and one and friendship and air and water and all things, he was uncertain whether any of these is the substance of things, since he recognized that all of them are something other. Therefore, he presupposed that the substance of things exists and that there is not more than one substance. However, like all the others, he was uncertain what this substance is. As he inquired, he encountered all those who gave substance various names; and he asked whether it had been rightly named by anyone. And, at last, it seemed to him that no one had named it correctly. For whoever named it, named something other (*aliquid aliud sive quid aliud*) and not that most simple quiddity-of-things, which Aristotle saw not to be able to be anything other. And he did not stray in this matter; but he stopped there, as had other men. For he saw that no rational mode of pursuit sufficed at all for acquiring that wise and so greatly desired knowledge.

FERDINAND: I see that there has happened to the Philosopher what you spoke of earlier.

NICHOLAS: What was that?

85 FERDINAND: That if someone seeks to see what the substance of visible things is, then if he seeks this substance among visible things and by means of sight, he does not attend to perceiving antecedently the light without which he could not either seek or

reperire visibile. Quodsi ad illam attenderet, in aliquo alio quae-
5 rere desineret. Nempe sic philosopho accidit, qui cum mente
rerum quidditatem quaereret, lumen quod per "non-aliud" significatur, illi sese obtulit, tamquam sine quo nequaquam reperiret.
|Ceterum ipse lumen ipsum, non aliud a quaesito, non esse aliud *37ʳ*
non attendit. Quia vero per non-aliud aliud quaesivit, non nisi
10 aliud ab aliis repperit; quocirca hinc quaerendo remotius nimis
adinvenit.
  NICOLAUS: Verum dicis. Nam si lumen ipsum, quod mente
medium esse vidit ad quaesitum perveniendi principium, etiam
ac finem esse attendisset, non deviasset profecto et tot labores
15 abbreviasset. Si enim dixisset: clarissime utique video rerum
quidditatem quid aliud esse non posse. Quomodo enim foret
rerum quidditas, si aliud foret? Aliud enim se ipsum quaesitum
negat. Quodsi non aliud esse debet, ab omni sane alio non aliud
esse necesse est. Sed hoc quod ab omni alio aliud esse non debet,
20 certe aliter nominari non potest. "Non-aliud" igitur recte nomina-
bitur. Esto igitur quod A per "non-aliud ipsum" significetur, A
profecto quaesitum erit.

86   CAPITULUM XIX

  FERDINANDUS: Utinam, ut dicis, attendisset! Magno quidem se
et nos labore liberasset. Nempe secretum hoc facillimis, clarissimis, ac paucissimis verbis tradidisset. Neque enim laboriosa logica
5 |nec difficili definiendi arte opus habuisset, quae, cum vir ille *38ʳ*
maximo labore investigasset, ad perfectum tamen perducere non
evaluit. Cessassent quoque omnes circa species et ideas difficul-
tates ac opinionum diversitates, humanamque scientiam gloriose
consummasset.

85 15 clarissime: clarissimo *S*   clarissime *U*

find what is visible. But if he were to attend to this light, then he would stop seeking |it| in something that is other. Surely, such a thing happened to the Philosopher; for when with his mind he sought the quiddity of things, the light which is signified by "Not-other" presented itself to him as that without which he could not at all make his discovery. Notwithstanding, he did not notice that the light, which was not *other* than what was sought, was not an other. But because through Not-other he sought an other, he found only what is other than others. Hence, in his inquiry he found |only| what is very far removed from this |i.e., from Not-other|.

NICHOLAS: You speak the truth. For surely he would not have gone astray, and he would have cut short such extensive efforts, if he had recognized that the light which he mentally saw to be the means of arriving at the sought-after beginning was also the end. For example, he might have said:

I see very clearly that the quiddity of things cannot be anything other. For how would it be the quiddity of things if it were other? For the very thing which is sought denies that it is other. Now, if it must not be other, then it must surely not be *other* than any other. But that which must not be *other* than any other must surely be named accordingly.[122] Therefore, it will rightly be named "Not-other." Therefore, if it be the case that A is signified by "Not-other," then surely A will be what is sought.

86   CHAPTER 19

FERDINAND: Would that Aristotle had been attentive, as you say! He would have spared us and himself great labor. Surely he would have handed down this hidden truth by means of words which are very simple, very clear, and very sparse. For he would not have had need either of an elaborate logic or of the difficult art of definition—neither of which this man was able to bring to perfection, even though he had studied the matter extensively. Moreover, all the difficulties and the diversities of opinions regarding species and Ideas would have ceased; and he would have gloriously perfected human knowledge.

87   NICOLAUS: Ostendis eximiam erga philosophum utique dili-
gendum affectionem, qui quidem ratione lucidissima dotatus
videtur fuisse. Verum idem fortasse de omnibus speculativis dici
philosophis posset. Difficilium enim haec est facilitas, quae ad
5 veritatem speculantes direxisset omni visui mentis indubitabilem,
qua meo quidem iudicio brevior nulla et artior vel tradi vel
apprehendi potest. Quae sola perfecta est; cui nihil addi per
hominem est possibile. Visum enim ad principium dirigit, ut ibidem contemplans delicietur assidueque pascatur et excrescat.
10 Neque ulla alia reperibilis est perfecta, absoluta, et completa tra-
ditio. Omnia enim quae oculi mentis acie non videntur, sed
ratione investigantur, tametsi verum admodum appropinquare
videantur, nondum tamen ad ultimam certitudinem pervenerunt.
| Ultima autem et omni ex parte cumulata certitudo visio est.   *38ʳ*

88   FERDINANDUS: Cuncta quae dicis, sic profecto se habent. Videtur sane philosophus ille omni suo tempore viam seu venandi
rerum substantiam artem ex ratione elicere studuisse, ac nullam
quae sufficeret adinvenisse. Nam nec ipsa etiam ratio ad id quod
5 rationem antecedit, pertingit; minusque omnes a ratione produc-
tae artes possunt viam praebere ad id quod omni rationi est
incognitum. Philosophus ille certissimum credidit negativae affirmativam contradicere, quodque simul de eodem utpote repugnantia dici non possent. Hoc autem dixit rationis via id
10 ipsum sic verum concludentis. Quodsi quis ab eo quaesivisset
"quid est aliud?" utique vere respondere potuisset "non aliud
quam aliud est." Et consequenter si quaerens adiecisset "quare
aliud est aliud?" sane quidem, ut prius, dicere valuisset "quia
non aliud quam aliud est." Et ita non-aliud et aliud neque sibi ut
15 repugnantia vidisset contradicere. Atque illud quod primum

87 NICHOLAS: You display extraordinary affection toward the admirable Philosopher, who seems indeed to have been endowed with very clear reasoning. But presumably the same |claim| can be made for all the speculative philosophers. For clear reasoning is a facility with difficult matters. |It is the facility| which directed speculating |philosophers| to the truth indubitable to all mental sight—|the truth| than which (in my judgment) none more brief or more concise can be either taught or apprehended.[123] Only this truth is perfect; no human being can possibly add anything to it. For it directs sight to the Beginning, so that one who meditates thereupon is delighted and is constantly nourished and grows. No other discoverable teaching is perfect, absolute, and complete. For whatever is investigated by reason but yet is not seen by the acute gaze of the mind's eye has not yet reached ultimate certainty, even though it may seem to come very close to the truth. But the certainty which is ultimate and entirely perfect is identical with seeing.

88 FERDINAND: All that you say is surely so. The Philosopher certainly seems throughout his lifetime (1) to have concerned himself with eliciting from reason a way, or an art, for pursuing the substance of things and (2) to have come upon none which sufficed. For not even reason attains to what precedes reason; and even less can any of the arts produced by reason furnish a way to what is unknown to all reason. The Philosopher held it to be most certain that an affirmation contradicts a negation and that both cannot at the same time be said of the same thing, since they are contradictories. He said this on the basis of reason's concluding it to be true. But if someone had asked Aristotle, "What is other?" he surely could have answered truly, "It is not other than other." And, if the questioner had thereupon added, "Why is other other?" Aristotle could rightly have answered as at first, "Because it is not other than other." And thus, he would have seen that Not-other and other do not contradict each other as contradictories. And he would have seen that that to which he gives the name "the first principle" (*primum princi-*

principium nominat, pro viae ostensione perspexisset non suffi-
cere ad veritatem quae supra rationem | mente contemplatur.   *39ʳ*

89 NICOLAUS: Tua equidem dicta laudo, addoque quod alio etiam
modo ad veritatem intuendam viam sibi ipse praeclusit. Aiebat
enim substantiae non esse substantiam nec principii principium,
ut supra tetigimus. Nam sic etiam contradictionis negasset esse
5 contradictionem. At si quispiam eum interrogasset, numquid in
contradicentibus contradictionem vidisset, veraciter se videre
respondisset. Deinde interrogatus, si id quod in contradicentibus
vidit, anterioriter sicut causam ante effectum videret, nonne tunc
contradictionem videret absque contradictione, hoc certe sic se
10 habere negare nequivisset. Sicut enim in contradicentibus contradictionem esse contradicentium contradictionem vidit, ita
ante contradicentia contradictionem ante dictam vidisset contradictionem, sicut Dionysius theologus deum oppositorum vidit
oppositionem sine oppositione. Oppositioni enim ante opposita
15 nihil opponitur. Verum etsi philosophus ille in prima seu mentali
philosophia defecerit, multa tamen in rationali ac morali omni
laude dignissima conscripsit. Quae quoniam praesentis specula-
tionis non sunt, haec de Aristotele dixisse sufficiat. |

90   CAPITULUM XX   *39ʳ*

PETRUS BALBUS PISANUS: Audivi te, pater, cum Ferdinando
multa et mihi quidem gratissima contulisse, sed maxime ex
Dionysii maximi theologi libellis recitata sum admiratus. Cum
5 enim Proculum illum Platonicum in libro de Platonis divini
theologia de Graeco verterem his diebus in latinum, ea ipsa
quasi eodem quoque expressionis tenore ac modo repperi, quam

89 6 contradicentibus: contrahentibus *S*   contradicentibus *U*

pium) does not suffice for showing the way to the truth which the mind contemplates beyond reasoning.

89   NICHOLAS: I laud your remarks. And I add that also in another manner Aristotle closed off to himself a way for viewing the truth. For, as we mentioned earlier,[124] he denied that there is a Substance of substance or a Beginning of beginning. Thus, he would also have denied that there is a Contradiction of contradiction. But had anyone asked him whether he saw contradiction in contradictories, he would have replied, truly, that he did. Suppose he were thereupon asked: "If that which you see in contradictories you see *antecedently* (just as you see a cause antecedently to its effect), then do you not see contradiction without contradiction?" Assuredly, he could not have denied that this is so. For just as he saw that the contradiction in contradictories is contradiction of the contradictories, so prior to the contradictories he would have seen Contradiction before the expressed contradiction (even as the theologian Dionysius saw God to be, without opposition, the Oppositeness of opposites; for prior to |there being any| opposites it is not the case that anything is opposed to oppositeness). But even though the Philosopher failed in first philosophy, or mental philosophy, nevertheless in rational and moral |philosophy| he wrote many things very worthy of complete praise. Since these things do not belong to the present speculation, let it suffice that we have made the preceding remarks about Aristotle.

90   CHAPTER 20

PETER BALBUS OF PISA: I have been listening to you, Father, discussing with Ferdinand many |points| which are very satisfying to me; I especially admired what you cited from the books of the greatest theologian, Dionysius. For I recently have been translating Proclus the Platonist from Greek into Latin. |While translating| in the book on the theology of the divine Plato, I discovered these very |points|, with virtually the same manner and tenor of expression. Accordingly, I would like to hear from

ob rem de Platonica etiam te audire theologia aliquid cupio.
NICOLAUS: Proculum tuum, Petre, Dionysio Areopagita tem-
10 pore posteriorem fuisse certum est. An autem Dionysii scripta
viderit, est incertum. Sed tu particularius narrato, quo in dicto
consentiant.

PETRUS: Sicut Dionysius inquit unum quod est posterius uno
simpliciter, ita et Proculus Platonem referens asserit.

91 NICOLAUS: Forte sapientes idem omnes dicere voluerunt de
primo rerum principio, sed varie id ipsum varii expresserunt.
Plato autem, quem tantopere Proculus extollit, tamquam deus
quidem fuerit humanatus, ad anterius semper respiciens conatus
5 est rerum videre | substantiam ante omne nominabile. Unde cum *40ʳ*
rem corporalem divisibilemque ex se subsistere non posse pers-
piceret, nec se ipsam propter debilitatem et fluxibilitatem suam
conservare: ante illam, animam, ante animam vero intellectum
vidit, atque ante intellectum, unum.

92 Posterius autem prioris participatione subsistit. Primum igitur
(cuius participatione omnia id sunt quod sunt) ante intellectum
videtur, cum omnia intellectu nequaquam participent. Intellectus
igitur "anterius sive senius se ipso," ut verbis eius utamur, non
5 attingit. Ex quo Platonem reor rerum substantiam seu principium in mente sua revelationis via percepisse—modo quo apostolus ad Romanos dicit deum se illis revelasse. Quam equidem
revelationem in lucis similitudine capio, quae sese per semetip-
sam visui ingerit. Et aliter non videtur neque cognoscitur quam
10 ipsa se revelat, cum sit invisibilis, quia est ante et supra omne
visibile. Haec Plato in epistolis sic se habere perbreviter exprimit,
deum ipsum dicens vigilantissime et constanter quaerenti se
demum manifestare. (Quae Proculus quoque in Parmenidis

you something about *The Theology of Plato* also.

NICHOLAS: It is certain, Peter, that your Proclus was later in time than Dionysius the Areopagite.[125] But it is uncertain whether he saw the writings of Dionysius. State more specifically in which saying they agree.

PETER: Just as Dionysius says that the *one* which exists is posterior to the unqualifiedly *One*, so also Proclus makes |the same point| in referring to Plato.

91 NICHOLAS: Perhaps all the sages wanted to make the same point about the first principle of things [*primum principium rerum*] and various of them expressed it variously. But Plato— whom Proclus so greatly exalts (as if he were a humanified god) and who was always looking to what is anterior—endeavored to see the substance of things before everything nameable. Hence, since he saw that a thing which is corporeal and divisible cannot exist from itself and cannot conserve itself (because of its weakness and fluxibility): prior to any material object he saw the soul, and prior to the soul he saw intellect, and prior to intellect he saw the One.

92 Now, what is posterior exists by means of participation in what is prior. Hence, what is the first (by participation in the first all things are what they are) is seen prior to intellect; for it is not at all the case that all things participate in intellect. Therefore, intellect does not attain to "what is earlier, or older, than intellect itself"—to use his words.[126] Wherefore, I think that Plato mentally viewed the substance, or the beginning (*principium*), of things by way of revelation—in the manner in which the Apostle tells the Romans that God has revealed Himself to them.[127] I understand this revelation by means of a likeness to light, which through itself presents itself to sight. It is not seen or known in any other way than it reveals itself, since it is invisible, because it is higher than, and antecedent to, everything visible. In his letters Plato very briefly declares that these matters are thus—saying that God eventually manifests Himself to one who seeks Him steadfastly and very vigilantly.[128] (Proclus, too, repeats

commentariis resumit.) Cum haec igitur vera supponat, animam
15 in|quit (quae quidem omnia posteriora se ipsam contemplans in *40ᵛ*
se animaliter complicat), ut vivo in speculo, cuncta inspicere
quae eius participant vitam et per ipsam vivunt vitaliterque subsistunt. Et quia illa in ipsa sunt, ipsa in sui similitudine sursum
ascendit ad priora, quemadmodum haec Proculus in eius recitat
20 theologia.

93   PETRUS: Declara id, quaeso, quod dixisti, ipsum idem dicere
scilicet quod tu de non-aliud praemisisti.

    NICOLAUS: Faciliter consideranti id ipsum clarescet. Namque,
ut ipse ait, omnium causam ab omnibus oportet participari. Ideo
5 ipsum unum quod dicit esse ante unum quod est unum, ab eo
non est aliud, cum eius sit causa. Quare causam ipsius unius
quod est, ideo unum nominat, ut non-aliud exprimat. Unde sicut
nominat unius quod est causam unum, sic entis causam ens nun-
cupat, et substantiae substantiam, et de omnibus eodem modo.
10 Per quod intelligi datur, omnia quae sunt et nominantur, id
quod sunt et nominantur habere ab omnium causa, quae in exis-
tentibus omnibus est id quod sunt et nominantur, et non aliud.
Vides igitur omnia nomina quae nominatorum nomina dicit
antecedere (sicut unum ante unum quod est et nominatur |
15 unum) ideo causae attribui: ut causam a causato non esse aliud *41ʳ*
designetur. In omnibus igitur nominibus, non-aliud est quod
significatur.

94   PETRUS: Video, pater, haec dubio carere. Sed dum ad li non
aliud me converto, non possum equidem, quid sit, mente
concipere.

    NICOLAUS: Si quidem posses id concipere, haud utique [esset]
5 omnium principium, quod in omnibus omnia significaret. Omnis
enim humanus conceptus, unius alicuius conceptus est. Verum
ante conceptum non-aliud est, quando quidem conceptus non

---

94 4 esset: *addidi cum Wilpert*

these |views| in his *Commentary on the Parmenides*.)[129] There-
fore, since |Plato| believes these |views| to be true, he says that
the soul—which contemplates itself and enfolds within itself (in
the way a soul does) the things posterior |to itself|—beholds, as
in a living mirror, all the things which participate in its life and
which through it live and exist vitally. And because these things
are in the soul, the soul, by means of the resemblance to itself,[130]
ascends upward toward the things which are prior |to it|—just
as Proclus cites these |doctrines| in his theology.[131]

93   PETER: Show, I ask, how what you have just said makes the
very same point as you have set forth about Not-other.

NICHOLAS: It will readily be clear to one who considers it. For
as |Proclus| says, it is necessary that the Cause of all things be
participated in by all things.[132] And so, the One (which he
says[133] to be prior to the one which exists as one) is not *other*
than the existing one, since it is the Cause of the existing one.
Therefore, to the Cause of the existing one he gives the name
"One," in order to express Not-other. Hence, just as he calls the
Cause of the existing one *One*, so he calls the Cause of being
Being, and |the Cause| of substance *Substance*, and |so on| in
the same way for all things. Hereby we are given to understand
that all the things which exist and are named have that-which-
they-are-and-are-named from the Cause-of-all-things, which in
all existing things is that which they are and are named but is
not an other. Therefore, you see that all the names which he
says precede the names of named things (as *One* precedes the
one which exists and is named "one") are ascribed to the Cause
in order to indicate that the Cause is not *other* than the caused.
Therefore, in all names Not-other is what is signified.

94   PETER: I see, Father, that these points are indubitable. But
when I turn to *Not-other*, I cannot mentally conceive what it is.

NICHOLAS: If you were able to conceive it, then by no means
would it be the *Beginning-of-all-things*, which signifies all in all.
For every human concept is a concept of some one thing. But
Not-other is prior to |every| concept, since a concept is not other

aliud quam conceptus est. Vocetur igitur ipsum non-aliud conceptus absolutus, qui videtur quidem mente, ceterum non con-
10 cipitur.

PETRUS: Ipsum ergo non-aliud, cum ab aliquo non sit aliud,
sed in omnibus omnia, nonne omni in conceptu omnia est?

NICOLAUS: Utique. Ideo cum omnis conceptus non aliud
quam conceptus sit, in omni conceptu non-aliud est quod-
15 cumque concipitur, manente sane conceptu, qui ipsum non-
aliud est, inconceptibili.

95   CAPITULUM XXI

PETRUS: Me certe li quam turbat, quando ipse definiendo dicis
"terra non est aliud quam terra." Id igitur ut explanares, vellem.

NICOLAUS: Plane tu quidem vides veram esse | hanc terrae *41ᵛ*
5 definitionem qua dicitur "terra non aliud quam terra est," hanc
vero falsam: "terra est aliud quam terra."

PETRUS: Video.

NICOLAUS: Veritas definitionis igitur unde dependet?

PETRUS: Adverto plane quomodo tam in vera quam falsa
10 definitione est "quam"; ideo nequeo ab ipso "quam" dicere veritatem dependere, sed ab "ipso non-aliud" potius.

NICOLAUS: Optime! "Quam" igitur non definit. Non ergo te
perturbet.

PETRUS: Quam ob causam apponitur?

15   NICOLAUS: Quia dirigit visum. Nam cum non-aliud dico non
aliud quam non-aliud, li quam in non-aliud visum simpliciter
dirigit, uti ante aliud est. Quando autem dico "aliud est non
aliud quam aliud," visum dirigit in non-aliud, ut est in alio
aliud. Et cum dico "terra non aliud quam terra est," dirigit obtu-
20 tum in non-aliud, ut est in terra terra, et pari de omnibus modo.

94 12 conceptu: concepto *S* conceptu *U*
95 5 non: aliter *post* non *scribit et del. S*

than a concept. Therefore, *Not-other* may be called the Absolute Concept, which is indeed seen mentally but which, notwithstanding, is not conceived.

PETER: Well, then, since Not-other is not *other* than anything, but in all things is all things, is it not everything in every concept?

NICHOLAS: Yes, indeed. And so, since every concept is not other than a concept, in every concept Not-other is whatever is conceived. But, without doubt, the concept *Not-other* remains inconceivable.

95   CHAPTER 21

PETER: When you say by way of definition "The earth is not other than the earth," the word "than" (*"quam"*) troubles me. So I would like you to explain it.

NICHOLAS: Clearly, you see to be true the definition of "earth" which says "The earth is not other than the earth"; and you see to be false |the definition which says| "The earth is other than the earth."

PETER: Yes, I do.

NICHOLAS: On what, then, does the truth of the definition depend?

PETER: I see clearly that "than" is present both in the true definition and in the false one; and so, I cannot say that the truth depends on "than." Rather, |it depends| on "Not-other."

NICHOLAS: Excellent! So "than" does not define. So don't let it trouble you.

PETER: Why is it added |to the definition|?

NICHOLAS: Because it directs our sight. For when I say that Not-other is not other than Not-other, the word "than" simply directs sight to Not-other insofar as it is prior to other. But when I say "Other is not other than other," |the word "than"| directs sight to Not-other insofar as in an other it is the other. And when I say "The earth is not other than the earth," |the word "than"| directs sight to Not-other insofar as in the earth it is the earth. And in like manner for all things.

96   PETRUS: Optime sane! Nam nunc video ad quaestionem "quid
est terra?" responsum hoc "terram non aliud esse quam terram"
mentis aciem explicare, qua mens quidem videt principium
omnium per "non-aliud" significatum terram definire—quod est
5 non-aliud in terra terram esse. Quodsi quaereretur "cur terra est
terra?" responderi debet "quia non aliud quam terra." Ideo
enim | terra est terra, quia ipsius principium seu causa in ipsa   *42ʳ*
ipsa est. Et sic si quaeratur "unde habet terra quod terra est?"
dici sane debet "ab ipso suo principio seu non-aliud id habere."
10 Ab eo enim a quo habet ut non aliud quam terra sit, habet quod
est terra. Quocirca si quaeratur "a quo habet bonum, quod est
bonum?" responderi potest "a non alio a bono." Nam cum
bonum ab alio a bono non habeat quod sit bonum, necesse profecto est quod id habeat a non alio a bono. Sic terra habet quod
15 est terra, a non alio a terra; et ita de singulis. Hoc modo prioriter
omnia in principio, quod non-aliud, video. Et per "non-aliud"
simplicissime et absolute significatur, quia A ab aliquo non est
aliud. Ideo "causa," "exemplar," "forma," "idea," "species," et
eiusmodi nomina ei per philosophos attribuuntur, quemadmo-
20 dum ante me videre fecisti.

97   NICOLAUS: Subintrasti, Petre, videsque omnium principium
per "non-aliud" significari, ideo non aliud ab aliquo atque in
omnibus omnia.

Sed tu nunc ad Platonem revertere, cuius utique erat intentio
5 principium, quod omnia est in omnibus, intueri. Unde ille
omnia quae habere se aliter possunt (ut est figura, nomen, | defi-   *42ᵛ*
nitio, ratioque, et opinio, et talia) quidditatem nequaquam vide-
bat ostendere, cum rerum essentia et quidditas haec omnia
praecedat. Anterioriter igitur vidit ad illa quae alia, instabilia, et

---

97 6 quae: se *post* que *scribit, del., et post* habere *rescribit,* S

96 PETER: Very good, indeed! For now I see that to the question "What is the earth?" the answer "The earth is not other than the earth" displays the acute mental gaze by which the mind sees the following: that the Beginning of all things—which is signified by "Not-other"—defines "earth" (i.e., that in the earth Not-other is the earth). But if the question "Why is the earth the earth?" is asked, then the answer "Because it is not other than the earth" ought to be given. For the earth is the earth because its Beginning, or Cause, is, in the earth, the earth. And if the question "From where does the earth have the fact that it is the earth?" is asked, then the answer "It has it from its Beginning, i.e., from Not-other" surely ought to be given. For the earth has the fact that it is the earth from that from which it has the fact that it is not other than the earth. Accordingly, if the question "From what does the good have the fact that it is good?" is asked, the answer "From not *other* than the good" can be given. For since the good does not have from any *other* than the good the fact that it is good, then, necessarily, it has it from not *other* than the good. Thus, the earth has from not *other* than the earth the fact that it is the earth. And similarly for each thing. In this manner I see all things antecedently in the Beginning, which is Not-other. And |the Beginning| is signified absolutely and very simply by "Not-other," because A is not *other* than anything. And so, "cause," "exemplar," "form," "Idea," "species," and names of this kind are ascribed to A by the philosophers—just as you previously made me see.

97 NICHOLAS: You have explored |the matter|, Peter; and you see that the Beginning-of-all is signified by "Not-other" and, consequently, is not *other* than anything but is all in all.

Turn back now to Plato, whose intention was to view the Beginning, which is all in all. Accordingly, he did not at all regard any of the things which can exist in different ways—e.g., figure, name, definition, concept (*ratio*), opinion, and the like— as showing quiddity; for the essence, and quiddity, of things precedes all these. Therefore, antecedently to these things which are

10 variabilia, ipsum quod quidem aliud praecedit, omnium substan-
tiarum substantiam et quidditatum esse quidditatem. Quae cum
in omnibus omnia sit, illa ipsum est quod per "non-aliud" significatur. Apud ipsum igitur primum, ipsum [esse] omnia, et ab
ipso vidit omnia ut a fonte seu causa et cuius gratia emanare.

15 PETRUS: Haec aperte de se ipso Plato in epistolis scribit.
Verum adicit illud: quo omnia prime apud regem primum sunt
et apud secundum secunde, tertie vero apud tertium.

98 NICOLAUS: Diversos modos essendi rerum vidit. Nam omnia
ante aliud ipsum principium intuitus est simplicissimum, in quo
quodlibet, quod in alio aliter, in ipso quidem non-aliud cernitur.
Quando enim de terra, quam rationis obtutu esse quid aliud a
5 non-terra video seu caelo sive igne, me ad intuendum ipsam in
principio transfero: ibi ipsam a non-terra aliam non video, quia
ipsam principium, quod ab aliquo non aliud est, video. Non
quod ipsam imperfectiori modo quam prius intuear, sed praeci-
sissimo modo | atque verissimo. Tunc enim quodlibet videtur *43*ʳ
10 praecisissime, quando non-aliud cernitur. Qui enim sic terram
videt, quod non-aliud ipsam videt, praecisissime intuetur. Et hoc
est quidditatis ipsius et omnium quidditatem cernere.

Namque alia est terrae quidditatis visio, quae intellectu a
quidditate aquae aut ignis videtur esse alia. Et illa non-aliud
15 sequitur, quia ab aliis alia est, et hic essendi quidditatis secundus
seu intellectualis est modus.

At tertius essendi est modus, quemadmodum per animam hoc
ab illo discernentem animaliter attingitur, prout res seu rei quidditas sentitur.

20 Quod quidem fortassis dicere voluit Plato aut altius quiddam.

97 13 esse: *supplevi*
98 2 intuitus: intutus *S* intuitus *U*
98 8-9 praecisissimo: preciosissimo *S* precisissimo *U*

other and changeable and variable, he saw that what is prior to other is the Substance of all substances and the Quiddity of all quiddities. Since in all things this |Substance or Quiddity| is all these things, it is that which is signified by "Not-other." Hence, he saw that within the First all things are the First; and he saw that all things emanate *from* the First (as from a fount or a cause) and *on account of* the First.

PETER: In his letters[134] Plato clearly writes these things about his views. But he adds the following: that all things exist first within the first King, and secondly within the second, and thirdly within the third.

98 NICHOLAS: He saw the different modes-of-being of things. For prior to *other*, he saw everything as the most simple Beginning, in which everything-that-exists-differently-in-another is discerned as Not-other. For example, when I turn my attention from the earth (which by rational sight I see to be something other than not-earth or sky or fire) to viewing the earth in the Beginning, I do not see it there as *other* than not-earth; for I see it as the Beginning, which is not *other* than anything. |I do| not |mean| that I see it in a more imperfect manner than at first; rather, |I mean that I see it| in a most precise and most true manner. For each thing is seen most precisely when it is seen as Not-other. For example, he who sees the earth in such way that he sees it as Not-other sees it most precisely. And this is to see the Quiddity both of its quiddity and of all things.

Another |kind of seeing| is the seeing of the quiddity of the earth. The earth's quiddity is seen by the intellect to be other than the quiddity of water or of fire. Moreover, the earth's quiddity is posterior to Not-other, because it is other than other |quiddities|; and this is the second, or the intellectual, mode-of-being of quiddity.

But the third mode-of-being is such as is attained by the soul's discriminating (in the way souls do) between this and that—according as the thing (or the thing's quiddity) is perceived.

Presumably, Plato wanted to make either the foregoing points

Suum enim hoc arcanum et secretum quam breviter et timide
Plato patefecit, et in paucis suis verbis acutissima multorum
ingenia excitavit.

99   CAPITULUM XXII

IOANNES ANDREAS ABBAS: Audivi te, pater, et antea saepe et
nunc maxime mentis tuae visionem nobis referentem, quodque
illam in ipsum primum, quod quidem omnia in omnibus est,
5 dirigis, quo prius quidquam concipi non | potest, quod "non- *43ᵛ*
aliud" nominas. Et tamen ipsum asseris primum videri ante
omne nominabile. Quae mihi profecto videntur esse contraria.
NICOLAUS: Pater abba, bene tenes audita. Sed "ipsum non-
aliud" non dico equidem illius nomen, cuius est super omne
10 nomen nuncupatio. Sed de ipso primo conceptus mei nomen
per "ipsum non-aliud" tibi patefacio. Neque mihi praecisius
occurrit conceptum meum exprimens nomen de innominabili,
quod quidem a nullo aliud est.

100   ABBAS: Equidem mirarer quonam modo ipsum quod tu vides
ante et supra omne aliud, non sit aliud, cum aliud ipsi, non-aliud
videatur opponi, nisi paene idem Plato quoque diceret in Parmenide et commentator Proculus hoc dubium enodaret. Etsi ibi
5 de uno et altero tam Plato quam Proculus disserant, dicentes
impossibile unum ab altero alterum esse, tu autem praecisiori
expressione tui conceptus per "ipsum non-aliud" clare me facis
intueri non-aliud ipsum ab alio aliud esse non posse, quocumque nominabili aut innominabili, cum omnia "ipsum non-
10 aliud" ita definiat, ut omnia in omnibus sit. Verum Dionysius
ille Areopagita dicebat etiam deum alterum dici, quod quidem
nega|tur in Parmenide.   *44ʳ*
101   NICOLAUS: Meministi, puto, Platonem negare quid rei defini-

---

99 2 IOANNES: Iohannes *S*   ABBAS: Albas *S*   Abbas *U*
99 5 dirigis: dirigit *SU*
99 8 abba: abbam *(?) S*   abbas *U*
100 11 Areopagita: Ariopagita *S*   Areopagita (*ex* Arcopagita *correctum*) *U*

or deeper ones. He disclosed his secret very tersely and cautiously; and with his few words he stimulated the sharpest intelligence of many |others|.

CHAPTER 22

ABBOT JOHN ANDREA: Often in the past and also especially just now, I have heard you, Father, conveying to us the vision of your mind. |I have heard| you directing this |mental vision| toward the First, which is all in all,[135] that than which something prior cannot be conceived, and that to which you give the name "Not-other." However, you also maintain that the First is seen prior to everything nameable. These |two claims| certainly seem to me to be opposed.

NICHOLAS: You remember well, Father Abbot, what you have heard. But I certainly do not mean that "Not-other" is the name of that whose name is above every name.[136] Rather, through "Not-other" I disclose to you the name of my concept of the First. There does not occur to me any more precise name which expresses my concept of the Unnameable, which, indeed, is not *other* than anything.

100   ABBOT: I would wonder—except for the fact that Plato also said almost the same thing in the *Parmenides* and that the commentator Proclus clarified his unclear statement—how that which you view before and above every other could be Not-other, given that Not-other seems to be opposed to other.[137] It is true that, in these respective works, both Plato and Proclus discuss *one* and *other*, stating that one |of them| cannot possibly be *other* than the other |of them|. Nevertheless, you, because of the more precise expression of your concept, make me see clearly by means of "Not-other" that Not-other cannot be *other* than any other, whether nameable or unnameable; for "Not-other" defines all things in such way that in all things it is all things. But Dionysius the Areopagite said[138] that even God is called Other—something which is denied in the *Parmenides*.

101   NICHOLAS: As you recall, I believe, Plato denies any attaining

tionem attingere, quia quidditati circumponitur, uti etiam Proculus explanat. Unde non fit ita, cum ipsum non-aliud se atque omnia definit. Non enim sic ipsum principium quidditativum
5 definit, quasi qui lineis circumpositis triangularem determinat seu definit superficiem, sed quasi superficiem, quae trigonus dicitur, constituat. Sed quod Plato et Dionysius sibi non repugnent atque adversentur, ipse quidem ex hoc vides: Dionysius enim ipsum alterum asserit, veluti communiter dicimus "amicus alter
10 ego," non sane propter separationem sed agglutinationem, et ad essentiam (ut sic dixerim) talem quod in omnibus omnia sit, ut ipse declarat. Nec aliud intendit Plato.

102   ABBAS: Video certe hanc quam asseris definitionem solum veram et quidditativam, non esse illam quam Plato mancam et defectuosam dicit. Et vehementer demiror, dum magis adverto, quomodo hic modus, quanto notior quidem clarior et facilior,
5 tanto ab omni obscuritate ac dubio est remotior atque absolutior. Quocirca cum dubitare nemo queat, quin hae tuae definitiones adeo sint verae, quod veriores esse non possint, | in ipsis   *44ʳ* utique rerum quidditas veraciter elucescit. Sed quid ad evangelium dices, ubi legitur Ioannem Baptistam, quo inter natos
10 mulierum nemo est maior, asserere quod deum nemo vidit umquam, quodque hoc filius dei, qui veritas in eodem nominatur evangelio, revelavit.

103   NICOLAUS: Idipsum sane aio, ipsum scilicet omni visionis modo invisibilem. Nam etsi quis assereret se ipsum vidisse, is utique nequiret exprimere, quid vidisset. Nam qui est ante visibile et invisibile, quo pacto est visibilis, nisi quia excellit omne
5 visibile, quod sine ipso nihil cernitur? Unde quando ipsum nec caelum nec a caelo aliud esse video et universaliter nec esse aliud, nec ab alio aliud esse, non video ipsum quasi sciens, quid

---

101 11 sit: fit *SU*
102 9 Ioannem: Iohannem *S*
102 11 quodque: *ex* quod *corr. S*

of a thing's definition, because (as Proclus, too, explains) the definition circumscribes the quiddity. Hence, this kind of defining is not what takes place when *Not-other* defines itself and all things. For *Not-other* defines the quidditative beginning not as does someone who determines, or defines, a triangular surface by means of circumscribing lines but *as if* someone constructed a surface which is called a triangle. But you see from the following |consideration| that Plato and Dionysius are not opposed to each other or at odds with each other: Dionysius asserts that God is other (1) in a sense comparable to our commonly saying "a friend is another I" (i.e., not on account of a separation but on account of an attachment) and (2) in relation to an "essence" (so to speak) of such a kind that it is all in all (as he says). And Plato did not intend anything else.

102   ABBOT: I certainly see that this definition which you assert to be the only true and quidditative definition is not the one which Plato calls incomplete and defective. And when I give the matter more thought, I am greatly amazed at how the more known, the more clear, and the more easy this mode |of seeing| is, the more free it is from all dimness and uncertainty. Therefore, since no one can doubt that these definitions of yours are so true that they cannot be truer, the quiddity of things truly shines forth in them. But what will you say with respect to the Gospel, where we read that John the Baptist (than whom no one among those born of women is greater)[139] asserts that no one has ever seen God and that the Son of God, who in the same Gospel is called Truth,[140] has revealed this |fact|?[141]

103   NICHOLAS: I say the very same thing, viz., that God is invisible to every mode of seeing. Even if someone asserted that he had seen Him, surely he would not be able to express what he had seen. For in what sense is He (who is prior to the visible and the invisible) visible except in the sense that He excels everything visible, which apart from Him is (seen to be) nothing? Hence, when I see that He is neither the sky nor *other* than the sky and is not at all either other or *other* than any other, I do not see

videam. Videre enim illud quod equidem ad deum refero, non
est videre visibile, sed est videre in visibili invisibile. Sicut cum
10 hoc esse verum video, quod nemo scilicet deum vidit, tunc sane
deum video super omne visibile non aliud ab omni visibili.
Actualem autem illam infinitatem omnem excedentem visionem, omnium quidditatum quidditatem, nequaquam visibilem
video, cum visibile quidem seu obiectum aliud sit a potentia,
15 deus autem, qui ab aliquo aliud esse non potest, | omne obiec- *45ʳ*
tum excedat.

104   CAPITULUM XXIII

IOANNES ANDREAS ABBAS: Non est mirandum deum creatorem,
esse invisibilem. Quippe cum mira intellectus opera in civitatum
aedificiis, navibus, artibus, libris, picturis, aliisque innumeris
5 videamus, intellectum tamen sensu visus non attingimus. Deum
itaque in creaturis suis cernimus, quamvis nobis maneat invisibilis. Sic quidem opera dei sunt caeli et terra, quem nemo
umquam vidit.

NICOLAUS: Visus se ipse non videt, licet in alio quod videt, se
10 videre attingat. Sed is visus qui est visuum visus, suum cernere
in alio non attingit, cum ante aliud sit. Cum igitur ante aliud
cernat, in ipsa visione non est aliud videns, aliud visibile, et
aliud videre ab ipsis procedens. Quare patet deum, qui theos
(quod est a "theoro" seu "video") dicitur, visionem illam ante
15 aliud esse, quam non possimus perfectam nisi trinam videre,
quodque ipsum videre infinitum et interminatum in alio est
videre non aliud ab aliquo. Se igitur et omnia unico et inenarra-
bili contuitu sapientes deum videre aiunt, quia est visionum
visio.

105   ABBAS: Quis non videret | hoc verum, quod tu te iam videre *45ᵛ*
ostendisti? Nemo profecto negat, nisi mentis carens acumine,

Him as if I knew what I saw. For the seeing which I direct toward God is not a visible seeing but is a seeing of the invisible in the visible. For example, when I see it to be true that no one has seen God, then I see God, above everything visible, as not *other* than everything visible. But that actual Infinity which excedes all sight and which is the Quiddity of all quiddities I do not at all see as visible—since what is visible, or is an object, is *other* than the power |of sight|, whereas God, who cannot be *other* than anything, transcends every object.

104   CHAPTER 23

ABBOT: We must not be surprised that God the Creator is invisible. Indeed, although in municipal buildings, in ships, artifacts, books, paintings, and countless other things we see the marvelous works of the intellect, nevertheless we do not make contact with the intellect by means of the sense of sight. In like manner, we discern God in His creatures, although He remains invisible to us. Thus, indeed, heaven and earth are the works of God, whom no one has ever seen.

NICHOLAS: Sight does not see itself, although it comes to be aware of itself in the other which it sees. However, *that* sight which is the Sight of sights does not come to discern itself in an other, since it is prior to other. Therefore, since it discerns prior to other: in its vision (1) the one who sees and (2) what is seeable and (3) the actual seeing that proceeds from these two are not distinct. Therefore, it is evident that God, who is called *theos* (|a word| which comes from *"theoro,"* i.e., *"video"*), is— prior to other—this vision which we cannot see as perfect unless |we see it| as trine. (And |it is evident| that to see God in an other—God, who is infinite and boundless—is to see |Him who is| not *other* than anything.) Therefore, the sages say that God sees Himself and all things by means of one indescribable viewing, because He is the Vision of visions.

105 ABBOT: Who would not see to be true what you have shown that you already see? Surely, no one maintains—unless he is

deum, qui principium ante aliud et omnia est, non esse privatum visu, qui quidem est ante privationem omnem. Quodsi visu pri-
5 vatus non est, sed a visu theos nominatur, perfectissimam habet visionem deus, se ipsam et omnia perficientem seu definientem eo modo, quo tu proxime explicuisti. Quod autem deus habet, hoc ante aliud est. Visus ergo qui et theos unitrinus, non alia sane visione sese et alia alia videt; sed ea visione qua se, simul et
10 omnia intuetur. Hoc videre definire est. Neque enim videre ab alio motum habet, sicut in nobis obiectum potentiam movet; sed illius videre constituere est, quemadmodum inquit Moyses deum vidisse lucem bonam et factam esse. Lux igitur non aliud quam lux—quae per visum est, qui non-aliud est—lux visa est. Ex quo
15 omnia una video ratione non aliud quam id quod sunt, esse, quia scilicet visus, qui non-aliud est, non aliud a se ipso vidit.

Sed reliquum est ut te de bono audiam, quod Moyses praemittit inquiens: "Vidit deus quod esset bonum, et mox creavit."

106   NICOLAUS: Legisti tu quidem in Parmenidis commentariis deum bonum | dici similiter et unum. Quae idem esse, quia illa *46^r* omnia penetrant, probat. Ac si diceret: quia deus est omnia in omnibus, hoc ei est attribuendum nomen, quod quidem omni-
5 bus centraliter adesse cernimus. Bonum autem relucet in omnibus. Omnia suum esse diligunt, quia bonum, cum de se ipso amabile sit bonum atque diligibile. Quando igitur Moyses universi voluit describere constitutionem, in quo deus se manifestaret, ad huius constitutionem singula creata bona dicit, ut uni-
10 versum esset gloriae et sapientiae dei perfecta revelatio. Id igitur quod ante aliud in se bonum vidit, in universi constitutionem,

devoid of intelligence—that God (who is the Beginning, who is prior to other and to all things, and who is even prior to all privation) is deprived of sight. But if He is not deprived of sight but because of sight is called *theos*, then He has most perfect sight, which perfects (or defines) itself and all things in the manner in which you explained a moment ago. But that which God has is prior to other. Therefore, it is not the case that Sight, which is the triune *Theos*, sees itself by means of one seeing and sees other things by means of another. Rather, by means of that seeing by which it sees itself it also sees all things. This seeing is defining. For |God's| seeing does not have its stimulus from another, as in our case an object moves the power |of sight|. Rather, His seeing is constituting; as Moses says, God saw that light was good, and light was created. Therefore, light that is not other than light—which exists through Sight, which is Not-other—is light that is seen. Hence, I see from one consideration that all things are no other than what they are: viz., |the consideration| that Sight, which is Not-other, saw what is not *other* than itself.

But it remains for me to hear you |discourse| about the good, which Moses mentions when he says: "God saw that it was good,[142] and straightway He created it."

106   NICHOLAS: You have read in the *Commentary on the Parmenides* that God is called both Good and One. |Proclus| proves them to be the same since they pervade all things. It is as if he were saying: because God is all in all, we ought to ascribe to Him the name which we see to belong basically to all things. Now, the good shines forth in all things. Since the good is desirable and lovable of itself and since |existence is| a good, all things desire their own existence. Therefore, when Moses wanted to describe the constitution of the universe, wherein God has manifested Himself, he said (with regard to the universe's constitution) that each created thing is good, so that the universe is the perfect revelation of the glory and the wisdom of God. Therefore, that which |God| saw as good in itself, prior to other,

quia bonum, pervenit. Deus vero cum ante aliud videret bonum,
ab illo utique aliud ipse non fuit. Quodsi quis bonum solum, ut
est ipsum non-aliud, posset intueri ante omne aliud, profecto is
15 intueretur quod nemo bonus nisi solus deus, qui est ante
non-bonum. Omnia quippe alia, quia aliud, esse aliter possent.
Idcirco de ipsis bonum ipsum, quod quidem, quia non-aliud,
aliter esse nequit, minime verificatur. At vero attende quomodo
principio bonum convenit, quia non-bonum praecedit, et non-
20 aliud praecedit aliud et principio convenit, et bonum, quod de
principio dicitur, non-aliud est; praecisius tamen | non-aliud, *46ᵛ*
cum sese bonumque definiat.

107   ABBAS: Attende an ita sit quod bonum non-bonum antecedit,
cum secundum Platonem non-ens praecedat ens et affirmationem generaliter negativa.

NICOLAUS: Cum dicitur non-ens praecedere ens, hoc non-ens
5 ente quidem melius est secundum ipsum Platonem—ita etiam
negativa quae affirmativam praecedit; ideo enim praecedit quia
melior. Verum non-bonum bono non est melius; quocirca
secundum hoc, bonum antecedit. Et solus deus bonum est, cum
bono nihil sit melius. Bonum vero quia aliud videtur a non-
10 bono, non est praecisum nomen dei. Et ideo negatur a deo, sicut
etiam alia omnia nomina, cum deus nec a bono nec a non-bono
aliud sit neque denique ab omni nominabili. Quare significatum
li non aliud praecisius in deum quam "bonum" dirigit.

108   CAPITULUM XXIV

ABBAS: Video nunc planissime cur magister veritatis aiebat
solum deum bonum. Sed tu, pater, unum adhuc, quaeso, adice:
quam ob causam idem magister deum spiritum dicat, et tibi
5 molesti esse desinemus.

---

106 14 omne: *non proprie scribit S*
108 1 Capitulum XXIV: Capitulum XXIIII et ultimum *S* Capitulum
XXIIII et ultimus *U*

entered (because it was good) into the constitution of the universe. But because God saw the good prior to other, surely He Himself was not *other* than the good. Now, if someone were able to behold the good in isolation and prior to every other, according as it is Not-other, then surely he would see that no one is good except God alone, who is prior to not-good. Indeed, all things other |than God| are able to exist differently because they are an other. Therefore, *good*—which (because it is Not-other) cannot exist differently—is not at all predicated truly of these things. But notice how it is that (1) the good befits the Beginning since good precedes not-good, and (2) Not-other precedes other and befits the Beginning, and (3) *good*, which is predicated of *Beginning*, is *Not-other*. Nevertheless, *Not-other* is more precise, since it defines itself and the good.

107 ABBOT: Determine whether it is true that good precedes not-good. For according to Plato not-being precedes being and, generally speaking, negation precedes affirmation.

NICHOLAS: When it is said that not-being precedes being, this not-being is better than being, according to Plato—and likewise for negation, which precedes affirmation (for it precedes because it is better). But not-good is not better than good. Hence, in accordance with this |consideration|, good precedes. Now, God alone is the good, since nothing is better than the good. But because *good* is seen as *other* than not-good, it is not a precise name for God. And so, it is not predicated of God (nor are any other names), since it is not the case that God is *other* than good or not-good or, indeed, than anything nameable. Therefore, the signification of "Not-other" more precisely directs |us| unto God than does |the signification of| "good."

108   CHAPTER 24

ABBOT: I now see very clearly why the Teacher of truth[143] said that God alone is good.[144] But add still one more point, I ask, Father—viz., why this same teacher says[145] that God is a spirit—and then we shall stop being a bother to you.

109   NICOLAUS: Spiritum quidem esse deum inquit quia, sicuti corpus, loco non clauditur, cum incorporeus | sit. Incorporeum *47ʳ* enim ante corporeum, illocale ante locale, incompositum est ante compositum. Quid enim omni in composito nisi simplex
5 dumtaxat cernitur seu incompositum? Compositum enim de se suum principium incompositum dicit. Nam si in composito compositum videretur, et in illo composito item compositum, unum utique magis compositum esse et aliud minus oporteret. Ad incompositum tandem deveniretur, cum ante compositum
10 sit componens. Nihil enim compositum se ipsum composuit. Erit ergo componens incompositum, quod ante partem et ante totum est et ante universum et ante omne; in quo anterioriter seu incomposite omnia sunt. Non igitur in compositis nisi incompositum dumtaxat videtur. Sic mens ante compositam lin
15 eam incompositum punctum contemplatur. Punctus enim signum est, linea vero signatum. Quid autem videtur in signato nisi signum?

110   Quippe signum est signati signum. Ideo principium, medium, et finis signati est signum, seu lineae est punctus, seu motus est quies, sive temporis est momentum, et universaliter divisibilis indivisibile. Non video autem indivisibile in divisibili qua|si eius *47ᵛ*
5 partem, quia pars, totius pars est; sed ipsum indivisibile ante partem et totum video in divisibili; et ipsum non aliud ab ipso video. Si enim ipsum non cernerem, nihil penitus cernerem. Universaliter ergo cum aliud in ipso video, non nisi non-aliud video. Deus igitur est spirituum spiritus, qui per ipsum non-aliud
10 cernitur ante omnem spiritum. Quo sublato nec spiritus nec corpus nec quidquam potest manere nominabile.

---

109 13 incomposite: incompositer *S*   incomposite *U*
110 6 et¹: ante *post* et¹ *scribit et del. S*

109 NICHOLAS: He says that God is a spirit for the following reason: since He is incorporeal, He is not enclosed within a space, as is a body. The incorporeal is prior to the corporeal; the nonspatial, to the spatial, the incomposite, to the composite. For in everything composite, what indeed is discerned except what is simple or incomposite? For the composite testifies about itself that its beginning is incomposite. For if in what is composite a composite were seen, and in this latter composite still another composite, then one |of these| would have to be more composite and the other less composite. At length, we would arrive at what is incomposite, since prior to what is composed there is what composes; for nothing which is composite has composed itself. Therefore, there will be something which composes but is incomposite and which is prior to part and to whole and is prior to the universe and to everything; and in it all things are antecedently and incompositely present. Therefore, to be sure, in things composite there is seen only what is incomposite. Thus, the mind beholds the incomposite point prior to the composite line. The point is a sign, but the line is something signified. Yet, what is seen in the signified except the sign?

110 Indeed, a sign is a sign for what is signified. And so, the sign is the beginning, the middle, and the end of what is signified; and the point is |the beginning, the middle, and the end| of a line; and rest is |the beginning, the middle, and the end| of motion; and the moment is |the beginning, the middle, and the end| of time; and, in general, the indivisible is |the beginning, the middle, and the end| of the divisible. But I do not see the indivisible in the divisible as its part. For a part is a part of a whole; but in the divisible I see the indivisible prior to part and whole, and I see it as not *other* than the divisible. For if I did not see the indivisible, I would not see anything at all. Therefore, when in what is divisible I see that which is altogether other, I see only Not-other. Hence, God is the Spirit of spirits, which by way of Not-other is seen prior to every spirit. If God were removed, neither spirit nor body nor anything nameable could remain.

111   Sicut frigiditas propter suam invisibilitatem activitatemque
quae in frigido seu glacie sentitur, dici spiritus potest, qua sublata esse glacies desinit (subtracto enim spiritu congelante seu
glaciente, cessat et glacies), sic cessante spiritu connectente in
5 compositis, compositum cessat; et cessante spiritu essentiante,
cessat ens; et cessante spiritu discernente sive discretiante (aut, ut
praecisius exprimam, non aliante), omnia pariter cessant. Spiritus enim qui omnia in omnibus operatur, per quem quodlibet
est non aliud quam est, per me non-aliud nominatur. Ille spiri-
10 tuum spiritus est, cum omnis spiritus non aliud quam spiritus sit.
Ille spiritus non nisi in spiritu seu mente in veritate conspicitur.
Solus enim ille rationalis creaturae spiritus, | quae mens dicitur, *48ʳ*
veritatem potest intueri. In ipsa autem veritate videt spiritum qui
est spiritus veritatis, qui quidem omnia veraciter efficit id esse
15 quod sunt. Et sicut ipsum videt, ita etiam ipsum adorat, in spiritu scilicet et veritate.

112   ABBAS: Duxisti me, pater, in spiritum quem omnium creatorem
video (ut propheta vidit, qui ad creatorem dixit "Emitte spiritum tuum, et creabuntur," ac si desiderans glaciem emitti spiritum
peteret spirantem glaciationem, ita universaliter de omni desi-
5 derato) atque ut mentem spiritum videam illius imaginem
spiritus. Etenim spiritus ille, qui de sua virtute ad omnia pergit,
omnia scrutatur et creat omnium notiones atque similitudines.
Creat, inquam, quoniam rerum similitudines notionales ex alio
aliquo non facit, sicut nec spiritus qui deus, rerum quidditates
10 facit ex alio, sed ex se aut non-alio. Ideo sicut ab aliquo creabili
non est aliud, ita nec mens est aliud ab aliquo per ipsam intelli-
113 gibili. Bene etiam in una video mente a corpore magis absoluta
perfectius spiritum relucescere creatorem et praecisiores creare
notiones.

111 6 discretiante: discreti ante *S*
111 8 quem: quam *S*   quod *U*

111   Now, coldness can be called *"spiritus"* on account of its invisibility and of the activity which is perceived in ice or in what is cold. If coldness is removed, the ice ceases existing; for if the congealing, or freezing, power [*spiritus*] is removed, the ice ceases to exist. Similarly, if the binding power ceases in composite things, what is composite ceases; and if the power-of-being ceases, the being ceases; and if the distinguishing, or separating, power ceases—or (to speak more precisely) if the not-othering power ceases—then all |the different| things also cease. The Spirit, or the Power, which works all in all and through which each thing is no other than it is, I call Not-other. It is the Spirit of spirits, since every spirit is no other than spirit. This Spirit is seen truly only by spirit, or mind. For only that rational spirit which belongs to a creature and which is called a mind can view truth. In the truth |the mind| sees the Spirit which is the Spirit-of-truth, which truly causes all things to be that which they are. And just as |the mind| sees this Spirit, so it also worships it in spirit and in truth.[146]

112   ABBOT: You have led me, Father, unto a Spirit which I see to be the Creator of all—just as was seen by the prophet who said to the Creator: "Send forth Your Spirit, and they will be created." [147] (It is as if one who desired ice were to ask that a spirit with congealing breath be sent forth—and so on for every desired thing.) And |you have led me| to see that the mental spirit is an image of this Spirit. For, indeed, this |mental| spirit— which of its own power goes forth unto all things—examines all things and creates the concepts and likenesses of all things. I say "creates" inasmuch as |this spirit| makes the conceptual likenesses of things from no other thing—even as the Spirit which is God makes the quiddities of things not from another but from itself, i.e., from Not-other. And so, just as |the Divine Spirit| is not *other* than any creatable thing, so neither is the mind *other*
113 than anything which is understandable by it. And in the case of a mind which is more free of a body, I clearly see a spirit (1) shining forth more perfectly as creator and (2) creating more precise concepts.

Sed quoniam tui propositi non est nisi nos tecum rapere et
5 ducere ad visionis primi viam, | quod omnia in omnibus est, *48*
quia in via alius alio citius currit, ut comprehendat, idcirco te
deinceps sinam amplius conquiescere. Sufficit enim nobis directio tua, qua nos nisus es dirigere ad ipsum principium, quod sese
et omnia definit, hactenus ab omnibus quaesitum semperque
10 quaerendum in posterum. Contentamur sane de via quam tu
nobis per ipsum non-aliud revelasti. Et ego tibi pro omnibus
immortales gratias ago, agemusque semper, quoad usque facie
ad faciem deum deorum in Sion semper benedictum videbimus.

113 13 Sion: Syon *SU*   videbimus: Finis. Laus deo *add. S*

But since it is your purpose only to take us along with you and to lead us to the pathway of the vision of the First—which is all in all—and because on this pathway one |person| is quicker to understand than is another, I shall now let you rest at more length. For we find to be sufficient the guidance by which you have endeavored to guide us to the Beginning, which defines itself and all things. |This Beginning| has hitherto been sought by all; and it is always to be sought in the future. We are indeed satisfied with the pathway which you have revealed to us by means of *Not-other*. I give you undying thanks on behalf of all; and we shall be grateful always, until such time as we see face to face [148] in Zion the God of gods,[149] blessed forever.[150]

Prima propositio: Definitio quae se et omnia definit, ea est
quae per omnem mentem quaeritur.

5 Secunda: Quisquis videt verissimum esse quod definitio est
non aliud quam definitio, is etiam videt ipsum non-aliud definitionis esse definitionem.

Tertia: Qui videt quod non-aliud est non aliud quam non-
aliud, videt non-aliud definitionis esse definitionem.

10 Quarta: Qui videt ipsum non-aliud definire se et definitionem
omnia definientem, is ipsum non-aliud videt non esse aliud ab
omni definitione et ab omni definito.

115 Quinta propositio: Qui videt ipsum non-aliud principium definire, cum principium sit non aliud quam principium: ipsum
non-aliud videt principium esse principii, sic ip|sum quoque *49ʳ*
videt medium medii et finem finis et nomen nominis et ens entis

5 et non-ens non-entis atque ita de omnibus ac singulis quae dici
possunt aut cogitari.

Sexta: Qui videt quomodo ex eo quod non-aliud se ipsum
definit, ipsum non-aliud est non aliud ipsius non-aliud, et quomodo ex eo etiam quod omnia definit et singula, est in omnibus

10 omnia et in singulis singula: ille quidem videt ipsum non-aliud
esse aliud ipsius aliud; et videt non-aliud, ipsi aliud non opponi—
quod est secretum, cuius non est simile.

Septima propositio: Qui videt quomodo subtracto ipso non-
aliud, non remanet nec aliud nec nihil, cum non-aliud sit nihil

15 ipsius nihil: ille sane videt ipsum non-aliud in omnibus omnia
esse et nihil in nihilo.

116 Octava propositio: Non est possibile quidquam in hominis
cogitationem posse venire absque ipso non-aliud, cum sit cogita-
tionum cogitatio. Et licet ipsum non-aliud non sit aliud | a cogi- *50ʳ*
tatione de se ipso cogitante, non est tamen ipsa cogitatio, cum

5 cogitatio non sit non-aliud simpliciter, sed non aliud quam cogi-

---

116 5 non-aliud: non aliud (non *supra lin.*) S

1. The definition which defines itself and all things is the definition which every mind seeks.

2. If anyone sees that "definition is not other than definition" is most true, he also sees that *Not-other* is the definition of definition.

3. He who sees that Not-other is not other than Not-other sees that *Not-other* is the definition of definition.

4. If anyone sees that *Not-other* defines itself and is the definition which defines all things, he sees that *Not-other* is not *other* than every definition and everything defined.[1]

115   5. If anyone sees that *Not-other* defines the beginning—since the beginning is not other than the beginning—he sees that Not-other is the Beginning of beginning; and he sees that it is also the Middle of middle, the End of end, the Name of name, the Being of being, the Not-being of not-being, and so on for each and every thing which can be spoken of or thought of.[2]

6. If anyone sees how from the fact that *Not-other* defines itself, |there follows that| Not-other is Not-other of Not-other, and |if he sees| how from the additional fact that it defines each and every thing, |there follows that| it is all in all and each in each, then he sees that Not-other is the Other|ness| of other and sees that Not-other is not opposed to other. This is a hidden truth of which there is not the like.

7. Suppose someone sees how if Not-other were removed, it is not the case that either other or nothing would remain, since Not-other is the Nothing|ness| of nothing. Then he sees that in all things Not-other is all things and in nothing it is nothing.

116   8. Without Not-other it is not possible that anything can come into human thought, for Not-other is the Thought of thoughts. Moreover, although Not-other is not *other* than Thought-thinking-of-itself, it is not thought itself. For thought is not unqualifiedly *Not-other* but is not other than thought; nor does

tatio; neque ipsum non-aliud aliter se habet in omnibus quae dici possunt.

Nona: Quidquid mens videt, sine ipso non-aliud non videt. Non enim videret aliud, si non-aliud non foret ipsius aliud aliud. 10 Sic nec ens cerneret, si non-aliud non foret ipsius entis ens, et ita de omnibus quae dici queunt. Ita videt mens omne aliud per aliud, quod non-aliud—quare sic etiam alia omnia. Aliam enim videt veritatem per veritatem quae non-aliud; aliam rationem per rationem quae non-aliud. Igitur quodlibet aliud, prioriter 15 non-aliud videt. Et eodem modo videt omnia et nomen et quidditatem et alia quaecumque habent, ab ipso non-aliud habere.

117 Decima propositio: Qui videt finitum non aliud quam finitum, et infinitum non aliud quam infinitum, pari modo de visibili et invisibili, de numerabili quoque et innumera|bili, mensur- *50*ᵛ abili et immensurabili, conceptibili et inconceptibili, imaginabili 5 et inimaginabili, intelligibili et inintelligibili, et ceteris talibus: ille videt deum per "non-aliud" significatum nec finito nec infinito finibilem, nec mensura mensurabili nec immensurabili mensurabilem, nec numero numerabili nec innumerabili numerabilem, ita nec conceptibilem, nec imaginabilem, nec intelligibilem, nec 10 nominabilem nomine nominabili nec nomine innominabili, licet a nullo omnium illorum et aliorum quae dici possunt, nec in ipsis aliud sit.

118 Undecima: Qui videt quomodo ipsum non-aliud se definiendo omnia definit, ille videt quoniam ipsum est omnium adaequatissima mensura, maiorum maior, minorum minor, aequalium aequalis, pulchrorum pulchra, verorum vera, et vivorum viva 5 mensura, et de omnibus eodem modo.

---

117 7 immensurabili: mensurabili *S* immensurabili *U*
117 8 numerabili: numerabilem *S* numerabili *U*

Not-other exist with any difference in any of the things which can be spoken of.

9. Whatever the mind sees, it does not see without Not-other. For example, it would not see other if Not-other were not the Other|ness| of the other. Thus, it would not see a being if Not-other were not the Being of the being—and so on for all things which can be spoken of. So the mind sees every other by means of the other which Not-other is—and thus also for all others. For example, by means of the truth which Not-other is, |the mind| sees an other which is a truth; by means of the form which Not-other is, |the mind sees| an other which is a form. Therefore, |the mind| sees whatever-is-other antecedently as Not-other. And, similarly, it sees that all things have from Not-other their names and quiddities and whatever else they have.

117 10. Suppose someone sees that the finite is not other than finite, the infinite not other than infinite—and in like manner with regard to the visible and the invisible, the numerable and the innumerable, the measurable and the immeasurable, the conceivable and the inconceivable, the imaginable and the unimaginable, the intelligible and the unintelligible, and other such things—then he sees that God, who is signified by "Not-other," is not limitable either by the finite or by the infinite; is not measurable either by a measurable measure or by an immeasurable measure; is not numerable either by a numerable number or by an innumerable number; and similarly is not conceivable, imaginable, or intelligible; and is not nameable by any nameable name or by any unnameable name. Yet, |God| is not *other* than any of these and others which can be spoken of; and in them He is not an other.

118 11. If anyone sees how it is that by defining itself *Not-other* defines all things, he sees that Not-other is the most congruent measure of all things—a greater measure for greater things, a lesser measure for lesser things, an equal measure for equal things, a beautiful measure for beautiful things, a true measure for true things, a living measure for living things, and so on in the same way for all things.

Duodecima: Qui videt quoniam ipsum non-aliud sui et omnium est definitio et definitum, ille in omnibus quae videt, non
nisi non-aliud videt se ipsum definiens. Nam quid videt in aliud
nisi non-aliud sese | definiens? Quid aliud in caelo quam non- *51ʳ*
10 aliud se ipsum definiens? Et de omnibus eodem modo. Creatura
igitur est ipsius creatoris sese definientis seu lucis, quae deus est,
se ipsam manifestantis ostensio—quasi mentis se ipsam definientis propalatio, quae praesentibus fit per vivam orationem et
remotis per nuntium aut scripturam. In quibus ostensionibus
15 mentis non est aliud nisi mens sese definiens, se clarissime et
vivaciter per propriam orationem audientibus manifestans, remotis per legatam orationem, remotissimis per scriptam. Ita
ipsum non-aliud, mens mentis, se in primis quidem creaturis
clarius, in aliis vero occultius ostendit.

119   Tertia decima: Qui videt quomodo li non aliud, quod est
ipsius non-aliud non-aliud, relucet in aeterno, ubi est aeternae
aeternitatis aeternitas, et in vero, ubi verae veritatis est veritas,
et in bono, ubi bonae bonitatis est bonitas, et ita in reliquis: ille
5 in omnibus deum videt, se ipsum definientem, unitriniter relu-
cere. Nam unitrinum non-aliud | in uno est unius unitatis unitas, *51ᵛ*
et in ente entis entitatis entitas, et in magnitudine magnae magnitudinis magnitudo, et in quanto quantae quantitatis quantitas, et
ita de ceteris.

10   Quarta decima: Qui videt in alio non-aliud aliud, is videt in
affirmatione negationem affirmari. Et qui deum videt ante
affirmationem et negationem, ille deum videt in affirmationibus
quae de ipso per nos fiunt, non esse negativam quae affirmatur,
sed affirmationis affirmationem.

118 17 scriptam: *ex* scripturam (*?*) *corr. S*
119 3 vero ubi: *om. S   habet U*   verae: vere *ex ? corr. S*

12. If anyone sees that *Not-other* is not only the definition of itself and of all things but also the object of its own definition and of the definition of all else, then in all the things which he sees, he sees only *Not-other* defining itself. For what does he see in other except *Not-other* defining itself? What else |does he see| in the sky except *Not-other* defining itself? And similarly for all things. Therefore, the creature is the manifestation of the Creator defining Himself—or the manifestation of the Light (which is God) manifesting itself. This is comparable to a proclamation of a mind which defines itself—|a proclamation| which through living speech is made to those who are present and through a messenger or a writing is made to those who are distant. In these manifestations of the mind there is no other than the mind defining itself, manifesting itself vitally and most clearly to listeners through its speech, to those far away through a delegated speech, to those farthest away through a writing. In this manner, Not-other, the Mind of mind, shows itself more clearly in the first creatures but more dimly in the others.

119 13. If anyone sees how it is that Not-other, which is Not-other of Not-other, shines forth (1) in the eternal, where it is the Eternalness of the eternal eternity, and (2) in the true, where it is the Truthfulness of the true truth, and (3) in the good, where it is the Goodness of the good goodness (and similarly in the remaining things), then he sees that God, who defines Himself, shines forth triunely in all things. For example, in what-is-one the triune Not-other is the Oneness of the one oneness; in a being it is the Being of the existing being; in a magnitude, the Magnitude of the great magnitude; in a quantity, the Quantitativeness of the quantitative quantity (and similarly for other things).

14. If anyone sees that in an other Not-other is the other, he sees that in an affirmation a negation is affirmed. And if anyone sees God prior to affirmation and negation, he sees that, in the affirmations which we make about God, God is not a negation which is affirmed but is the Affirmitiveness of the affirmation.

120   Quinta decima: Qui videt in alio non-aliud aliud, ille videt in
calefacto non-calefactum calefactum et in frigefacto non-frigefactum
frigefactum et in formato non-formatum formatum et in facto
non-factum factum et in divisibili indivisibile divisibile et in
5 composito incompositum compositum et generaliter in affirmato
non-affirmatum affirmatum. Et videt negativam tale principium
affirmationis, quod ea sublata est affirmatio. Negationes igitur
dirigunt visum | mentis in quid, affirmationes autem in tale quid. *52ʳ*

121   Sexta decima: Qui videt quomodo negationes, quae mentis
visum in quidditatem dirigunt, sunt priores affirmationibus, ille
videt omne nomen significare tale quid. Nam "corpus" non signifi-
cat quidditatem, quae incorporalis est, sed talem scilicet corpo-
5 ream; sic "terra" terrestrem, et "sol" solarem, et ita de omnibus.
Nomina igitur omnia ex aliquo sensibili signo impositionem
habent significativam, quae signa sequuntur rerum quidditatem.
Non igitur ipsam, sed talem significant. Mens autem, ipsam
anterioriter contemplans vocabulum negat esse proprium ipsius
10 quam videt quidditatem.

122   Septima decima: Videt mens quomodo ipsum non-aliud est
actus ipsius actus et ipsius maximi maximum et ipsius minimi
minimum. Et ideo videt actum purum, qui purior esse non
potest, numquam fuisse in potentia; nam per puriorem actum in
5 actum devenisset. Quare videt omnia | quae alia esse possent, *52ᵛ*
semper posse alia esse, et ideo in recipientibus magis seu maius
numquam deveniri ad actum maximum, quo maius esse nequit,

---

120 7 sublata: *bis S*

120 15. If anyone sees that in an other Not-other is the other, he sees that in something hot What-is-not-hot is the hot thing; in something cold, What-is-not-cold is the cold thing; in what is formed, What-is-not-formed is the formed thing; in something created, What-is-not-created is the created thing; in something divisible, What-is-indivisible is the divisible thing; in something composite, What-is-incomposite is the composite thing; and, in general, in something affirmed, What-is-not-affirmed is the affirmed thing. And he sees that negation is the following kind of beginning of affirmation: viz., such that if the negation is removed, the affirmation results. Therefore, negations direct the mind's sight unto *what* (*quid*), whereas affirmations |direct it| unto *what is such* (*tale quid*).

121 16. If anyone sees how it is that negations (which direct the mind's sight unto quiddity) are prior to affirmations, then he sees that every name signifies what-is-such (*tale quid*). For example, "body" does not signify quiddity, which is incorporeal, but |signifies a quiddity which is| such as to be corporeal. In like manner, "earth" |signifies a quiddity which is such as to be| terrestrial; "sun," |a quiddity which is such as to be| solar; and similarly for all things. Therefore, all names signify in accordance with some perceptible sign; these signs are subsequent to the respective quiddity of the things. Hence, they signify not *what* [*quidditas*] but *what is such* [*talis quidditas*]. But the mind, which beholds the quiddity antecedently, denies that the name is the proper name of the quiddity which it sees.

122 17. The mind sees how it is that Not-other is the Actualness of actuality, the Maximality of maximum, and the Minimality of minimum. And so, it sees that pure actuality, which cannot be purer, was never in |the state of| potency. For |otherwise| it would have come into actuality by means of a still purer actuality. Hence, |the mind| sees (1) that all the things which *could* be other can *always* be other and (2) that, consequently, in the case of things which admit of being more, or of being greater, we never come to an actual maximum, than which there cannot be

et quae aliud esse possunt, quia numquam ad ipsum non-aliud
attingunt, semper possunt esse aliud.

123   Decima octava: Qui videt quomodo non-aliud, quod est aliud
ipsius aliud, non est ipsum aliud, ille videt aliud ipsius aliud,
quod est aliud aliorum. Sic aequalis videt aequale, quod aequalium est aequale; et bonum ipsius boni, quod est bonum bon-
5 orum; et ita de omnibus.

Ille sane videt quomodo non-aliud, quod est aliud ipsius
aliud, non participatur per ipsum aliud, quia ab ipso non est
aliud, sed in ipso ipsum, sed aliud ab aliis participatur. Sic de
aequali et bono et ceteris. Bonum igitur, a quo non-aliud non est
10 aliud, ab omnibus aliis bonis participatur et in aliis aliter. Numquam igitur erunt duo aeque bona aut aeque aequalia, quae
meliora esse non possint aut aequaliora; de similibus eodem
modo. Oportet enim omne aliud ab alio esse aliud, cum solum
non-aliud sit non aliud ab | omni alio.   *53ʳ*

124   Decima nona: Qui videt deum non esse aliud nec ab omni eo
quod intelligit, nec ab omni eo quod intelligitur, ille videt deum
dare intellectui quod est non aliud quam intellectus intelligens,
et intelligibili quod est non aliud quam intelligibile ab intellectu,
5 et quod intellectus intelligens non sit aliud ab intellecto. Ipsum
igitur non-aliud clarius relucet in intellectu, qui non aliud est ab
intellecto, sicut scientia non aliud a scito, quam in sensibus.
Visus enim non sic clare non aliud est a viso et auditus ab
audito. Intelligentiae autem in quibus clarius ipsum non-aliud
10 relucet, citius et clarius intelligibilia, a quibus minus sunt alia,

123 2 est: esse *SU*
123 11 erunt: *om. S   habet U*
124 6-7 qui . . . scito: *ut verba interposita S*

a greater. Those things which *can* be something other can *always* be something other because they never attain to Not-other.

123 18. If anyone sees how it is that Not-other (which is the Other|ness| of the other) is not the other, then he sees the Other-|ness| of the other—i.e., the Other|ness| of other things. In this manner, he sees the Equal|ity| of the equal—i.e., the Equal|ity| of equal things. |Or he sees| the Good|ness| of the good—i.e., the Good|ness| of good things. And similarly for all things.

Assuredly, he sees how it is that Not-other, which is the Other|ness| of the other, is not participated in by the other (for |Not-other| is not *other* than other but in other is the other); yet, other is participated in by others. (The same holds true regarding the equal and the good and so on). Therefore, the Good (than which Not-other is not *other*) is participated in by all other goods; and it is differently participated in by different |goods|. Therefore, there will never be two equally good things (or two equally equal things) which cannot be better (or more nearly equal). And similarly for similar things. For everything which is an other must be other than another, since only Not-other is not *other* than any other.

124 19. If anyone sees that God is not *other* than anything which understands and |is not *other*| than anything which is understood, then he sees that God (1) bestows upon the intellect the fact that it is not other than an intellect which understands and (2) bestows upon what is understandable the fact that it is not other than what is understandable by an intellect and (3) causes that the intellect which understands is not *other* than what is understood. Therefore, Not-other shines forth more clearly in the intellect than in the senses; for the intellect is not *other* than what is understood—even as knowledge is not *other* than what is known. For |compared with the intellect| seeing is not as clearly not-*other*-than-what-is-seen; nor hearing, |not-*other*-| than-what-is-heard. But the intellects, in which Not-other shines forth more clearly, understand intelligible objects more quickly and more lucidly; for it is less the case that they are *other* than these

intelligunt. Hoc est enim intelligere, scilicet intelligibilia a se non alia facere, sicut lumen illuminabilia citius non alia a se facit, quando est intensius. Relucere autem videtur ipsum non-aliud in omnibus, quando constat quod omnia se in omnibus nituntur
15 definire. Sicut calor omnia nititur calida talia facere, ut ipse sit non aliud ab ipsis et se in omnibus definiat, | sic intellectus, ut *53ʳ* omnia sint intellectus et se in omnibus definiat; ita et imaginatio et omnia cetera.

125 Vicesima: Quando mens considerat non-calidum calefieri et frigidum calefieri, per intellectum attingit non-calidum, per sensum frigidum, et videt non esse idem, quando per diversas potentias attingit. Et dum considerat non-frigidum per mentem
5 videri, sicut non-calidum, ac quod non-calidum potest calefieri et non-frigidum frigefieri et quod frigidum potest calefieri et calidum frigefieri: videt quomodo idem est non-calidum et non-frigidum. Et dicitur non-calidum quia, licet non sit actu calidum, potest tamen calefieri; et sic dicitur non-frigidum quia, licet non
10 actu frigidum, potest tamen frigefieri. Ideo cum actu est calidum, adhuc manet potentia frigidum; et cum actu est frigidum, manet potentia calidum. Potentia autem non quiescit, nisi sit actu, cum sit finis et perfectio eius, alias frustra foret potentia. Ideo non foret potentia, cum nihil sit frustra. Quia autem poten-
15 tia se ipsam non producit in actum—hoc enim repugnat—ideo est motor necessarius, qui potentiam ad actum moveat. Ita videt mens naturam et naturalem motum et ipsum non-aliud, naturae naturam in ipsa relucentem.

125 18 relucentem: Finis propositionum. Laus deo optimo. Scripsi Hartmannus Schedel, arcium et utriusque medicine doctor, anno domini 1496, die 6, mensis Aprilis Nueremberge *add. S*

|intelligible objects|. Indeed, |for the intellect| to understand is |for it| to make intelligible objects to be not *other* than itself— just as light, when it is more intense, more quickly makes the illuminable objects to be not *other* than itself. But Not-other is seen to shine forth in all things by virtue of the fact that all things endeavor to define themselves in all things. For example, hotness endeavors to make all things so hot that it is not *other* than they and that it defines itself in all things. Similarly, the intellect |endeavors to bring it about| that all things are intellect and that it defines itself in all things. And similarly for the imagination and all other things.

125 20. When the mind considers what-is-not-hot becoming hot and what-is-cold becoming hot, the mind makes contact through the *intellect* with what-is-not-hot, through the *sense* with what-is-cold. And |the mind| sees that |not-hot and cold| are not the same thing, since it makes contact with them by different powers. And when |the mind| considers the fact that (1) what-is-not-cold is seen by the mind (even as is what-is-not-hot) and that (2) what-is-not-hot can become hot and what-is-not-cold can become cold and that (3) what-is-cold can become hot and what-is-hot can become cold, then |the mind| sees the sense in which the same object can be both not-hot and not-cold. This object is called not-hot for the following reason: although it is not actually hot, it can become hot. And, likewise, it is called not-cold for the following reason: although it is not actually cold, it can become cold. And so, when it is actually hot, a potency for being cold still remains; and when it is actually cold, a potency for being hot still remains. Now, a potency does not cease unless it is actualized. For |actuality| is the end and the perfection of potency; otherwise, the potency would be in vain. And so, there would be no potency, since nothing is in vain. But because potency does not bring itself into actuality (for this would be inconsistent), a mover is needed in order to move the potency to actuality. In this way, the mind sees nature and natural motion and Not-other, which is the Nature-of-nature, which shines forth in nature.[3]

abbreviations

DI	*De Docta Ignorantia: On Learned Ignorance*
DP	*De Possest: On Actualized-possibility*
NA	*De Li Non Aliud: On Not-other*
VS	*De Venatione Sapientiae: On the Pursuit of Wisdom*
S	Codex Latinus Monacensis 24848
U	Codex Latinus Tolletanensis 19-26

The abbreviations of the books of the Bible are the standard ones.

Abbreviations in the Latin notes:

add.	*addit; addunt*
cf.	*confer*
coni.	*conicit*
corr.	*corrigit; corrigunt*
del.	*delet; delent*
in marg.	*in margine*
lin.	*linea; lineam*
om.	*omittit; omittunt*

praenotanda

1. Where, for clarification, words from the Latin text have been inserted into the translation, the following rule has been employed: when the Latin term is noted exactly as it appears in the Latin text, parentheses are used; when the case endings of nouns have been transformed to the nominative, brackets are used.

2. Strokes are used in place of brackets, as an aid to readability. *English* words and phrases thus "bracketed" are supplied by the translator to fill out the meaning implied by the Latin text.

3. Quotation marks are employed when Nicholas mentions a word rather than uses it. On occasion, however, he both mentions and uses a word in the same sentence. In such cases the word is italicized in the translation. (E.g., 37:7-8: "It is certain that *Not-other* defines itself and all |other| things.")

4. When words such as "beginning," "being," "truth," "absolute," "wisdom," "form," etc., refer to God, they are capitalized. Where used as a noun, the words "not other" are hyphenated, and the hyphenated expression is capitalized irrespective of whether or not it is being used as a name for God.

5. Throughout this dialogue Nicholas uses three expressions which, in translation, the reader needs to construe properly: (a) "*x* is not other than *x*"; (b) "God (or Not-other) is not *other* than *x*," which always means "God is not other-than-*x*, i.e., is not not-*x*," for God transcends all differentiation between x and not-*x*; and (c) "In *x* God (or Not-other) is not other than *x*," which always means "In *x* God is *x*." (See n. 46 of the Notes to the Introduction and n. 1 of the Notes to

177

the Propositions.) To exhibit an instance of each expression: (a′) the sky is not other than the sky; (b′) Not-other is not *other* than the sky; and (c′) in the sky Not-other is not other than the sky. [In expressions *b* and *c* Nicholas's characteristic use excludes the possibility of instantiating "*x*" by "God" (or "Not-other").]

In order to eliminate ambiguity I have, where necessary, italicized "other" for emphasis and used "no other" or "none other" in place of "not-other."

PRAENOTANDA FOR THE LATIN TEXT

1. The printed Latin text follows Manuscript *S* (Codex Latinus Monacensis 24848, fol. 1ᵛ - 54ʳ); it was copied in Nuremberg on April 6, 1496 by Hartmann Schedel. Regarding Manuscript *U*, see the comments in the Preface to the Third Edition of the present work.

2. The boldfaced section numbers in the left-hand margin (but not the roman line numbers) correspond to those found in the second edition of Paul Wilpert's German translation *Vom Nichtanderen* (Hamburg: Felix Meiner Verlag, 1976).

3. Strokes in the Latin text indicate the end of one ms. folio and the beginning of another. The number of the beginning folio is placed in the right-hand margin and is italicized.

4. In the text itself spelling, punctuation, and capitalization are editorialized. In the notes to the text, punctuation, but not spelling, is editorialized, as is also capitalization.

PRAENOTANDA FOR THE ENGLISH NOTES

1. All references are to the Latin texts. See the list of texts at the beginning of the Notes.

2. The numbering of the Psalms accords with the Douay Version of the Bible and, in parentheses, with the King James Version.

notes

All references to Nicholas of Cusa's works are to the Latin texts—specifically to the following editions (unless explicitly indicated otherwise):

   A. Heidelberg Academy edition of the *Opera Omnia Cusana: De Concordantia Catholica; Sermones; De Coniecturis; De Deo Abscondito; De Quaerendo Deum; De Filiatione Dei; De Dato Patris Luminum; Idiota* (1983 edition) *de Sapientia, de Mente, de Staticis Experimentis; De Venatione Sapientiae; Compendium; De Apice Theoriae.*

   B. Text authorized by the Heidelberg Academy and published in the Latin-German editions of Felix Meiner Verlag's Philosophische Bibliothek: *De Docta Ignorantia* (Book I, 3rd ed., 1979; Book II, 2nd ed., 1977; Book III, 1977); *De Beryllo.*

   C. Paris edition (1514) of the *Opera Cusana: Complementum Theologicum; De Aequalitate; De Principio* (=Paris edition, Vol. II, Part I, fol. 7ʳ - 11ᵛ).

   D. Strasburg edition (1488) of the *Opera Cusana* as edited by Paul Wilpert and republished by W. de Gruyter (Berlin, 1967, 2 vols.): *De Ludo Globi.*

   E. Banning Press editions: *De Visione Dei; De Possest; De Li Non Aliud.*

N. B.: For some treatises the references in the notes indicate book and chapter; for others, section and line; for still others, page and line. Readers should have no difficulty determining which is which when they consult the particular Latin text. E.g., "*DI* II, 6 (125:19-20)" indicates *De Docta Ignorantia*, Book II, Chap. 6, margin number 125, lines 19-20. And "*Ap.* 8:14-16" indicates *Apologia Doctae Ignorantiae*, p. 8, lines 14-16. Citations of *De Possest* are in terms either of margin numbers alone or of both margin and line numbers.

PREFACE

1. See *A Concise Introduction to the Philosophy of Nicholas of Cusa*

179

(Minneapolis: Banning Press, 3rd. edition, 1986). The bibliography found there will also be of service to readers of the present work. It is supplemented by the bibliographies in my *Nicholas of Cusa on Learned Ignorance: A Translation and an Appraisal of De Docta Ignorantia* (Minneapolis: Banning Press, 1985, 2nd edition) and in my *Nicholas of Cusa's Dialectical Mysticism: Text, Translation, and Interpretive Study of De Visione Dei* (Minneapolis: Banning Press, 1985).

2. The present translation is literal without being altogether *mot-à-mot*. For the sake of my students, however, I have used "brackets" (i.e., strokes) to indicate where I supplied words whose meanings are implicit in the Latin constructions.

3. In "A Translation of *De Non Aliud* by Nicholas de Cusa with an Introduction and Critical Notes" (Columbia University doctoral dissertation, 1966) Rose Finkenstaedt once denies that, for Nicholas, Not-other is God (p. 35: "although Not Other is not God . . . "), once asserts that "only God is Not Other" (p. 28), and once again implies that Not-other and God are distinct (p. 121, n. 42: "Cusa applies the verb *videtur* to the Not Other as well as to God"). In general, her discussion is philosophically uncritical and her translation unreliable. For example, she misconstrues the use of the word "*li*" (pp. 33, n. 19; 138, n. 6); misstates the argument from *DI* I, 4 about the coincidence of the Absolutely Maximum and Minimum (p. 41); claims that in *DI* Nicholas did not emphasize the priority of God *vis-à-vis* the universe (p. 49); and speaks of a concept as being a method (pp. 35 and 89). She repeatedly mistranslates the word "*ipse*" (and its variants), translates "*absoluta*" as "absolute" where it should be translated as "free from" or "independent of" (pp. 175 and 141), and so forth.

INTRODUCTION

1. At the end of *NA* 19 Nicholas refers to *De Li Non Aliud* as a *speculatio*; and, in the manuscript, an alternate title for the work is "*Directio Speculantis*," i.e., "Guidance for One Who Is Speculating."

The date of composition, 1461, is ascertainable from several considerations. In the preface of *VS*, Nicholas indicated that he had concluded his sixty-first year; and at the end of Chapter 14 of *VS* he stated: "Last year at Rome I wrote more extensively about Not-other in a tetralogue." See the preface of *Nicolai de Cusa Opera Omnia*, Vol. 12 (1982), F. Meiner Verlag, for further discussion.

2. *NA* 4 (12:7).
3. See *NA* 1 (5:3-4) and the beginning of *NA* 21 (95:5).
4. *NA* 8 (30:5-7).
5. *NA* 17 (82:14-15).

6. *NA* 16 (79:5-6). Cf. *NA* 10 (36:4-17). Also note the following: *NA* 16 (76:14-15): "Time is participated in in different ways, while remaining unable to be participated in in different ways." *NA* 9 (32:26-28): "Hence, I see this incomprehensible Ground because it shines forth comprehensibly in comprehensible things." *NA* 14 (68:13-14): Things "imitate Him who cannot possibly be imitated clearly."

7. *NA* 14 (65:13).

8. Proposition 5 (*NA* 115:4-5). Cf. *NA* 7 (23:21-22).

9. *NA* 6 (20:19-20).

10. See *A Concise Introduction to the Philosophy of Nicholas of Cusa* (Minneapolis: Banning Press, 3rd ed., 1986), pp. 23-27.

11. Quoted from pp. 182-183 of Richard Campbell's *From Belief to Understanding: A Study of Anselm's Proslogion Argument on the Existence of God* (Canberra: The Australian National University, 1976). Also see Rudolf Haubst, " 'Am Nichtteilnehmbaren teilhaben'. Zu einem Leitsatz der cusanischen 'Einheitsmetaphysik' und Geistphilosophie," pp. 12-22 in Norbert Fischer *et al.*, editors, *Alte Fragen und neue Wege des Denkens* [Festschrift für Josef Stallmach] (Bonn: Bouvier Verlag Herbert Grundmann, 1977).

12. N. B.: The use of these analogies does not *ipso facto* show that Nicholas subscribed to the doctrine of *analogia entis*.

13. On p. 224 of *Die verborgene Gegenwart des Unendlichen bei Nikolaus von Kues* (Munich: Anton Pustet, 1968), Mariano Alvarez-Gómez attributes to Herbert Wackerzapp's *Der Einfluss Meister Eckharts auf die ersten philosophischen Schriften des Nikolaus von Kues (1440-1450)* the view that *with respect to their being*, things do not differ from God. However, this does not seem to me to be a precise statement of Wackerzapp's interpretation of Cusa.

14. *DI* II, 3 (110). Cf. *DI* II, 2 (103:1-9).

15. Note the phrase *"essentia essentiarum"* in *NA* 10 (37:14) and the phrase *"entitas omnis esse"* at *DP* 67:13. On p. 291 of "The Principle of *Contractio* in Nicholas of Cusa's Philosophical View of Man," *Downside Review* 93 (October 1975), Mark Fuehrer asserts that "Cusa is consistent with his thesis that creatures have no essence of their own." Fuehrer stands with Vincent Martin, who on p. 234 of "The Dialectical Process in the Philosophy of Nicholas of Cusa," *Laval théologique et philosophique*, 5 (1949), tells us that Cusa's logic commits him to the view "that God and the creature have the same proper nature; that the most unique of all beings, the universal cause, is also the most common of all, the universal predicate; the very being of God is the intrinsic being of the creature." Neither Martin nor Fuehrer takes adequate account of Nicholas's statement in *Apologia Doctae Ignorantiae* (26:4-12): "Therefore, if God is the Form of forms, He gives being—even though the

form of earth gives being to earth, and the form of fire [gives being] to fire. Yet, the Form which gives being is God, who forms every form. Hence, just as (1) an image has a form which gives to it that being through which it is an image, and (2) the form of the image is a formed form, and (3) whatever truth [the image] has, it has it only from [that] form which is its truth and exemplar, so, in God, every creature is that which it is. For in God every creature—[each of] which is the image of God—is present in its Truth. Nevertheless, the individual existence of things *through their own forms* is not thereby destroyed." Just as God would not be the Form of forms unless created things had their own forms, so He would not be the Essence of essences unless they had their own essences. In *NA* 10 Nicholas qualifiedly rejects Ferdinand's interpretation: "You seem to mean," says Ferdinand, "that the essences of things are not plural but are one essence, which you call the Constituting Ground." Nicholas explains: "You know that 'one,' 'essence,' 'Idea,' 'form,' 'exemplar,' and 'species' are not applicable to Not-other. Therefore, when I look at things, beholding their essences: since things exist in accordance with their essences, then when I behold these essences through the understanding, prior to |the things' existence|, I maintain that they are different from one another. But when I view them above the understanding and prior to other, I do not see different essences but see no other than the simple Constituting Ground of the essences that I was contemplating in these things. And I call this Ground *Not-other* or the *Essence of essences*, since it is whatever is observed in all the essences."

On a careful reading, even the passage at the end of *DI* I, 17, where Nicholas is making a point about conceivability and about learned ignorance, does not teach that each thing in its being is God: "From these [considerations] the intellect can be helped; and by the illustration of an infinite line, it can in sacred ignorance very greatly advance beyond all understanding and toward the unqualifiedly Maximum. For here we have now seen clearly how we can arrive at God through removing the participation of beings. For all beings participate in Being. Therefore, if from all beings participation is removed, there remains most simple Being itself, which is the Essence of all things. And we see such Being only in most learned ignorance; for when I remove from my mind all the things which participate in being, it seems that nothing remains. Hence, the great Dionysius says that our understanding of God draws near to nothing rather than to something. But sacred ignorance teaches me that that which seems to the intellect to be nothing is the incomprehensible Maximum."

16. *NA* 14 (54:2).
17. At the end of *NA* 1 Nicholas openly acknowledges this influence.
18. *NA* 14 (66:6-7).
19. *NA* 2 (6:8).

20. See pp. 10-17 of Ludwig Baur's *Cusanus-Texte. III. Marginalien. 1. Nicolaus Cusanus und Ps. Dionysius im Lichte der Zitate und Randbemerkungen des Cusanus.* (*Sitzungsberichte der Heidelberger Akademie der Wissenschaften. Philosophisch-historische Klasse*, 1941.) Also see p. 186, n. 5 of Paul Wilpert's German translation of *NA, Vom Nichtanderen.* (Hamburg: F. Meiner Verlag, 1976, 2nd edition). Finally, see *Dionysiaca*, 2 vols. (Paris: Desclée de Brouwer, 1937 and 1950 respectively).

21. *Nikolaus von Cues und die griechische Sprache (Sitzungsberichte der Heidelberger Akademie der Wissenschaften. Philosophisch-historische Klasse*, 1938). p. 51.

22. See René Roques, "Traduction ou interprétation? Brèves remarques sur Jean Scot, traducteur de Denys," in his *Libres sentiers vers l'érigénisme* (Rome: Edizioni dell'Ateneo, 1975). For instance, Roques points out that Erigena systematically mistranslates *"oukoun"* as *"non igitur"* instead of as *"igitur."* Also see J. Uebinger, *Die Gotteslehre des Nikolaus Cusanus* (Münster: Schöningh, 1888), p. 177 n.: "Versagt habe ich mir, die vorbezeichneten Stellen im Originale mitzuteilen. Ein Vergleich derselben mit diesem zeigt, dass die Übersetzung des Ambrosius viel, *sehr viel* zu wünschen übrig lässt."

23. See Nikolaus M. Häring, editor, *Commentaries on Boethius by Thierry of Chartres and His School* (Toronto: Pontifical Institute of Mediaeval Studies, 1971).

24. *De Dato Patris Luminum* 2 (98:9-10).

25. *Ibid.*, 2 (98:12-16). Also see *Ap.* 26:4-7. Cf. *NA* 10 (39:5-7).

26. *Summa Contra Gentiles* (Leonine edition), Book I, Chapters 53-54. For one aspect of Nicholas's teachings on this topic, see *VS* 27 (81:4-8).

27. "Zur Seinsmetaphysik gehört die Unterscheidung des Seins (d. h. Gottes) und der Seienden, dazu gehört die Seinsanalogie, die Unterscheidung von Seinsstufen, die Lehre von der Zusammensetzung aller Seienden aus Wesenheit und Seinsakt und der Wesenheit alles körperlichen Seienden aus Form und Stoff, dazu gehört die Anerkennung des Widerspruchsprinzips als Seinsgesetz usw. All das wird nun von Cusanus weder genannt noch bekämpft, aber Stück für Stück durch seine Einheitsmetaphysik ersetzt." *Die Ars coniecturalis des Nikolaus von Kues* (Cologne: Westdeutscher Verlag, 1956), p. 16. (Heft 16 of *Arbeitsgemeinschaft für Forschung des Landes Nordrhein-Westfalen.*)

28. "Seinsmetaphysik ist ihrer Natur nach 'Metaphysik von unten', d. h. sie geht von dem Seienden, zu dem wir selbst gehören, aus und versucht, mit Hilfe analoger Begriffe (seiend, eines, wahr, gut usw.) zum Sein selbst, d. h. Gott, aufzusteigen und über ihn Aussagen zu machen. Einheitsmetaphysik neuplatonischer Prägung ist immer 'Metaphysik von oben', d. h. sie geht von der absoluten Einheit als dem Erstgegebenen aus und steigt von da zum Verständnis der Welt herab." *Ibid.*, p. 23.

29. Cf. Kurt Flasch's verdict: "Auch die Unterscheidung einer seinsphilo-sophischen von einer einheitsphilosophischen Phase im Denken des Cusanus lässt sich in dieser Form nicht halten . . . . " *Die Metaphysik des Einen bei Nikolaus von Kues. Problemgeschichtliche Stellung und systematische Bedeu-tung.* (Leiden: E. J. Brill, 1973), p. 219n. See also 163n.

30. N. B. *De Coniecturis* I, 5 (19:10), where God is called *entitas omnium entium.*

31. Note his statement to this effect in *NA* 18 (83:9).

32. See the end of *NA* 19 (89:15-16).

33. *NA* 13 (49:15-17): "Although coldness is not found as separate from cold things, nevertheless the intellect beholds it prior to the cold things and as their cause."

34. *NA* 16 (78:17-18).

35. This statement is reminiscent of St. Anselm's appeal to *rationes necessariae* in the *Cur Deus Homo*. Nicholas's use of *"ratio"* seems to draw upon Anselm's further statement in the *Cur Deus Homo*: "For in the case of God, just as an impossibility results from any unfittingness, however slight, so necessity accompanies any degree of reasonableness, however small, provided it is not overridden by some other more weighty reason" [*Cur Deus Homo* I, 10 (Schmitt edition, Vol. II, p. 67, lines 4-6)]. On the whole, however, Nicho-las's conception of rational consideration is broader and looser than Anselm's.

36. Similarly, his notion of certainty seems more attenuated than ours. Consider, for example, the context of the statement in *NA* 20 (94:1): "I see, Father, that these points are indubitable."

37. *NA* 5 (19:9-12).

38. *DI* III, 11 (244:8-9). See also *Sermo* IV (26:13-14), *Opera Omnia* XVI, 1. See, finally, the edition of Nicholas's sermons published under the title *Predigten. 1430-1441*, translated by J. Sikora and E. Bohnenstädt (Heidelberg: F. H. Kerle, 1952), p. 372. Nicholas's reading of Isaiah 7:9 is not from the Vulgate but from the Old Latin version.

39. *DI* III, 11 (244:9-12).

40. *DP* 15:2.

41. *DP* 38:6.

42. *DP* 38:11.

43. Cf. *DP* 40-41.

44. Cf. *NA* 22 (103) with Nicholas's speech in *NA* 23 (107).

45. *NA* 14 (68:9-10).

46. Note *Apologia Doctae Ignorantiae* (*Opera Omnia* II, pp. 16-17): "Per hoc enim, quod omnia sunt in Deo ut causata in causa, non sequitur causatum esse causam,—licet in causa non sint nisi causa, sicut de unitate et numero saepe audisti. Nam numerus non est unitas, quamvis omnis numerus

in unitate sit complicitus sicut causatum in causa; sed id, quod intelligimus numerum, est explicatio virtutis unitatis. Sic numerus in unitate non est nisi unitas."

Nicholas's reasoning throughout *NA* seems to be the following:

(a) It is not the case that God is x, and it is not the case that God is not-x (where x is anything except God).

(b) If God were *other* than x, He would be not-x; and if God were *other* than not-x, He would be x.

So (c) it is not the case that God is *other* than x, and it is not the case that God is *other* than not-x.

So (d) God is not *other* than anything, whether x or not-x; He is unqualifiedly Not-other.

As Nicholas maintains, the Creator is not identical with the things He has created [cf. *NA* 6 (20:14-15)]. But in that case it must follow that God, the Creator, is other than His creation and hence is not unqualifiedly Not-other. Nicholas would reply that even though God is not identical with His creation, He is not *other* than His creation since *in any created thing He is none other than that created thing*. (Cf. n. 18 of the English translation of *NA*.) No matter how we may attempt to render intelligible this italicized claim, Nicholas is still wrong in speaking of "Not-other, which cannot in any way be an other." [*NA* 6 (20:5-6)]. He should rather maintain that Not-other is in some respect other, though not in such way as to be deprived of what it is other than.

47. *NA* 6 (21:5-6); 22 (100:1-4). Proposition 6 (*NA* 115:7-11).

48. Rom. 1:20.

49. I Cor. 15:28.

50. Eph. 1:21.

51. I Cor. 13:12.

52. *NA* 2 (7:20-24). See Phil. 2:9. Not-other can even be said to precede God insofar as God can be *spoken* of.

53. *DP* 15.

54. One is reminded of the difficulties with the principal manuscript of *DP* (viz., *Codex Cusanus* 219), at the end of which we read a redactor's irritated words: "Correctum per Episcopum Acciensem maximo labore diebus duobus, quia librarius qui descripsit omnium est eiusmodi hominum mendosis-simus et abiectissimus."

55. The reference numbers cited here are the numbers of the sections and lines in my text. The section numbers, but not the line numbers, are the same in my text as in Wilpert's.

56. Typical of such translators is Anton Pegis, who professes: "After publishing *What Plato Said* in 1933, Paul Shorey had intended to write a sequel,

What Plato Meant. There is a lesson here for translators; at least there is a lesson for the present translator in relation to St. Thomas. In translating Book One of the SCG, I have thought it my business to set down what St. Thomas said, not what he meant." It comes as no surprise that Pegis adds: "This is harder to do than is sometimes imagined." See p. 50 of *On the Truth of the Catholic Faith: Summa Contra Gentiles. Book I: God* (Garden City, N. Y.: Image Books, 1955).

57. Paul Wilpert, in his German translation, construes the meaning along these lines.

58. In *VS* 14 (40:9-10) Nicholas uses the word "other" in this formula, thus making explicit what elsewhere is only implied.

59. See n. 56 above.

60. N. B.: Erigena uses "*ipsum*" to translate the definite article in Greek. See I. P. Sheldon-Williams, editor, *Iohannis Scotti Erivgenae Periphyseon*, Book I (Dublin: Dublin Institute for Advanced Studies, 1968), p. 243, n. 242.

61. See *NA* 4 (12:6-7). Also see n. 2 above.

62. Note also *VS* 21 (59:7 and 14-15).

63. Viz., it functions as a substitute for the definite article, which Latin lacks. A further function of "*ipsum*," but not of "*li*," is to indicate, by its endings, the case of "*non-aliud*," which Nicholas tends to use indeclinably in *NA*.

64. *NA* 8 (28:3-4).

65. Cf. Proposition 20 (*NA* 125:1 and 3-4). *DP* 38:2-3.

66. Cf. *DP* 12:5-6. *DP* 14:10.

67. *DI* II, 2 (100:6). This proposition is borrowed from Pseudo-Hermes Trismegistus's *Book of the Twenty-four Philosophers*, by way of Meister Eckhart.

68. Proposition 13 (*NA* 119:1-9).

69. *NA* 7 (24:10).

70. *NA* 5 (17:11-12).

71. "Here we stand, then, before the paradoxical situation that the experience of the failure of his powers does not discourage the human being or cripple his striving. On the contrary, it gives him a feeling of liberation and, in fact, actually stimulates him." Theo van Velthoven, *Gottesschau und menschliche Kreativität. Studien zur Erkenntnislehre des Nikolaus von Kues* (Leiden: E. J. Brill, 1977), p. 30.

Cf. Mariano Alvarez-Gómez, *Die verborgene Gegenwart des Unendlichen bei Nikolaus von Kues* (Munich: Anton Pustet, 1968), pp. 241 and 244 respectively: "Das Streben nach Gott bedeutet ein Streben nach sich selbst, das wiederum ein Sein-in-Gott, eine Ekstase besagt." "Gott ist der immer Gesuchte und nie Gefundene, das bei allem Erstrebte und in keinem Erreichte. Seine

Nähe kommt dadurch zum Vorschein, dass wir in allem nach ihm streben—
seine Ferne darin, dass er nicht zum fassbaren Gegenstand der Erkenntnis und
des Strebens werden kann. Da er das Eigentlichste von uns ist, erweckt seine
Abwesenheit eine schmerzliche und leidenschaftliche Sehnsucht nach ihm.
Dabei erfährt der Mensch sein Bedürfnis und seine Leere. Erst in diesem leid
offenbart sich Gott. Daher ist das Leid von der Hoffnung begleitet, diese aber
ist nur als Sehnsucht lebendig."

72. See my translation of this passage—in *Nicholas of Cusa's Dialectical
Mysticism, op. cit.*

73. "A Translation of *De Non Aliud* by Nicholas de Cusa with an Introduction and Critical Notes" (Columbia University doctoral dissertation, 1966),
pp. 128-129.

74. *NA* 6 (20:4-5).

75. *DP* 15.

TRANSLATION

1. The *incipit* reads: "Here begins the book of the most reverend lord
and father-in-Christ Nicholas of Cusa, cardinal of St. Peter in Chains—|a
book| which is entitled *Guidance for one who is speculating*. With the Cardi-
nal are the interlocutors Abbot John Andrea Vigevius, Peter Balbus of Pisa,
and Ferdinand Matim of Portugal."

John Andrea Vigevius, who also appears as one of the interlocutors in *DP*,
was abbot of the monastery of St. Justine of Sezadium; Ferdinand Matim of
Portugal was Nicholas's personal physician; and Peter Balbus of Pisa was a
translator of Proclus and, later, bishop of Tropea. For further information see
pp. 142-148 of Johann Uebinger's *Die Gotteslehre des Nikolaus Cusanus*
(Münster: F. Schöningh, 1888) and pp. 99-103 of Paul Wilpert's German
translation *Vom Nichtanderen* (Hamburg: F. Meiner, 1976, 2nd edition).

2. Cf. the opening sentences of the prologue to Anselm of Canterbury's
Monologion [J. Hopkins, *A New, Interpretive Translation of St. Anselm's
Monologion and Proslogion* (Minneapolis: Banning Press, 1986)].

3. In *Compendium* 9 (25:8-9), Nicholas writes: *"Oratio enim est rei
designatio seu definitio."* And he thinks that to define something is to specify
or determine it through genus and differentiae [*VS* 14 (39:11-12)]. In this
respect he is following Aristotle and Thomas, both of whom regard a definition as a *logos* (*oratio*) signifying an essence.

In the present passage Nicholas supposes that just as a given definition
defines a given kind of thing, so definition as such defines everything. For a
fuller discussion of Nicholas's views on definition see Nikolaus von Kues, *Vom
Nichtanderen*, translated by Paul Wilpert (Hamburg: F. Meiner Verlag, 1976,

2nd edition), pp. 110-112; and Gerhard Schneider, *Gott—das Nichtandere* (Münster: Aschendorff, 1970), pp. 109-117.

In *VS* 33 ("The Meaning of a Word") Nicholas mentions both Aristotle and Thomas, uses *"ratio"* in the sense of *concept* and *"oratio"* in the sense of *definition by words*, asserts that human words can suitably be predicated of God only if their meanings are transferred, and so on. I here translate the entire chapter:

"If with deep meditation you ponder all things, you will find that the pursuers |of wisdom| looked carefully at a word's meaning, as if a word were a precise representation of things. But because the first man assigned words to things in conformity with the concept which he conceived, it is not the case that words are precise and thus that a thing cannot be named by a more precise word. For the concept which a man conceives is not that Concept of a thing's essence which precedes every thing. If anyone knew the name of that Concept, he would name all things correctly and would have a most perfect knowledge of all things. Hence, there is no disagreement in the substantifying Concept of things but only in the words variously assigned to things in conformity with the various concepts. And the entire difference of opinion among those who dispute has to do with the representation of a thing's essence—a representation which likewise varies. As Plato in his letters to the tyrant Dionysius writes most elegantly: truth precedes words, *orationes* (i.e., definitions by words), and perceptible representations. He gives as an example a depicted circle, its name, its definition [*oratio*], and the concept of it. And for this reason Dionysius the Areopagite instructs us to turn to the concept rather than to the word's meaning—although in *The Divine Names* he himself, like Plato, places much emphasis upon the signification of a word.

"Moreover, no one was more intent than Aristotle upon seeking out a word's meaning—as if the one who assigned the names for all things had been most skilled and had expressed in his words that which he knew, and as if |for us| to attain to his knowledge were |for us| to attain to a perfect knowledge of all things knowable. And for this reason Aristotle asserted that the light of knowledge is in the definition, which is the unfolding of the word.

"I believe that these points hold true for the human knowledge which the one called the first Adam, or first man, excellently possessed in the beginning. And for this reason knowledge which is consolidated in the meaning of a word is most pleasing to man, as conforming to his nature. But the pursuer of divine Wisdom must refuse to predicate of God human words according to their human assignment. For example, the life which extends to all living things does not reach unto God, who is the cause of all life—and similarly for all words.

"Also, the distinctions made by pursuers who interpret words should be carefully heeded. For example, St. Thomas, in his commentary on Dionysius's book *The Divine Names*, maintains that three things must be noticed with regard to the substances of existing things: First, |there is| the particular (e.g., Plato); it includes—in itself and actually—individuating and last principles. Second, there is the species or the genus (e.g., *man* or *animal*), in which the last principles are included actually but particulars potentially. For example, 'man' signifies 'who has humanity'—apart from any distinguishing because of individuating principles. The essence (e.g., humanity) is third; by the word 'humanity' only the principles of the species are signified. For no individuating principle belongs to the concept of humanity; for 'humanity' signifies exclusively that in virtue of which a man is a man, and no individuating principle is of such kind. Hence, by the word "humanity" no individuating principle is signified, whether actually or potentially; and to this extent |the humanity| is said to be the nature. See that by distinguishing this word, |that| very learned man clarified many things which elsewhere are obscure. How greatly Aristotle, too, labored to distinguish words is shown by his *Metaphysics*. Hence, through the distinctions of words, with which task many very learned men have been engaged, many differences among writers are harmonized.

"But our quest for the ineffable Wisdom which precedes both the assigner of names and everything nameable takes place in silence and by seeing rather than in talkativeness and by hearing. Our quest presupposes that the human words which it uses are neither precise nor angelic nor divine. But it adopts them because otherwise it could not express what is conceived. |It adopts them| on the assumption, however, that (1) it does not intend for them to signify any such thing as that for the sake of which they received their meaning, but to signify the cause of such things, and that (2) the verbs are timeless, since eternity is intended to be represented by them."

4. In *VS* 14 ("The Third Field, viz., Not-other") Nicholas states unequivocally that God is this definition: "Therefore, the trine and one God is the definition defining itself and all things." (Throughout *NA* Nicholas attempts to elucidate the sense in which God is not *other* than anything even though these things are *other* than God.) Since Chapter 14 captures many of the main themes of *NA*, I here present it in translation:

"In his *Metaphysics* Aristotle writes that in the first place Socrates turned his intellect to definitions. For the definition imparts knowledge. For the definition expresses the agreement in genus, and the difference in species, of the thing defined; and this agreement and this difference are enfolded by the word in its signification. Therefore, what we are seeking is seen—in the way in which it can be known—in its definition. Therefore, the intellect which pursues that which precedes the possibility-to-become must consider the fact that it also precedes other. For that which precedes the possibility-to-become cannot become other, because other is subsequent to it. And because of this fact no other terms can define it, i.e., specify or determine it through genus and differentiae, which it precedes. Hence, it must be the definition of itself. This point is also clear from the foregoing, since |that which we are seeking| precedes the difference between the definition and the defined. And not only |must it be the definition of itself|, but also all things must be defined through it, since they cannot exist unless they exist and are defined through it. Dionysius saw this point very clearly in the chapter on the Perfect and the One, in *The Divine Names*, where he says: That One—the Cause of all—is not a one out of many; rather, it is prior to everything one, prior to all multitude, and is the definition of every one and of all multitude.

"Now, to the field where there is the most delightful pursuit of that which defines itself and all things I give the name 'Not-other.' For Not-other defines itself and all things. For when I ask 'What is Not-other?' the following answer will be the most suitable: 'Not-other is not other than Not-other.' And when I ask 'What, then, is other?' the following answer will be correct: 'Other is not other than other.' And, in like manner, the world is not other than the world; and similarly about all other things which can be named.

"You now see that the Eternal, that Most Ancient, can be sought in this field by a very delectable pursuit. For inasmuch as it is the definition of itself and all other things, it is not found more clearly in any other field than in Not-other. For in this field you come upon the trine and one Most Ancient, who is the definition of Himself. For Not-other is not other than Not-other. The intellect marvels over this mystery when it notices attentively that *trinity*, without which God does not define Himself, is *oneness*, because the definition is the defined. Therefore, the trine and one God is the definition defining itself and all things. Hence, the intellect finds that God is not *other* than other, because He defines other. For if Not-other is removed, other does not remain. For if other is to exist, it will have to be not other than other. Otherwise, it would be other than other and hence would not exist. Therefore, since Not-other is prior to other, it cannot become other, and it is actually everything which is at all possible to be.

"But notice that 'Not-other' does not signify as much as does 'same.' Rather, since same is not other than same, Not-other precedes it and all nameable things. And so, although God is named 'Not-other' because He is not *other* than any other, He is not on this account the same as any other. For example, it is not the case that just as He is not *other* than the sky, so He is the same as the sky. Therefore, it is true of all things, as being not other than they are, that God defines them; and from Not-other they have the fact that they beget no other in species but produce what is similar to themselves. Therefore, goodness is good-making, and whitness is white-making; and similarly for all other things.

"Pursuers who are philosophers did not enter this field, in which, alone, negation is not opposed to affirmation. For Not-other is not opposed to other, since it defines and precedes other. Outside this field negation *is* opposed to affirmation—for example, immortal to mortal, incorruptible to corruptible, and so on for all other things except Not-other alone. Therefore, seeking for God in other fields, where He is not found, is an empty pursuit. For God is not someone who is opposed to anything, since He is prior to all difference from opposites. Therefore, it is not the case that God is named *animal*, to which not-animal is opposed, and *immortal*, to which what is mortal is opposed, in as perfect a way as He is named *Not-other*, to which neither other nor nothing is opposed. For Not-other also precedes and defines nothing, since nothing is not other than nothing. The divine Dionysius said, most subtly, that God is *all in all and nothing in nothing*.

"Last year at Rome I wrote more extensively about Not-other in a tetralogue. And so, enough about this |topic| at this time."

5. *VS* 14 (40:9-10) shows that Nicholas intends for the reader to supply the word "other" here and elsewhere.

6. *The Mystical Theology* 5 [*Dionysiaca* (Paris: Desclée de Brouwer, 1937) I, 599-600].

7. Passages like this one have led interpreters such as Rudolf Haubst to the conclusion that Nicholas subscribes to the doctrine of *analogia entis*. See Haubst's "Nikolaus von Kues und die Analogia Entis," pp. 686-695 in Paul Wilpert, editor, *Die Metaphysik im Mittelalter. Ihr Ursprung und ihre Bedeutung* [*Vorträge des II. internationalen Kongresses für mittelalterliche Philosophie, Köln, 31. August - 6. September 1961* (Berlin: W. de Gruyter, 1963)].

8. Throughout his works Nicholas generally uses "*omnia*" to indicate all things other than God. That is, God is not among the *omnia*. The *omnia* are the *principiata*, whereas God is the *principium*. That is, God is the Principle, the Beginning, the Foundation, the unoriginated Source of all originated things. Although there is much to be said for translating "*principium*" as "principle" and "*principiatum*" as "principiate," I tend to favor the non-Scholastic expressions "beginning" and "what is originated." Both of these expressions are used in the opening speech of *NA* 2.

9. See Phil. 2:9.

10. Not-other, which is identified with God, is here said to precede God insofar as God can be *spoken* of.

11. Generally, when Nicholas uses "*non-aliud*" as a noun or a name, he uses it indeclinably. (Often, it is used with a form of "*ipsum*" to indicate its case.) However, this practice is not uniform, as the present sentence and the

sentences at 19:18-22 and 25:9 through 26:6 show.

12. See Acts 17:27.

13. Cf. Anselm of Canterbury, *Proslogion* 15. [J. Hopkins, *A New, Interpretive Translation of St. Anselm's Monologion and Proslogion* (Minneapolis: Banning Press, 1986)].

14. Although Nicholas deems the *via negativa* to be superior to the *via positiva* since it furnishes a more *fitting* concept of God, even this more fitting concept falls infinitely short of representing God as He is in Himself. See J. Hopkins, *A Concise Introduction to the Philosophy of Nicholas of Cusa* (Minneapolis: Banning Press, 1986, 3rd edition), pp. 21-27.

15. That is, we commonly use the expression "it must be one thing or the other."

16. In *DP* Nicholas refers to the Trinity as Actuality, Possibility, and their Union.

17. Cf. *DI* I, 9 (25:7).

18. In *DI* II, 4 (115:14-16), Nicholas asserts: "It is not the case that God is in the sun sun and in the moon moon; rather, [in them] He is that which is sun and moon without plurality and difference." However, throughout *NA* he makes such statements as the following: "In the sky He is not other than the sky" (*NA* 6). "Through this Constituting Ground |the sky| is constituted as the sky; and in the sky this Constituting Ground is the sky" (*NA* 6). "Indeed, Not-other is not an essence; but because in the essences it is the essence, it is called the Essence of essences" (*NA* 10). "When I say 'The earth is not other than the earth,' |the word 'than'| directs sight to Not-other insofar as in the earth it is the earth" (*NA* 21).

Is it possible to reconcile the statements in *NA* with the statement in *DI*? Or has Nicholas simply changed his mind during the interval between 1440 and 1461? Cf. *VS* 14 (41:1-6): " 'Not-other' does not signify as much as does 'same.' . . . And so, although God is named 'Not-other' because He is not *other* than (*non aliud ab*) any other, He is not on this account the same as any other. For example, it is not the case that just as He is not *other* than the sky, so He is the same as the sky." In accordance with this distinction it might seem that, for Nicholas, in the sky God is (not other than) the sky and yet that in the sky God is not (identical with) the sky. But this interpretation would not accurately reflect either the sense of the passage from *VS* or the distinction between "*non aliud a*" and "*non aliud quam*".

19. The allusion is to *NA* 2 (7:3-4).

20. Nicholas also discusses *ratio* in *NA* 9.

21. Cf. *DP* 11, the example of the sun.

22. Here, as in *DP* and *DI*, *materia* is identified as *possibilitas essendi*. Cf. *DP* 28.

23. Here Nicholas distinguishes *potentia* (possibility) and *non-ens*. In *DP* 73 he states, not inconsistently, that in God "not-being is everything which is possible to be."

24. For this meaning of *"motus"* see also *NA* 23 (105:11).

25. *"Quantitas"* may also be translated as "extension." An image, Nicholas goes on to say, must be the image of something extended.

26. I Cor. 13:12.

27. More literally: "Just as someone does when he sees snow through a red glass (he sees the snow and attributes the appearance of redness not to the snow but to the glass), so does the mind when it sees the unformed through a form."

28. See Pseudo-Dionysius, *The Celestial Hierarchy* IV (*Dionysiaca* II, 801-802). This passage is cited in *NA* 14.

29. Cf. *De Coniecturis* II, 6 (98:4-5).

30. II Cor. 4:18.

31. For a limited discussion of Nicholas's view of universals see my *Concise Introduction to the Philosophy of Nicholas of Cusa, op. cit.*, pp. 32-36. Also see my review article "A Detailed Critique of Pauline Watts' *Nicolaus Cusanus: A Fifteenth-Century Vision of Man,"* Philosophy Research Archives*, 9 (1983), Microfiche Supplement.

32. Literally: "You seem to mean that there are no essences of things but that there is one Essence, which you affirm to be the Constituting Ground."

33. The light which is in the eye is sight, *das Augenlicht*. Note Stephanus page 266c of Plato's *Sophist*, as well as 46a of his *Timaeus*.

34. I John 1:5.

35. Here and in Chapter 13 matter is identified with *possibilitas essendi*— i.e., with the possibility-of-existing, or the possibility-of-being.

36. I.e., Not-other is to intelligible substances as intelligible substances are to perceptible substances.

37. Cf. Proposition 16 (*NA* 121:3-7).

38. See the opening speeches of *NA* 1.

39. See the citations referenced by notes 43-45 below.

40. Regarding the translations with which Nicholas was familiar, see the section of the present Introduction where note 20 occurs. In *NA* 14 Nicholas's citations of Ambrose's translations are not always exact.

41. Ambrose Traversari (1386-1439) entered the Camadolese monastery of St. Mary of the Angels, at Florence, in 1400. He attended the Council of Basel (1431-1437), which sought the reunification of Eastern and Western Christendom.

42. *Dionysiaca* II, 735.

43. *Ibid.*, II, 745.

44. *Ibid.*, II, 758.
45. *Ibid.*, II, 801-802.
46. *Ibid.*, II, 809.
47. *Ibid.*, II, 962.
48. *Ibid.*, II, 1084-1085.
49. *Ibid.*, II, 1089-1090.
50. *Ibid.*, I, 9-11.
51. *Ibid.*, I, 19.
52. *Ibid.*, I, 22-24.
53. *Ibid.*, I, 33.
54. *Ibid.*, I, 34-35.
55. *Ibid.*, I, 49-50.
56. *Ibid.*, I, 77-78.
57. *Ibid.*, I, 106-107.
58. *Ibid.*, I, 108.
59. *Ibid.*, I, 115.
60. *Ibid.*, I, 145-146.
61. *Ibid.*, I, 159-160.
62. *Ibid.*, I, 162.
63. *Ibid.*, I, 163.
64. *Ibid.*, I, 172-173.
65. *Ibid.*, I, 174-175.
66. *Ibid.*, I, 178.
67. *Ibid.*, I, 182-183. The subject here is Supersubstantial Beauty.
68. *Ibid.*, I, 185.
69. *Ibid.*, I, 185.
70. *Ibid.*, I, 198.
71. *Ibid.*, I, 334-335. From this point on Nicholas's numbering of the chapters in *The Divine Names* does not follow the order of the editions printed in *Dionysiaca*.
72. *Ibid.*, I, 335.
73. *Ibid.*, I, 336.
74. *Ibid.*, I, 336-337.
75. Cf. *NA* 15 (74).
76. *Dionysiaca* I, 338-340.
77. *Ibid.*, I, 341-342.
78. *Ibid.*, I, 342.
79. *Ibid.*, I, 366.
80. *Ibid.*, I, 376-377.
81. *Ibid.*, I, 383.
82. *Ibid.*, I, 385-386.

83. *Ibid.*, I, 400-401.
84. *Ibid.*, I, 404.
85. *Ibid.*, I, 405.
86. *Ibid.*, I, 417-418.
87. *Ibid.*, I, 421.
88. *Ibid.*, I, 428.
89. *Ibid.*, I, 433.
90. *Ibid.*, I, 452.
91. *Ibid.*, I, 454.
92. *Ibid.*, I, 454-455.
93. *Ibid.*, I, 456-457.
94. *Ibid.*, I, 458.
95. *Ibid.*, I, 460-461.
96. *Ibid.*, I, 468-469.
97. *Ibid.*, I, 471-472.
98. *Ibid.*, I, 472.
99. *Ibid.*, I, 483.
100. *Ibid.*, I, 484.
101. *Ibid.*, I, 485-486.
102. *Ibid.*, I, 520-521.
103. *Ibid.*, I, 538-539.
104. *Ibid.*, I, 541-542.
105. *Ibid.*, I, 542.
106. *Ibid.*, I, 544.
107. *Ibid.*, I, 545.
108. *Ibid.*, I, 545.
109. *Ibid.*, I, 548-549.
110. *Ibid.*, I, 549.
111. *Ibid.*, I, 549.
112. *Ibid.*, I, 549-550. Note the various Latin translations given for the Greek phrases "τὸ ἕν ὄν" and "τὸ ὂν ἕν."
113. *Ibid.*, I, 599-600. This is a passage from Pseudo-Dionysius which stimulated Nicholas's views regarding *non-aliud*. See the end of *NA* 1, where this fact is mentioned.
114. *Ibid.*, I, 600-601.
115. *Ibid.*, I, 606-607.
116. Nicholas refers to Dionysius as "the Theologian" in the way that Thomas refers to Aristotle as "the Philosopher."
117. Cf. *NA* 14 (70:15-16 and 70:18-19).
118. Vansteenberghe [*Le Cardinal Nicolas de Cues* (Frankfurt: Minerva GmbH, 1963; reprint of the 1920 Paris edition), p. 419] and Wilpert, translator

[Nikolaus von Kues, *Vom Nichtanderen* (Hamburg: F. Meiner Verlag, 1976, 2nd edition), p. 192, n. 5] regard the use of "A," to signify God, as indicative of the influence of Raymond Lull. "It was Lull's idea," writes Wilpert, "to derive from several first principles the entire domain of knowledge and thereby to obtain mathematical certainty in all branches of knowledge. Cusa, to be sure, is not thinking of mathematical certainty; nonetheless, the thoughts of Lull made a great impression on him."

119. Literally: "Let these statements now have been made in this way concerning our admirable theologian."

120. *Metaphysics* 996^{a}5-9 (Loeb Library edition).

121. *Metaphysics* 1028^{b}2-4 (Loeb Library edition).

122. Literally: "But that which must not be *other* than any other surely cannot be named in another way."

123. That is, the truth about Not-other.

124. Nicholas's understanding of Aristotle is not always precise. For example, in *NA* 10 he mentions that though Aristotle disallowed a quantitative infinity, he nonetheless traced all things back to a First Mover, which is of infinite power. Now, in *Metaphysics* 1066^b Aristotle does reject the view that there can be an actual infinity. But he does not, as Nicholas supposes, trace all things back to a First Mover having infinite power. Aside from the problem that the *Metaphysics* contains conflicting accounts about the number of Unmoved Movers, Aristotle nowhere teaches that the Mover (or Movers) is of unlimited power—though it is the ultimate power behind everything caused to be or to occur.

125. Nicholas does not realize that the author of *The Divine Names* and of the other works cited is not the Dionysius mentioned in Acts 17.

126. See *The Theology of Plato*, Book II, Chapter 4—especially the last sentence, where Plato is cited. [*The Six Books of Proclus on the Theology of Plato*. Translated by Thomas Taylor (London, 1816, Vol. I)].

127. Rom. 1:19.

128. See the last line of Epistle 6 (323d).

129. Wilpert takes this reference to correspond to p. 924, lines 27 ff. of the text edited by Victor Cousin [viz., *Procli Philosophi . . . continens Procli Commentarium in Platonis Parmenidem* (Hildesheim: Olms, 1961; reprint of the 1864 Paris edition)].

130. That is, the soul regards all things as participating in the One analogously to the way in which whatever is known or envisioned by the soul participates in the soul.

131. Proclus, *The Theology of Plato*, Book III, Chap. 2 [*The Six Books of Proclus on the Theology of Plato*. Translated by Thomas Taylor (London, 1816), especially p. 163 of Vol. I]. Proclus, *Elements of Theology*. Text and translation by E. R. Dodds (Oxford: Clarendon Press, 1933), pp. 160-185.

132. Cf. *Elements of Theology, op. cit.* Proposition 12.
133. In the English translation of *NA* see the passage marked by n. 117. Also see Proclus, *Elements of Theology, op. cit.*, Proposition 2.
134. Plato, Epistle 2 (312e); Loeb Library edition.
135. I Cor. 15:28.
136. Phil. 2:9.
137. That is, Not-other seems to be diametrically other than other. Because of the punctuation of this sentence in the manuscript, I take *"ipsi"* with *"aliud"* rather than with *"non-aliud."* The Latin sentence at 100:7-8 best shows that Nicholas does not uniformly place *"ipsum"* before *"non-aliud"*; and 6:16 shows the same thing about *"ipsum"* and *"aliud."*
138. See *Dionysiaca, op. cit.*, I, 460-461. This passage is also cited in *NA* 14—at the place marked by n. 95 of the English translation.
139. Matt. 11:11.
140. John 14:6.
141. John 1:18.
142. Gen. 1:10, 12, 18, 21, 25, 31.
143. Viz., Jesus.
144. Matt. 19:17.
145. John 4:24.
146. John 4:24.
147. Ps. 103:30 (104:30).
148. I Cor. 13:12.
149. Ps. 83:8 (84:7).
150. The manuscript adds: "The end. Praise to God."

PROPOSITIONS

1. In the Latin sentence I regard an *"esse"* as having to be understood. Cf. 3:10-11 and 118:6-7. See the discussion of this passage in my introduction. In contrast to Paul Wilpert, Rose Finkenstaedt recognizes that this is the correct rendering. See p. 292 of "A Translation of *De Non Aliud* by Nicholas de Cusa with an Introduction and Critical Notes" (Columbia University doctoral dissertation, 1966).

When Nicholas uses *"non-aliud"* to express identity, he generally adheres to the following stylistic forms: "x *est non aliud quam* x"; "x *est non aliud quam* y." [But he also writes: *"Sensibile igitur caelum non est . . . quid aliud a caelo"* (22:11-12 of *NA* 6). Note *DI* II, 4 (115:4-6); *DI* I, 21 (63:15-18). See the switch from *"aliud quam"* to *"aliud a"* at 20:18 of *NA* 6.] For example, in *NA* 6 (20:16) he states that *in caelo |deus est| non aliud quam caelum*. Here the phrase *"non aliud quam"* suggests an identification: viz., that in the sky God is the sky.

Accordingly, Nicholas distinguishes the statements *"Deus est non aliud a caelo"* and *"|In caelo| deus est non aliud quam caelum."* In general, he uses *"non aliud a"* in order to avoid expressing identity. In the English translation of *NA "non aliud a"* has been rendered as "not *other* than" and *"non aliud quam"* as "not other than," "no other than," or "none other than."

2. Nicholas uses expressions such as "Being of being" and "Substance of substance" in a vague way. Sometimes he seems to mean that God is the very being itself of all beings, the very essence of all essences, the very substance of all substances. Accordingly, at the end of Chap. 10 he indicates that we may call God either "Form of form" or "Form of forms." (Note also Proposition 13.) At other times, he seems to regard these expressions as functioning as do the titles "King of kings," "God of gods," "Lord of lords"—i.e., as pointing to God's supremacy, loftiness, and priority. "Mind of mind" and "Beginning of beginning" appear to be titles. (See Propositions 5 and 12.) Similarly, "Actuality of actuality" seems to express the belief that God is the purest of all actualities—even purer than can be conceived. (See Proposition 17.)

3. The manuscript adds: "End of the propositions. Praise to the best God. I, Hartmann Schedel, doctor both of arts and of medicine, copied |this| in Nuremberg on April 6, 1496."

appendix

VARIANT READINGS FROM LATIN MS. 19-26
OF THE CATHEDRAL LIBRARY IN TOLEDO, SPAIN

1 1-2 Eiusdem de non aliud ac etiam de diffinitione omnia diffinienti.
Capitulum primum *in rubro habet U*   3 Abbas: *om. U* colloqui: loqui *U*
6 graeca: greco *U*   7 Areopagita Dionysio: Arcopathica Dionisio *U*   8 Gauderemus: Gaudaremus *U*   9 tibi clariorque: clariorque tibi *U*   12 hii quos:
hos *U*   visum: missum *U*

2 1 veritate: veritati *U*   6 considerasti: consciderasti *U*   7 colloquar:
coloquor *U*   8 compellaris: compellaris *ex* compellans *corr. U*   10 mei:
om. U

3 4 respondes: *om. U*   6 definiendo: *non proprie abbreviat U*

4 2 aciem: actiem *U*   8 Nequaquam: Neque quid *U*   16-17 omnia
definire: diffinire omnia *U*

5 1 cognitu: cognitu *ex* cogitu *corr. (n supra lin.) U*   Quid: equidem *add. U*
2 quis: si *add. U*   quid est: quidem *U*   3 quid: quidem *U*   8 praecisissimus:
precissimus *U*   10 humanitus: humanitas *U*   14 Dionysius: Dyonisius *U*
15 varie: bene *U*   17 pervenit: pervenerint *U*   affirmat: affirmant *U*   19 magni:
magis *U*   20 secretum: decretum *U*

6 2-3 appellent: appellant *U*   3 significari: significare *U*   7 se: sese *U*
12 antecedat: antecedit *U*   16-17 terminatur: *bis U*

7 9 li: si *U*   10 et: in *add. U*   13 clare: *om. U*   21 ut viam: viam ut *U*
23 pretiosiori: precisiori *U*

8 4 ostendas: ostendes *U*   5 Dicunt: Dicunt (*non* Dicut) *habet U*   6 quia:
qui *U*   7 deus: est *add. U*   8 nominabilem: nobilem *U*   10 lucet: licet *U* (u
pro i *supra lin. coni. U²*) lumine: luce *U*   11 aliqualiter: aliquando *U*   15 sive:
sine *U*   definitionem: diffinitione *U*   ut: hec *add. U*   iris: ius *U*   17-18 Ita . . .
cognoscendi: *om. U*

9 1 se: etiam *add. U*   2 sensibili: sensibile *U*   5 neque[1]: nec *U*   neque[2]:
nec *U*   6 iris: ius *U*   aut: *om. U*   8 nec: neque *U*   Ista: Ita *U*   10 tenes: te
nes (nes *ex* nos *correctum*) *U*   13 igitur: ergo *U*

10 5 sive: *om. U*   7 consideratur: conscideratur *U*   10 minime quaeri:

199

queri minime *U*   attrectare: actractare *U*   11 Paulus: apostolus *add. U*   14 ut: uti *U*   15-18 Neque . . . videatur: Neque enim opus est lucem queri, que se ipsam alioquin inreperibilis sua sponte offert, licet sit incomprehensibilis, oporteret enim lucem queri. Lux igitur invisibilis ubi percipiant exquiritur, ut sic saltem attractabiliter videatur *U*

11 4 tu: *om. U*   5 quod: per *add. U*   8-9 quonam modo: natura modo *U* 9 Omnes: Dicimus *(?) U*   10 supersubstantialem: supersubstantialiter *U* 11 affirmarunt: affirmaverunt *U*   11-16 neque . . . substantiam[2]: neque aliud per supersubstantialem et substantiam sine substantia, aliud per in, aliud per non, et substantiam insubstantialem, et substantia non-substantialem, et substantiam ante substantiam *U*   18 idem: id *U*   aliudque: aliud quam *U*

12 3-5 et . . . ostendunt: *om. U*   7 positionem: acquisitionem *U* ablationem: oblationem *U*   11 non-ens: est *add. U*   14 nec: neque *U*   16 ipsum: *om. U*   18 videntur: videtur *U*

13 1 omnem: omne *U*   quemcumque: quecumque *U*   3 miror: maior *U* 8-9 cum . . . est: *om. U*   10 Enimvero: Bene vero *U*   10-11 quidam: quidem *U*   12-13 Parmenide: Permenide *U*   13 Areopagita Dionysio: Arcopagita Dionisio *U*   15 alio: illo *U*   16 item: ita est *U*

14 1 considera: conscidera *U*   7 dicuntur: dicitur *U*

15 2 FERDINANDUS: Ferdinandus *ante* Capitulum quintum *scribit U* 8 neque: non *U*   9 effugere: effligere *U*   10 intelligereve: intelligerene *U* quippiam: *aut* quippiam *ex* quispiam *aut* quispiam *ex* quippiam *corr. U*   extra: esse *U*   sed: sequi *U*   13 enim: erit *add. U*   15 in[2]: *om. U*

16 1-2 discretioque: descriptioque *U*   3 sint: sunt *U*   3-4 sic . . . sic: *om. U*   5 ut[1]: et que *U*   ut[2]: et que *U*   6 eiusmodi: huiusmodi *U*

17 1 aciem: actiem *U*   3 tibi: *om. U*   4 nunc quidem: quidem nunc quidem *U*   Tantum autem conceditur: *om. U*   6 nunc: *om. U*   6-8 per . . . se: *om. U*   8 visibilem: reperibilem *U*   10 quia: que *U*   se: sic *U*   17 Placet: Placuit *U*

18 4 Nicolaus: *om. U*   unica: unita *U*   7 quod: quid *U*   7-9 est . . . vides: *om. U*   9 est: et *U*   12-13 tamen quoniam: nunquam *U*   14 et unitas: *om. U* 15-16 trinitas[1] . . . quam: *om. U*   16 simplex principium: principium simplex *U* 18 ante: an *U*   18-20 aliud . . . nihil: *om. U*   21 nisus: visus *U*

19 1 fide: fidei *U*   2 exsuperet: exuperet *U*   3 medio: modo *U*   5 nominant: nominat *U*   7 unitatem: unitatemque *U*   9 litteris: libris *U*   hi: quinque *U*   12 consideranti: consciderandi *U*   15 Sic: Sed *U*   in: *om. U* 17 nostram: viam *U*   18 se definit: dese finit *U*   21 definitio quae: definitioque *U*

20 2 FERDINANDUS: Ferdinandus *ante* Capitulum sextum *scribit U* 4 Non-aliud: Nichil aliud *U*   5 alia: *om. U*   15 et[2]: si *add. U*   20 quod: quo *U*

21 4 est[1]: *om. U*   7 affirmarunt: affirmaverunt *U*   9-10 innominabilem: innobinabilem *U*   10 omnia[1]: *om. U*

22 2 perspicitur: prospicitur *U*   4 intueor: intuor *U*   5 prioriter: preoritur *U*   9 consideraremus: conscideremus *U*   11 sive: sine *U* quae: qua *U*   12 quid: quod *U*   14 omnia: *om. U*   16 pari: ratione *add. U*   17 modo: modis *U*   19 nullo nomine: *om. U*   20 ante: autem *U*

23 2 FERDINANDUS: Ferdinandus *ante* Capitulum septimum *scribit U*   7 videtur: videntur *U*   11 essendi: potest *ante* essendi *scribit et del. U*   14 necessitari: necessari *U*   15 nihil: *om. U* non: *bis U* ab: *om. U*   16 aquam: aque *U*   17-18 confusissimaque . . . ipsum: vigo aut omnipotentie ipsum confussimaque omnipotentie tamen necessitare obedire *U*   18 cessaret: tamen *add. U*   21 et[1]: *om. U*

24 1-2 est non: non est *U*   3-4 confusissimum: confussimum *U*   9 nonaliud: non *U*   11 quantumcumque: quandocumque *U*   12 sensibili: sibili *U*   13 recto: recte *U*   14 intuitu: intuenti *U*

25 2 quam: quod *U*   3-5 et . . . videre[2]: *om. U*   10 non: *om. U*

26 2 nec: et *U*   4 utique non vides: *om. U*   9 dicerem: dicere *U*

27 2 FERDINANDUS: Ferdinandus *ante* Capitulum octavum *scribit U*   5 non-aliud: non aliquid *U*   5-6 in omni: omni in *U*   9 ipsius aliud: aliud ipsius *U*   10 occumbunt: accumbit *U*   11 quae[1]: quia *U*   12 est prioris: prioris est *U*

28 1 ante: *bis U* quantitatem: quantitate in *U*   3 queunt: possunt *U*

29 3-4 a grossa: acrassa *U*   6 verior: vero *U*   9 imaginabiliter: y-magnabiliter (y *supra lin.*) *U*   10 sine: relucentia ymaginaria *add. U*   11 est: et *U* relucentia: *om. U*   12 imaginabiliter: *om. U*

30 1 relucet: relucens *U*   2 magnam dicimus: dicimus magnam *U*   3 et: *om. U*   5 modum: modum *ex* motum *corr. U*   5-6 incomprehensibiliter: incomprehensibiliter *ex* comprehensibiliter *corr.* (in *supra lin.*) *U*   8-9 attrectatur: attingitur *U*   9 imaginabilis: inmaginabilis *U*   10 imaginabilis: inmaginabilis *U*   11-12 in imaginabili: inmaginabili *U*   13 est: esse *U*   14 foret: neque *add. U*   15 ante: autem *U*   17 relucet: ut *add. U*   19-20 cognoscibilis: cognoscibilibus *U*

31 1 universaliter: utiliter *U*   7 et . . . quidditatis: *om. U*   8 utique: *om. U*   12 cognito: *om. U*   13 iridis: iridis *ex* iribis *corr. U*

32 2 FERDINANDUS: Ferdinandus *ante* Capitulum nonum *scribit U*   3 subintrem: subintram *U*   5 his: hiis *U*   9 comperio: comperio *ex* compereo *corr. U*   10 hisque: hiis *U*   11 vivacius: innatius *(?) U*   15 incomprehensibilem: comprehensibilem *U* haesito: exito *U*   20 sol[1]: sol [solum *aut* solis] *habet U*   21 quod: *om. U*   22 et: *om. U*   23 creativa: creatura *U*   26-27 Ipsam . . . incomprehensibilem: *om. U*   28 perspicio: prospicio *U*

32 29 - **33** 14 FERDINANDUS . . . informatum: *om. U*

34 1 videbo: video *U*   4 atque: *bis U*   5 quae: est *add. U*   8 ordinem: et talia *add. U*   10 Traiani: Troiam *U*   11 columna: columpna *U*   12 Traianus: Trianus *U*   13-14 gloriae suae: sue glorie *U*   14 exhibere: exhiberi *U* 15-16 id . . . voluntate: *om. U*   17 quidquid: quid *U*   21 Traiani: Triani *U*

35 1 iuvabis: invicibus *U*   5 anima: omnia *U*   9 speculando: speculandi *U*   10 ista: illa *U*   11 desiderari: desciderari *U*   17 desideratur: descideratur *U*

36 2 FERDINANDUS: Ferdinandus *ante* Capitulum decimum *scribit U* 3 dei: de *U*   participationem: participatione *U*   percupio: percupiam *U* 7-8 igitur . . . participatur: *om. U*   8 quae obscure: obscureque *U*   9 sunt quae: suntque *U*   9-10 sunt[2] quae: suntque *U*   12-13 intelligentiam: intelligentia *U*   14 At quae: Atque *U*

37 2 quonam id modo: quo nam modo id *U*   verum: *bis U*   4 ipsum: *om. U*   11 praecedit: prececedit *U*   12 in alterabili: materiabili *U*   12-13 radicatur: indicatur *U*   18 et tamen sunt: *om. U*   22-24 Sin . . . incorruptibilem: *om. U*

38 1 Videris: Videns *U*   2 sive: sine *U*   speciem: specie *U*   6 esse: *om. U*   emanant: emaneant *U*   9 et[1]: in *U*   10 numeratur: nominatur *U*

39 1 Videris: Videns *U*   2 quam: rerum *add. U*   rationem: rationes *U* 5 intueor: intueor *ex* intuor *corr.* (e *supra lin.*) *U*   6 quidem per ipsas: per ipsas quidem *U* (per *om. U et supra lin. supplet U*[2]) sint: sunt *U*   prioriter: *om. U*   7 vero: ratio *U*   9 quam: nominis *U*   contemplabar: contemplabat *U*

40 1 FERDINANDUS: *om. U*   2 ob: ab *U*; causa *post* ab *add. U* in: *om. U*   4 in: *om. U*   5 pertransiri: pertransiri *ex* pertransire *corr. U* 7 eiusmodi: ehuiusmodi *U*   refutavit: refutant *U*   9 participari: participare *U* 10 dico: equidem *U*   11 sive: sine *U*   12 eo quod: quo *U*

41 2 FERDINANDUS: Ferdinandus *ante* Capitulum undecimum *scribit U* Velis: Felix *U*   3 velis: vellis *U*   5 rubinum: rubinum *ex* turbinum *(?) corr. U (?)*   6 in: ex *U*   7 exserere: exercere *U*   8 occurreret: occurent *U* 9 sentiretur: sentieretur *U*   11 defert: deffert *ex* deffer *corr.* (t *supra lin.*) *U* illo: *om. U*   11-12 Considero: Conscidero *U*   12 alius[2]: aliud *U*   13 perfectior: perfectior *ex* perfectio *corr. U*   14 ignobilior: ignobilice *U*   15 perspicio: prospicio *U*   17 ergo: autem *U*   molis: molis *ex* mollis *corr. U*[2] *(?)* 18 est: *om. U*   21 de: *om. U*   23 sit: est *U*

42 2 nihil habet: habet nihil *U*   4 substantialis: substantialiis *U*   6 est: *om. U*   7 est[1]: et *U*   7-8 similitudo: similiter *U*   11 penitior: penitror *U* est: *om. U*   12 ipsam: ipsum *U*   13 substantiam: substantia *U*   videt: *om. U* 15 aliis[2]: *om. U*   18 lucem videt: videt lucem *U*   18-19 invisibilem: *om. U* 20 et: atque *U*   21 intelligibilem: intelligibile *U*

43 1 deinde: de in *U*   6 ipsa quae: ipsaque *U*   7 est: et *U*   10 non-aliud: aliud *U*   13 Ioannes: Iohannes *U*   13-14 deum lucem dicit: dicit deum lucem *U*   16 creaturae: create *U*   18 a: *om. U*   est: et *U*

44 2 FERDINANDUS: Ferdinandus *ante* Capitulum XII *scribit U* e-quidem: quidem *U*   7 videtur: videntur *U*   Unde: Bene *U*

45 2 at quae: atque *U*   6 illo: alio *U*   iste: ille *U*   7 altero: altro *U* igitur: in *U*   9 secundum: *om. U*   11 vero: ideo *U*   12 forma: est *add. U* 13 non: *om. U*

46 1 igitur: ita *U*   4 consequuntur: consequitur *U*   6 non est: est non *U* 8 ipsorum: ipsarum *U*   11 et: *om. U*

47 1 nonne: non hic *U*   2 et alias: *om. U*   5 igitur: in *U*   6 iste: ille *U* 7 Nicolaus: *om. U*   10 sicut … substantia: *om. U*   11 quae: *om. U*   12 tum: tam *U*   15 ipsum: et *add. U* et aliud: *om. U*   19 considerandum: consciderandum *U*   20 enim: cum *U*   esset: substantia *add. U*   24 sive: sine *U*

48 2 FERDINANDUS: Ferdinandus *ante* Capitulum XIII *scribit U* in: bis *U*   3 ipsos: eius *U*   6-7 quemlibet esse carbunculum: bis *U*   7-8 in-ternum: intermini *U*

49 2 ipsique: ubique *U*   4 confusam: consussam *U*   5 determinatam: determinata *U*   specificatam: specificata *U*   6 absolutum vidisti: vidisti ab-solutum *U*   7 quoniam: quando *U*   8 consideret: conscideret *U*   9 quem: que *U*   10 videt: *om. U*   11 est: *om. U*   12 quae in: quem *U* con-cretam: concreatam *U*   15 a: autem *U*   19 frigidabilium: frigidalium *U* 21 frigidabilis: et *add. U*   22 alioquin: alioquim *U*

50 1 consequenter: consequentes *U*   3 pruinam: pruinam *ex* parvinam *corr. U*   7 conspici: perspici *U*   8 praemisso: premissio *U*   9 substantiis: substancis *U*   10 erigo: erigo *ex* ergo *corr.* (i *supra lin.*) *U*

51 3 considerando: consciderando *U*   7 illius: numquam *add. U*   non: *om. U*   10 ut: uti *U*   11 sentiente: sciente *U*   14 acriter: et *add. U* ante: autem *U*   14-15 consideras: descideras *U*   16 anterioriter[1]: anteriter *U* An-terioriter[2]: Anteriter *U*   17 insensibiliter: sensibiliter *U* in: *om. U*   18 in[2]: *om. U* frigidum: frigus *U*   19 sentitur: sentiter *U*

52 3 Aliaque: Alia *U*   7 dixerim: dixerunt *U*   8 quoniam: quomodo *U* eorum: *om. U* regione: regionum *U*   9 quidquam: quicquid *U*   10 in: *om. U*   14 frigida intelligit: intelligit frigida *U*   16 non-aliud: vero aliud *U*

53 2 FERDINANDUS: Ferdinandus *ante* Capitulum quartum decimum *scribit U*   7 neque: nec *U* intelligetur: intelligitur *U*   8 omne[1]: sibi *add. U* 10 frigefacere: frigescere *U*   11 nunc: non *U*   12-13 Dionysium: Dyoni-sium *U*   13 quam: *om. U*

54 2 Dionysius: Dionisius *U*   3 sensibilium: insensibilium *U*   4 form-arum: *om. U* hominem: hominum *U*   6 Deum: Dum *U*   9 esse: hec *U* 11 tibi: sit *U*   13 ego: ego *ex* ergo *corr. U* Ambrosii: auxilii *U* Camal-

dulensium: Camaldunensium *U*   14 interpretis: interpretis *ex* interpretus *corr. U*   15 subiungam: submergam *U*; alias subiungam *in marg. add. U³*
55 1 Ex: Frater Ambrosius *ante* Ex   *add. U* Caelestis: hac *add. U* 2 spiritualium: spiritualem *U* ascendere: alscendere *U*   5 rerum: in *add. U* 8 Ex¹: In *U* ipsam: ipse *U*   20 umquam: umquam *ex* numquam *corr. U* 21 Admonebatur: Admovebatur *U*   23 eminentiam: eminentiam *ex* emanentiam *corr. U*
56 1 hierarchia: iera *U* proprie: proprior *U*   6 capitulo: in *add. U* 7 unica: unita *U*   8 bonitatis: bonitas *U*   9 transcendenti: trascendenti *U* 11 sibi: si *U* perspecto: profecto *U*
57 2 et²: etiam *U* qui: quoniam *U*   5 tactui: tactui *ex* tatui *corr.* (c *supra lin.*) *U*   7 supersubstantialis: substantialis *U* omnes: omnis *U*   8 eminentior: eminentior *ex* emanentior *corr. U*
58 1 ferme: ferme *ex* forme *corr. U*   3 in omnibus ferme: *om. U* 4 sanctis: sacris *U*   5 unicam: unitam *U*   6 illius: unius *U*   7 Dividuisque: Divinisque *(?) U* alteritatibus: altaribus *U*
59 2 praesubsistunt: presupsistunt *U*   3 possumus: possimus *U* sit: si *U* 4 et: ut *U*   5 scientiae: scientis *U*   7 sit: sic *U* percipiat: participat *U* 10 omnia: divina *U*   12 custodia: substantia *U*   15 cuncta: conta *U*   16 positio omnium: positionum *U* positionem: *bis U*
60 1 Hierothei: Hierotheii *U*   2 ut quae: utque *U*   2-3 comprehendat: comprehendent *U*   3 et: ut *U*   4 quidem: quid est *U* in imperfectis: in inperfectis *U* utpote: utputa *U*   5 imperfecta: perfecta *U* perfectionem: perfectionum *U*   5-7 temporeque . . . eadem: *om. U*   9 In eadem: *om. U* neque: nec *bis U* particeps: particeps *ex* particepes *corr. U*   10 super: supra *U*
61 1 Eodem . . . quarto: Eodem capitulo quarto de divinis nominibus *in folio 66ʳ, lineis 8-9 habet U. Confusionem in foliis perpetuat U. Transitum facio ex fine folii 65ʳ ad verbum* Eodem *in folio 66ʳ, linea 8*   3 appellantes: appellentes *U*   5 ita: igitur *U*   11 etc. Nota exemplum: et infra non extra *U*
62 11 esse: *om. U*   12 Eodem: *om. U* aliquid: aliud *U*   13 item: idem *U*   15 enim: in *U* etc.: et ita *U*   16 quae: ut *add. U*   18 sunt et bono: et bono sunt *U*   19 etc.: et scilicet *U*
63 3-4 Ipse . . . est: *om. U*   5 octavo: *om. U* dicamus: dicamus *ex ? corr. U*
64 1 ante: autem *U*   3 est: *om. U*   6 velis: vellis *U* initium: ipsum *add. U*   7 etc.: et ita *U*   11-12 participia sunt: sunt participantia *U*   14 Eodem: Eodem libro de divinis nominibus capitulo nono *in folio 65ᵛ, linea 1 habet U. Propter confusionem in foliis facio transitum ex folio 66ᵛ, linea 12 ad folium 65ᵛ, lineam 1 in U*
65 1 nono: decimo *U*   2 decimo: *om. U* ex: in *U*   3 et: in *add. U*

5 excedentes: excedente *U*   8 vero: idem *U*   9 causa: causam *U*   tandem:
tandem *ex* tandam *corr. U*   13 capitulo: undecimo *add. U*
66 1 undecimo: *om. U* et: *om. U*   5 percipiendae: percipiendi *U*   6 Eodem capitulo: *om. U*   7 aliquid: aliud *U* ulla: nulla *U*   8 quique quae:
quecumque *U*   9 habeat: habet *U* his: is *U*   10 excellentis: excellentiis *U*
67 7-8 Eodem . . . numero: *om. U*   9 molem: molem *ex* mollem *corr.*
U²(?)   16 Eodem: *om. U*
68 6 deo: ideo *U*   8 est: *om. U*   15-16 inferiora: in feriora *U*   16 eo:
longe *add. U*
69 3 Eodem: *om. U*   4 Eodem: *Propter confusionem in foliis facio tran-*
situm ex folio 66ʳ, linea 8 ad verbum Eodem *in folio 66ᵛ, linea 12 in U*   5 ac:
at *U*   6 eum: cum *U*   7 et: ut *U*   8 in: a *U*   13 principia: *om. U*
cuncta: conta *U*
70 5 sed: si *U* unum: ita *add. U*   7 erunt: *om. U*   8 toto: totum *U*
13 etc.: et ita *U*   14 ipsumque: ipsum *U* determinat: determinant *U*
71 1 theologiae: in eadem epistola ad Caium *add. U*   2 cuiquam: quicquam *U*   3 aliquid: aliud *U*   4 In eadem: *om. U*   5 In: prima *add. U*
Gaium: Caium *U*
71 9 - **72** 1 cognoscuntur. Capitulum XV: cognoscuntur. Sequitur de
libello de definitione Capitulum quintum decimum *U*
72 2 Haec: Hoc *U*   3 in: *om. U*   5 quomodo: quo *U*   7 considerasti: considerasti *et non* consciderasti *scribit U*   9 duc: due *U*
73 1-2 considerasti: consciderasti *U*   4 Consideravi: Conscideravi *U*   12-
13 omnem terminans infinitatem: *om. U*   14-15 multitudinis . . . sane: *om. U*
16 A: *om. U*
74 2 ut: et *U*   3 sit¹: sic *U*   4 cum ante: *om. U*   6 praecedat: pre-
cedit *U*
75 7 saeculum: secundum *U*   8 videtur: *bis U*   9-11 ipsum² . . . saeculo:
om. U   12 in: *om. U*   15 per: ipsum *add. U*   16 praestitit: prestit *U*
17 intueris: intuens *U*   20 posse: esse *U*
76 4-5 ipsum non-aliud: non aliud ipsum *U*   5 intelligere: intelligitur *U*
7-8 omnia . . . omnibus: *om. U*   10 definiat: defineat *U*   12 maiori: *om. U*
13 venit: evenit *U*   14 minusve: minusne *U*
77 5 mones: moves *U*   8 indivisibilitatem: simplicitatem *U*   8-9 inal-
terabilitatem: alterabilitatem *U*   14 sive: *aut* sive *aut* sine *scribit U*   16 quae:
queque *U*
78 1 te: *hic om. et post* velle *scribit, U*   3 quoniam: quomodo *U*   6-7 et
. . . futura: *om. U*   10 absque: ab *U*   12 ipsam: *om. U (supra lin. add.*
U²)   13-14 cum . . . ipsum²: *bis U (in linea 14* vero aliud *pro* non-aliud *bis*
habet *U)*   16 praesentia: substantia *U*   17 praesentiam: presentia *U*
79 1 FERDINANDUS: *om. U* iam: ita *U* equidem: quidem *U*   3 Di-

onysius: Dionisius *U* ipse: *om. U* 6 sublato: sublata *U* cessent: cessant *U* 8 gaudeo: gaudio *U* 13 omnia: *bis U* 14 Dionysius: Dionisius *U* 19 considerasti: consciderasti *U*

80 2 Consideravi: Conscideravi *U* 6 elementata: elementa *U* summoto: sumoto *U* 7 modo: moto *U* intimiore: in timore *U* (*ex* in amore *corr. U*) 8 elementata: ellementa *U*

81 1 David: Quid *U* Dynanto: Dinanto *U* 2 is est: est iis *U* errarunt: erraverunt *U* 3 physin: phisyn *U* nuncuparunt: nuncupaverunt *U* 4 hylen: hylien *U* 9 nihil te moveant: te moveant nihil *U* 12 FERDINANDUS: *om. U* 13 admodum: id *add. U* est gratum: gratum est *U* Gaium: Cayum *U* 17 deum: *om. U* 18 non: nam *U* 19 David: dicendum *U* Dynanto: Dinanto *U* esse: a *add. U*

82 1 id: *om. U* 2 considerasti: consciderasti *U* 3 FERDINANDUS: *om. U* 4 NICOLAUS: *om. U* 6 aliud[1]: *om. U* non esse: esse non *U* 8 nec: et *U* aliquid[2]: aliud *U* 9 non: *om. U* videretur: videtur *U* 10 Ast: Ac *U* 11 non-aliud[2]: non *U* 13 excellens: excelles *U* et: ac *U* 16 est: et *U*

83 2 Nunc: Hunc *U* 3 hoc: hec *U* 9 fatear: fateatur *U* 11 dicit: dicit *habet U* Sic: Sicut *U* 13 ut Pythagorici: Pithagorici ut *U* 15 aquam: aqua *U*

84 1 utique: *om. U* 1-2 aestimanda: exstimanda *U* 4 considero: conscidero *U* 6-7 quaesivit: que sunt *U* 10 illa omnia: illud omnia *U* (alias preter illa omnia *in marg. add. U*[2]) esse[1]: *om. U* igitur: in *U* 15 nominavit: nominaverit *U* 16 nominarunt: nominaverunt *U* 20 desideratam: descideratam *U* 21 philosopho: profecto *U* praedixisti: dixisti *U*

85 2 illam: illa *U* visibilia: visibilium *U* 10 remotius: remotus *U* nimis: minus *U* 11 adinvenit: adiunxit *U* 14 attendisset: et *add. U* 18 alio: alia *U* aliud[2]: alia *U* 20 recte: certe *U* 21 Esto: *hic incipit novum capitulum in U*; Capitulum decimum nonum *ante* Esto *scribit U* significetur: significent *U* 22 erit: *textus in U continuat* Ferdinandus: Utinam *etc.*

86 1 Capitulum XIX: *vide notas pro 85 21 et 22* 3-4 clarissimis: clarissimisque *U* 4 Neque: Nempe *U* 7 Cessassent quoque: Cessassentque *U*

87 1 philosophum: prophetum *U* 6 artior: certior *U* 7-8 addi per hominem: per hominem addi *U* 8 est: *om. U* 9 contemplans: contemplatis *U;* animus *post* contemplatis *supra lin. add. U*[2] 10 ulla alia: alia ulla *U* 12 tametsi: etsi *U* verum: vero *U* 14 omni ex parte: ex omni parte *U*

88 8 utpote: *om. U* 9 possent: possent *ad* posse *corr. U*[2] *(?)* 12 est: *om. U* quaerens: quereres *(?) U* 15 quod: quo *U* 16 viae: me *U*

89 1 equidem: quidem *U* 2 ipse: ipsi *U* 7 respondisset: respondisset *ex* respondissent *corr. U* 10 nequivisset: quisset *U* 13 Dionysius: Dionisius *U* 16 tamen: enim *U* 18 Aristotele: Aristotile *U* dixisse sufficiat: sufficiat dixisse *U*

90 2 Audivi: Nundini *U* 4 Dionysii: Dionisi *U* 5 illum: *om. U* Platonicum: Platonicum *ex* Platonicam *corr. U* 6 verterem: veterem *U* 9 Dionysio Areopagita: Dionisio Arcopagita *U* 10 Dionysii: Dionisii *U* 13 Dionysius: Dionisius *U* quod: uno *add. U*

91 3 tantopere: tanto opere *U* 5 videre substantiam: substantiam videre *U* 8 ante animam: *om. U* (*in marg. add* U^3)

92 2 cuius: unus *U*; *ad* unius *corr.* (i *supra lin.*) U^2 3 participent: participant *U* 7 equidem: quidem *U* 10 invisibilis: invisibillis *ex* invisibilles *corr. U* 14 resumit: resumenit *U* animam: anima *U* 16 complicat: compleat *U* cuncta: cunta *U* inspicere: prospicere *U* 17 quae: que *ex* qui *corr. U*

93 3 consideranti: consideranti *U* 5 unum[2]: esse *add. U* eo: quod *add. U* 8 ens: eius *U* 12 est . . . aliud: id quod aliud est *U* 13 nominatorum: nominativorum *U* dicit: appellat *U* 15 ut: et *U* esse: est *U*

94 4 haud: a̅n̅t (=? a̅u̅t=autem) *U* 12 in[2]: *om. U*

95 2 PETRUS: Petrus *ante* Capitulum vicesimum primum *scribit U* 8 NICOLAUS: *om. U* 10 est: li *add. U* ipso: li *add. U* 12 Optime: li *add. U* 14 PETRUS: Nicolaus *U* 18 visum . . . non-aliud: *om. U*

96 3 aciem: atiem *U* 4 definire: indefinire *U* 9 ab: a *U* ipso: *om. U* suo: primo *add. U* 12 a[2]: *om. U* 13 a: *om. U* 15 a[2]: *om. U* 16 non-aliud[1]: non est aliud *U* 17 significatur: significant *U* 18 Ideo: Ideo *ad* Idea *corr. U* 19 attribuuntur: attribuunt *U*

97 6 habere se: se habere *U* 7 ratioque: ratio que *U* et[1]: *om. U* 12-13 significatur: significant *U* 16 adicit: addicit *U* quo: quomodo *U*

98 4 de: de *ex ? corr. U* 8 sed: si *U* 9 modo atque verissimo: atque verissimo modo *U* 12 omnium quidditatem: omnia ipsa *U* 13 Namque: Nam *U* intellectu: intellectum *U* 17 est: *om. U* 18 attingitur: attinere *U* 20 aut: autem *U* quiddam: quidam *U* 23 excitavit: exacuit *U*

99 3 mentis tuae: tue mentis *U* 5 dirigis: dirigit *U* 7 videntur: viderentur *U* 8 abba: abbas *U* 11 patefacio: patefatio *U* 12 occurrit: occurrunt *U* 13 a nullo: *om. U*

100 5 altero: altero *ex* altro *corr.* U^2 6 altero: altro *U* 7 ipsum: *om. U* 9-10 non-aliud ita: ita non aliud *U*; ipsum *post* aliud *add. U* 10 Dionysius: Dyonisius *U* 11 Areopagita: Areopagita (*ex* Arcopagita *correctum*) *U*

101 1 rei: reii *U* 3 fit: sit *U* 7 Dionysius: Dionisius *U* 8 Dionysius: Dyonisius *U* 10 propter: per *U* 11 sit: fit *U*

102 9 quo: quod *U* 10 asserere: esserere *U*

103 2 invisibilem: visibilem *U* 3 est: cum *U* 4 quia: sic *add. U* 9 in visibili: invisibile *U* 16 excedat: excedit *U*

104 4 aedificiis: hedificiis *U* 5 visus: visus *ex* visu *corr.* (s[2] *supra lin.*) *U* 6 cernimus: cernitamus *U* 9 videt[1]: vidit *U* 10 is: his *U* visuum: visibilium *U* cernere: cernerem *U* 14 est: *om. U* theoro: theo theoro *U*

17 unico: unito *U*　　18 est: *om. U*

105　2 ostendisti: *om. U*　　4 qui: quod *U*　　8 ergo: autem *U*　et: est *U*
12 inquit: nequit *U*　Moyses: dosis *U*　　13 igitur: est *add. U*　　14 quae: qui *U*
16 visus: visu *U*　est: *om. U*

106　2 unum. Quae: unumque *U* (unum *ex* bonum *corr. U*)
14 is: si *U*　　19 convenit quia non-bonum: *om. U*

107　6 quae affirmativam: affirmativaque *U*　　8 bonum[2]: bonus *U*　　12 neque: nec *U*　Quare: Quia *U*

108　1 Capitulum XXIV: et ultimus *add. U*

109　1 NICOLAUS: *om. U*　　4 enim: *om. U*　composito: composita *U*
5 dumtaxat: dumtaxit *U*　　6 incompositum: compositum *U*　si: *om. U*　　8 o-
porteret: oportet *U*　　9 incompositum: igitur *add. U*　　10 composuit: com-
ponit *U*　　14 videtur: vident *U*

110　1-2 Quippe . . . signum: *om. U*　　3 temporis: tempus *U*　　4-6 quasi
. . . divisibili: *bis U* (*in linea 5 semel* totus *et semel* totius *scribit U; in linea 6
semel* divisibili *et semel* divisibile *scribit U*)

111　1 propter: *non proprie abbreviat U*　　2 quae: qua *U*　　3 desinit:
potest *U*　　7 praecisius: *om. U*　aliante: aliente *U*　　8 enim: *om. U*　qui:
quia *U*　quem: quod *U*　　12 creaturae spiritus: spiritus creature *U*

112　3 ac: at *U*　　4 spirantem: spiritantem *U*

113　4 rapere: recipere *U*　　8 nisus: visus *U*　　13 Sion: Syon *U*　videbimus: Finis *add. U; et in rubro continuat* Prestantissimus dyalogus de diffinitione sive directione speculantis explicit

114　1-2 Propositiones . . . Non-aliud: Incipiunt propositiones *in rubro U*
3 propositio: *om. U*　　6 is: his *U*　　9 definitionem: se definientem *add. U*
10 definitionem: non *add. U*　　11 is: his *U*

115　1 propositio: *om. U*　　2-3 quam . . . non-aliud: *om. U*　　5 quae: que
ex qua *corr. U*　　8 est: et *U*　　8-11 non-aliud[2] . . . ipsius: *om. U*　　11 videt:
vidit *U*; et *post* vidit *add. U*　　13 propositio: *om. U*　　14-16 cum . . . nihilo:
ipsius nihil, ille sane vidit ipsum non aliud esse aliud ipsius aliud, et quomodo
ex eo etiam quod omnia definit et singula etiam omnibus omnia et in singulis
singula, ille quidem vidit ipsum non aliud esse aliud ipsius aliud et vidit non
aliud nisi aliud non opponi, quod est secretum cuius non est simile. Octava:
Qui videt quomodo subtracto illo non aliud non remanet nec aliud nec enim
quomodo aliud nihil sit ipsius [*ex* ipsum *correctum*] nihil, ille sane videt ipsum
non aliud in omnibus omnia esse et nihil in nichilo *U*

116　1 Octava propositio: Nona *U*　　4 se: *om. U*　　5-6 simpliciter . . .
non-aliud: *om. U*　　8 Nona: Nam *U*　　9 aliud aliud: aliud *U*　　12 sic: si *U*
alia omnia: omnia alia *U*　　13 videt: vidit *U*　　15 videt[2]: vidit *U*

117　1 propositio: *om. U*　　3-5 et[1] . . . inintelligibili: *om. U*　　6 nec in-
finito: *bis U*　　10 nec nomine innominabili: *om. U*

118 6 quoniam: quomodo *U*   7 videt: vidit *U*   8 videt[1]: vidit *U*   8-9 Nam . . . definiens: *om. U*   11 definientis: definiens *U*   14 remotis: remotisque *U* aut: et *U*   18 quidem: *om. U*   19 vero: vero *ex* non *corr. U*

119 4 ubi: nisi *U*   5 videt: vidit *U*   11 videt: vidit *U*   12 deum: dum *U* videt: vidit *U*   13 fiunt: finit *U* negativam: negativa *U*

120 1 videt[1]: vidit *U* aliud: *om. U* videt[2]: vidit *U*   3 frigefactum: *om. U* facto: factum *U*   4 factum: *om. U* indivisibile: *om. U*   6 Et: ut *U* videt: vidit *U*   7 sublata: *bis U*

121 1 videt: vidit *U*   3 videt: vidit *U*   5 sic: si *U*   6 impositionem: impositionum *U*   10 videt: vidit *U*

122 1 Videt: Qui *ante* videt *scribit U* ipsum: ipso *U*   3 videt: vidit *U*   5 videt: vidit *U*   6 posse: *om. U* maius: minus *U*   7 maius: magis *U*   8 quae: *om. U*

123 1 videt: vidit *U*   2 est: esse *U* videt: vidit *U*   3 videt: vidit *U*   6 videt: vidit *U*   10 bonis: *om. U*   10-11 Numquam: Nunquid *U*   12 possint: possunt *U*

124 1 videt: vidit *U*   2 videt: vidit *U*   5 intellecto: intellectu *U*   5-7 Ipsum . . . intellecto: *om. U*   7 quam: quomodo *U*   14 constat: costat *U*

125 1 considerat: consciderat *U*   1-2 et frigidum calefieri: *om. U*   4 considerat: consciderat *U*   5 quod: per *U*   7 videt: vidit *U*   9-10 et . . . frigefieri: *om. U*   10 Ideo: Idem *U*   14 sit: *om. U*   14-15 potentia: potentiam *U*   15 non: *om. U*   18 relucentem: Finis propositionum *in rubro add. U*

index of persons

Adam, the first man, 188n3
Alvarez-Gómez, Mariano, 181n13, 186
n71
Anselm (St.), 16, 184n35
Aquinas, Thomas, 11, 186n56, 187n3,
188n3, 189n3, 195n116
Aristotle (*called* the Philosopher), viii,
13, 31, 79 125, 127, 129, 131, 133,
187n3, 188n3, 189n3n4, 195n116, 196
n124
Augustine (St.), 16
Balbus, Peter, of Pisa, 187n1 *et ubique*
Campbell, Richard, 7, 181n11
David, of Dinant, viii, 123
Dionysius, Pseudo- (*called* the Theolo-
gian), viii, 3, 5, 9, 10, 14, 17, 18, 31,
35, 47, 95, 113, 115, 117, 121, 123,
125, 133, 135, 145, 147, 182n15, 188
n3, 189n3, 191n4 195n116, 196n125
Dionysius, the Tyrant, 188n3
Eckhart, Meister, 3, 186n67
Empedocles, 125
Erigena, John Scotus, 3, 10, 183n22,
186n60
Finkenstaedt, Rose, 26, 180n3, 197n1
Flasch, Kurt, 184n29
Fuehrer, Mark, 181n15
Gerson, John, 3
Goethe, Johann, 26
Grosseteste, Robert, 10
Harries, Karsten, vii
Haubst, Rudolf, 181n11, 191n7
Hauke, Hermann, ix
Hegel, Georg, 14
Honecker, Martin, 10
Hummel, 26
Jesus, 16, 101, 197n143
John, the Baptist, 147

John, the Evangelist, 83
Koch, Josef, 12, 13
Lull, Raymond, 196n118
Martin, Vincent, 181n15
Matim, Ferdinand, of Portugal, 187n1 *et
ubique*
McTighe, Thomas P., vii
Milton, John, 26
Moses, 121, 151
Paul, the Apostle, 9, 43, 75, 135
Pegis, Anton, 185n56, 186n56
Plato, viii, 47, 125, 133, 135, 137, 141,
143, 145, 147, 153, 188n3, 189n3, 196
n126
Proclus, viii, 3, 31, 133, 135, 137, 145,
151, 187n1
Reinhardt, Klaus, ix
Roques, Réné, 183n22
Sarrazin, John, 10
Schedel, Hartmann, 178, 198n3
Schneider, Gerhard, 188n3
Shorey, Paul, 185n56
Socrates, 75, 189n4
Thierry, of Chartres, 3, 10
Thomas (St.), *see* Aquinas
Tillich, Paul, 10
Trajan, the Emperor, 71
Traversari, Ambrose, 10, 95, 183n22,
193n40n41
Trimegistus, Hermes (Pseudo-), 186n67
Uebinger, Johann, 183n22
Vansteenberghe, Edmond, 195n118
Van Velthoven, Theo, 26, 186n71
Vigevius, John Andrea, 187n1 *et ubique*
Wackerzapp, Herbert, 181n13
Wilpert, Paul, 19-21, 24, 185n55, 186
n57, 195n118, 196n118n129, 197n1

211